DISCARD

DISCARD
Y0-BRV-010

Guernsey
Memorial Library
Norwich, New York

Presented by

MISS JEAN NEWTON

Early
American
Inns
and
Taverns

**ELISE
LATHROP**

FRAUNCES' TAVERN

# Early American Inns and Taverns

*By*

### ELISE LATHROP

AUTHOR OF *"Where Shakespeare Got His Stage,"*
*"Sunny Days in Italy,"* etc., etc.

ILLUSTRATED

"Whoe'er has traveled life's dull round,
Where'er his stages have been found,
May sigh to think he still has found
His warmest welcome at an inn."

TUDOR PUBLISHING COMPANY
*New York*                    MCMXXXVI

COPYRIGHT, 1926,
BY ROBERT M. McBRIDE & COMPANY


*New Edition November, 1935*

EARLY AMERICAN INNS AND TAVERNS
———
PRINTED IN THE UNITED STATES OF AMERICA

*To*

EDWARD HALE BIERSTADT

*Whose kind suggestions and advice*
*are responsible for this book.*

# INTRODUCTION

The demands of modern travelers for the latest conveniences and equipment are undoubtedly in part responsible for the disappearance or conversion to other uses of some of the historic inns or taverns of colonial and later times. Yet when these have survived, their stout construction, the solid beams and planks used in building by our forefathers, insured far longer lives than will fall to many modern structures. Occasionally, old inns have survived by virtue of historical societies which have therein enshrined themselves, and carefully preserved the houses from the inroads of time. Recently, the automobile has given inns a new lease of life.

The tavern played a very important rôle in colonial times, and enjoyed real repute. Edward Field, in his delightful book, *The Colonial Tavern,* speaks of the intimate relation between such inns and the old meeting-houses in New England. The inn or tavern was the place where people went to warm and refresh themselves after long services in meeting-houses, where, during cold winter months, the only heat came from foot-warmers brought by members of the congregation. This explains why the tavern was always close to the church.

Mr. Field further says that beer was the common drink of

these first settlers, who drank water only from necessity, and early arranged to import stronger liquors from the mother country, of which liquors women and children, as well as men, partook.

Licenses for taverns were easily obtained on condition that "good rule and order be maintained." Selectmen were indeed anxious that taverns be opened, but there was much grumbling when occasionally in those early days a tavern-keeper showed prohibition tendencies.

Thus, when in 1660 the selectmen of Concord, Massachusetts, "prevailed upon Serjeant Buss to keep a public house," but the worthy man "desireth to be free from any engagement to sell wine and strong waters," it was not long before there was much complaint.

The terms: tavern, inn, and ordinary were not always interchangeable. The name tavern was usually given in New England and New York State; in Pennsylvania, inn was more common; in the South, ordinary was the general term. Sometimes inn and tavern were employed to distinguish between a mere drinking place and one where meals also were served. Coffee house was another term which by no means meant that only coffee was sold. Some localities scorned the word inn as "too English." Not until after the Revolution was hotel or house in general use.

Old inns or taverns have sometimes played a prominent part in the affairs of our country. Thomas Jefferson wrote the Declaration of Independence in the Indian Queen Tavern, Philadelphia, where he was staying at the time; many stirring meetings were held before the outbreak of the War of the Revolution in taverns whose landlords were in sympathy with the cause of the patriots. Fraunces' Tavern was one such, and there were many others. The Green Dragon, in Boston, was headquarters for the Whig Party; The Ohio Land Company originated in another Boston

# Introduction

tavern, The Bunch of Grapes; Frankfort was chosen as Kentucky's seat of government in Brent and Love's Tavern in Lexington.

Fortunately, increase in travel with the automobile has awakened the proprietors of some of these old buildings, still used as inns, to their historic value. New proprietors have furthermore hunted out and leased other houses of Revolutionary or earlier period, and, opening them as inns or tea-rooms, boast of their age and interest. The motorist often comes across these in most unexpected spots. Equally of course, many are left unvisited because they are slightly off the beaten track, or because the speed at which the average motorist travels barely permits a glimpse of "1711" or "1777" on a signboard, or over the door. Perhaps some of these hurried travelers would pause if they knew just where some of these old inns were located, and what of interest they offer.

Because of the necessity for setting a definite age for the term "old" to cover, practically no inn of the eastern and southern sections of this country less than one hundred years old has been included. The majority are much older. But in more recently settled states, the age limit has been fixed at approximately seventy-five years, although a few still older will be found.

As to states omitted, California's state historian is responsible for the statement that, to the best of his knowledge, not a single old inn survives in that state. Here, as in Florida, New Mexico, Arizona and much of Texas and Louisiana, during Spanish occupation, such travelers as passed usually found lodgings in convents or monasteries, in private homes or in the governors' residences, sometimes involuntarily in the dungeons of the latter.

Colorado dates practically from the gold discoveries, and in other states, if travelers were not lodged in private homes,

[ix]

# Introduction

they stayed in such temporary, makeshift shacks that these have long since disappeared from the memories of even the oldest inhabitants.

In the index, two signs will be found prefixed to the names of many inns. An asterisk indicates that the old inn—or in a few cases the old residence now used as such—is still in operation either as a hotel or tea-room. Occasionally, as mentioned, a new building now occupies the old site. A dagger indicates that the former tavern is owned and occupied by some patriotic or civic society, in which case those interested can usually arrange to see its interior. Many former inns have been converted into private residences or apartments, often so completely altered that their age would never be suspected. These, of course, are not open to the general public.

Of the other inns or taverns listed in the index, many are not mentioned in the text, for the reason that they are no longer standing or are so transformed into private residences that it is difficult now to recognize them as old inns.

Although much effort has been expended to make this record complete, it can not possibly be so, for there undoubtedly existed many more old inns, and probably some of these, in out-of-the-way spots, or so altered long ago as to have ceased to be remembered as inns, are still standing.

For reference purposes, all of the inns along the "Old Pike" mentioned by Mr. Thomas B. Searight, in his *The Old Pike* and by Dr. Julius F. Sachse in his *Wayside Inns on the Lancaster Road* have been included in the index.

# ACKNOWLEDGMENT

To historical societies and patriotic associations in almost all of the states covered—except those of the State of Louisiana, which were unwilling to furnish any information whatsoever, and those of Mississippi, which apparently had none—and to individual members of these societies; to librarians, postmasters and postmistresses, and to Chambers of Commerce; to owners and proprietors of many old inns, as well as to the authors who kindly loaned their historical pamphlets and articles, the author wishes to express her grateful thanks. Also to:

Mrs. Fred F. Blaisdell, Dr. Anna Broomall, Mr. Peter A. Brannon, Miss Louise Butler, Messrs. Richard M. Carpenter, Robert W. Chambers, H. E. Cole, Curtis Chappelaer, Prof. V. Lansing Collins, Mr. Samuel Craig Cowart, Dr. P. C. Croll, Messrs. Charles E. Eckels, H. T. Deats, Mrs. C. F. Fendrick, Mr. Cyrus T. Fox, Miss Jane S. Hall, Messrs. Richard Herrmann, George L. Hopper, Mrs. Zephine Humphreys, Mr. Clifton Johnson, Miss Grace King, Col. Samuel L. King, Mr. J. H. A. Lacher, Judge Landis, Dr. Preston A. Laury, Miss Marion B. Longfellow, Mr. George A. Macaltioner, Mayor Park Marshall, Messrs. Curtis Marshall, J. Appleton McKin, John C. Mendenhall,

# Acknowledgment

Mrs. E. K. Morton, Messrs. Fred C. Neuman, Stephen O'Higgins, Thomas Overington, Jr., George R. Powell, J. Nick Perrin, Mrs. William T. Rafferty, Miss Mary Rawlings, Capt. H. M. M. Richards, Dr. Charles E. Reed, Messrs. J. E. Reed, John R. Sampson, T. E. Smith, L. D. Scott, Horatio S. Shull, Miss Emma T. Thackara, Dr. W. E. Vail, Mrs. C. A. Ward, Messrs. Henry S. Wardner, Richard Webber, Clifford C. Wilber, Miss Janice Craft Woodin, and Judges Samuel C. Williams and J. P. Young, all of whom, and many others whose names even are unknown, have rendered much valuable assistance to

E. L.

# CONTENTS

[xiii]

# Contents

[xiv]

# Contents

[xv]

# Contents

[xvi]

# Contents

[xvii]

# ILLUSTRATIONS

[xix]

# Illustrations

# Illustrations

[xxi]

# Alabama and Georgia

# STAGES,

**W**ILL leave Montgomery every Monday, Wednesday, and Friday morning, at 4 o'clock· and arrive at Milledgeville early on the morning of the following Thursdays, Saturdays, and Mondays.

Good Horses and suitable Carriages have at great expense been provided — The excellent condition of the roads, and the convenient stands established throughout, render this as pleasant and is expeditious a route as any in the Southern States.

The attention of Travellers is respectfully solic ted by

## The Proprietors.

*⁎* The *Mobile Commercial Register* and the *Louisiana Advertiser* will insert the above four times. and forward their bills to this office for payment.

June 1. 1827.

A Bill Poster of 1827 Announcing Stage Route from
Montgomery, Alabama, to Milledgeville, Georgia

# EARLY AMERICAN INNS AND TAVERNS

## CHAPTER I

*Inns from New York City to Springfield, Massachusetts*

NEW YORK CITY is chosen as starting point for this series of visits to old inns because it is one of the oldest settlements in the United States, as well as the terminus of one of the oldest and most frequented highroads in the country, the famous Boston Post Road. Boston, with her many radiating roads leading to old inns, might equally have been selected, but Boston is younger than New York.

The first buildings on Manhattan Island, where No. 41-45 Broadway now stands, were probably some huts set up in 1613 to house for the winter the crews of Adrian Block's ships, of which one, the *Tiger,* had been burned. Although there was a trading-post for some years on the island, the first permanent settlement was not made until 1626. An old map drawn in 1642, reproduced in *Valentine's Manual,* shows a tavern on or near the East River, not far from Bowling Green. Broadway, *De Heere Straat* of the early Dutch settlers, and another along the East River known as Great Queen, now Pearl Street, were the first streets running north and south in Manhattan. The name of Broadway, for but a short stretch of the present street, was first used in 1642. Famous Wall Street took its name from a palisade running from the East River to the Hudson, built originally to keep out encroachments on the part of English settlers and Indians in the Bronx and Westchester. Eventually this palisade was leveled, giving its site and name to the present financial center.

[25]

# Early American Inns and Taverns

Almost as soon as there were Dutch settlers on the Island there were taverns. That one shown on the early map mentioned may have been the tavern built on Pearl Street in 1642 by Governor Kieft, and which Mrs. Van Rensselaer mentions in her *History of the City of New York*. The Governor, she says, had tired of being obliged always to entertain travelers in his own home, so he built this tavern, the *Staat's Herberg*, for the powerful West India Company, and leased it for 300 guilders to Philip Giraerdy (or Gerritsen), with the stipulation that the landlord sell only the company's liquors. Later this building became New Amsterdam's and then New York's City Hall, and was used as such until the new one was built.

During this same year of 1642, the first ferry to Long Island was operated, and very primitive the boat must have been. Increasing travel induced the building of a second tavern during the following year, when Broadway was beginning to resemble a street. This second one stood at what is now 9-11 Broadway, and was kept by Martin Cregier. Later known as Atlantic Gardens, it survived until 1860. Another early Dutch tavern-keeper was Solomon La Chair, and by 1649 there were "seventeen taphouses." A year before this, one tavern was closed after a man had been murdered within its walls.

Another early tavern-keeper by the name of Litsche must have been in business for some time when in 1653 he exchanged his house and grounds "near the Fort" for the Jansen homestead, "just outside of the palisades or town wall," which was nine feet high, and lived on this land until "the property was condemned by the authorities because it stood too near the fortifications."[1]

In 1664, Mrs. Van Rensselaer states, Wolfert Webber built his tavern on a small hill near the present Chatham Square.

---

[1] *A Century of Banking in New York*, Henry W. Lanier.

She gives some information as to the appearance both within and without of the early Dutch houses in New Amsterdam. They had high, steep roofs of varicolored tiles; stoops raised several feet above the ground. Within were enormous stone fireplaces, large enough to roast an ox whole, and framed in blue and white tiles. Great bedsteads were built into the walls, and the large kitchen was the common living-room. If there was a best room, it contained as chief article of furniture a great bed for honored guests. The housewife's treasures of silver and pewter were displayed; the chairs were straight-backed, their seats covered with Russia leather, or with velvet and silver lace. The floors were usually sanded, often in patterns, and occasionally there were a few small rugs. The New York Historical Society has a painting of one of these early houses which stood on Beaver Street. It was almost square, its main story topped by a very high, pointed roof, pierced by dormer windows for the upper half-story, and beneath the eaves was the date 1679.

When Dutch days on the Island came to an end, there were two taverns on the west side of Bowling Green; one, a gray stone building with flower garden stretching down to the Hudson River, stood near the Fort, and was known as the King's Arms; another, the Province Arms, later the City Arms, then Burns' Coffee House, still later was known as Cape's Tavern.[2] Here, in 1783, the French Minister was entertained. Until his death in 1770, Burns managed his house, and was succeeded by Bolton, who came there from the Queen's Head, later known as Fraunces' Tavern. On the site of the old Burns' Coffee House was built the City Hotel, a hostelry where many distinguished men stayed, and which became famous for its banquets. This hotel was torn down in 1850.

The Black Horse, first of at least three taverns of that

2 See later.

[27]

name in New York City, stood on what is now Fulton Street. It was first kept by Robert Todd, and was noted for its drinks made of West India rum. "On the evening of Jan. 19th, 1736, a ball was therein given in honor of the Prince of Wales' birthday. The healths of the Royal Family, the Governor and Council had been pledged loyally and often at the Fort through the day, and the very great appearance of ladies and gentlemen, and an elegant entertainment ended the celebration. The ladies were said to be magnificent. The ball opened with French dances, and then proceeded to country dances, upon which Mrs. Morris led up to two new country dances made up for the occasion, the first of which was called the Prince of Wales, the second the Princess of Saxe-Gotha." [3]

Montagne's Tavern stood on Broadway, near Murray Street. In front of this house, on January 16, 1770, were piled the fragments of the fourth Liberty pole, which the soldiers of the 16th regiment had just chopped down. At that time, the tavern was headquarters for the Sons of Liberty. [4]

When the English were in possession of the Island of Manhattan, Colonel Francis Lovelace established a monthly mail service between New York and Boston. On January 1st, 1672, the first post-rider was announced to start from the Fort, New York. This fort, as Mrs. Van Rensselaer tells, stood "on the southern extremity of the island," between what are now Bridge, Whitehall and State Streets, and Bowling Green, "overlooking a reef of rocks which at a later time was filled in, extended and fortified, and called the Battery."

"Each first Monday of the month he sets out from New York, and is to return within the month from Boston to us again," the Colonel wrote Governor Winthrop of Connecticut. This post-rider traveled by bridle-paths and In-

[3] *History of the City of New York,* Mrs. Van Rensselaer.
[4] *New York Old and New,* Rufus Rockwell Wilson.

[28]

dian trails, but only a few trips were made until much later, after the Boston Post Road was laid out.

Although as early as 1679 an attempt at lighting New Amsterdam had been made, for the Dutch decreed that a lantern must hang on a pole outside every seventh house, and in this lantern a candle must burn, except on moonlight nights, none of Broadway was paved until 1707, and this first paving consisted of a ten-foot strip of cobblestones in front of the house, leaving a gutter in the middle, which in bad weather became almost impassable mud.

However, stage-lines are said to have been running in 1733 between New York and Philadelphia, by way of Perth Amboy and Burlington; there is an authentic record that, in November, 1756, "a new stage left John Butler's Sign of the Death of the Fox, in Strawberry Alley, Philadelphia, for New York," and Mr. Rufus Rockwell Wilson states that, "stage lines after 1785 connected New York with Albany, Boston and Philadelphia. The route to Albany was by the Bowery Lane and Kingsbridge Road to Kingsbridge, and thence along the Hudson River. Stages left both ends of the route twice a week. Three days were required for the trip in summer, and four or more in winter, a day's journey lasting from five o'clock in the morning until ten in the evening. The Boston stages left New York three times a week, by way of the Bowery Lane and Post Road, Harlem, and thence eastward, covering the distance between the two cities in six days, by traveling from three o'clock in the morning until ten at night. Stages for Philadelphia left Paulus Hook, now Jersey City, every morning and afternoon, and the journey was made in three days. The stages on all the routes were drawn by four horses, and could accommodate twelve passengers, while the fare was four pence a mile, fourteen pounds of baggage being carried free."

Two years before this, on the other hand, a traveler, Josiah Quincy, is quoted on stage journeys as follows:

[29]

"The journey to New York from Boston took up a week. The carriages were old and shackling, and much of the harness made of ropes. One pair of horses carried the stage 18 miles. We generally reached our resting place for the night, if no accident intervened, at ten o'clock, and after a frugal supper, went to bed, with a notice that we should be called at three the next morning, which generally proved to be half past two." [5]

Another early traveler, an Englishman, Thomas Twining, who in 1795 journeyed from Philadelphia to Baltimore, Washington and return, wrote:

"The vehicle was a long car, with four benches. Three of these in the interior held nine passengers. A tenth passenger was seated by the side of the driver on the front bench. A light roof was supported by eight slender pillars, four on each side. Three large leather curtains suspended to the roof, one at each side, and the third behind, were rolled up or lowered at the pleasure of the passengers. There was no place nor space for luggage, each person being expected to stow his things as he could under his seat or legs. The entrance was in front over the driver's bench. Of course the three passengers were obliged to crawl across all the other benches to get to their places. There were no backs to support and relieve us during a long and fatiguing journey over a newly and ill made road."

Furthermore, these coaches, not content with the advertised early hour for starting, often left before the hour, so that "many a time an indignant passenger, on time but left behind, was sent off after the coach in a chaise, with a single swift horse at full gallop." The hour of departure from Boston to New York was sometimes 2 A.M.!

Not until 1827 was the first Concord stage made. These were a great improvement over the former ones, for they had side entrances. Some of them had seats on top for more

---

[5] *Stage Coach and Tavern Days,* Alice Morse Earle.

passengers, and they soon became so popular that they were shipped all over the country.

As to the inn accommodations for travelers in early days, a brief extract from the diary of that noted early traveler, Madame Sarah Knight, will suffice to show what must often have been encountered. This indefatigable woman made the journey alone from Boston to New York, traveling with the post-drivers. One night she stopped in Rye, New York, and:

"Being very hungry, I desired a Fricassee, wh. the land-lord undertaking managed so contrary to my notion of Cook-ery that I hastened to Bed superless. Being shew'd the way up a pair of Stairs wh. had such a narrow passage that I had almost stopt by the Bulk of my Body. But arriving at my Apartment I found it to be a little Leanto Chamber, furnisht among other Rubbish with a High Bedd, and a Low one, a Long Table, a Bench and a Bottomless Chair. Little Miss went to scratch up my Kennell, whch. Russelled as if shee'd bin in the Barn among the Husks and supose such was the contents of the Tickin—nevertheless being exceedingly weary down I laid my poor Carkes never more tired, and found my Covering as scanty as my bed was hard. Anon I heard an-other Russelling noise in the room—called to know the mat-ter—Little Miss said she was making a bed for the men, who when they were in Bed complain'd that their Leggs lay out of it by reason of the shortness. My poor bones complained bitterly not being used to such Lodging, and so did the man who was with us, and poor I made but one Grone wh. was from the time I went to Bed to the time I riss, wh. was about three in the morning, Setting up by the fire till light."

After successfully accomplishing her journey to New York —which she did not like so well as Boston—and returning, Mme. Knight opened an inn herself, on the road between Norwich and New London, Connecticut.

There is scarcely a more traveled road than the old Boston

Post Road between New York City and Boston, but one may search in vain for its original starting-point in New York City: the old fort mentioned by an English visitor in 1822 as standing, but "entirely useless," opposite Bowling Green. From here the road ran along what is now Park Row, then east to Bowery Lane, up to Chatham Street, then along Bloomingdale Road, later known as Broadway, to 23d Street, where it turned east, then north, and crossed our Central Park near McGown's Pass. Thence, by Harlem Lane or by Kingsbridge Road, it crossed Spuyten Duyvil Creek, now merged in the Ship Canal, proceeded up what is now Sixth Street, Mount Vernon, through Pelham, and with slight deviations from the present road, through the old Huguenot settlement of New Rochelle, on through Mamaroneck and Rye into Connecticut.

Along this road in 1769, milestones were set from the old City Hall, New York, then located at Nassau and Wall Streets, as far as Mamaroneck, or farther. Benjamin Franklin set some of these stones, attaching to the wheel of his horse-drawn vehicle an apparatus, invented by himself, which indicated each mile.

There was a middle road from New York to Harlem, but it ran through the woods and was not very good. In 1671, a new road was laid out on the east side, running to the vicinity of Third Avenue and 130th Street.

When the post road reached Connecticut, it linked up with the "New Connecticut Road," and later with the "Old Connecticut Road," from Cambridge, Massachusetts to Albany, New York. This latter very old road was made a permanent thoroughfare by the General Court of Massachusetts, after it had established, in 1639, the "Plymouth Trail" from Boston to Plymouth, earliest of Massachusetts roads.

With the laying out of the Post Road and the inaugurating of a regular stage service, New York's taverns increased

[32]

YE 1711 CLUB INN, MERIDEN, CONNECTICUT

[*See page* 63.

INTERIOR AND FIREPLACE, YE 1711 CLUB INN, MERIDEN, CONNECTICUT

SHELDON TAVERN, LITCHFIELD, CONNECTICUT

[See page 58.

until soon they were found at short distances apart along the entire route.

The first Tammany Club in New York City met in Martling's Tavern, which stood on the site later occupied by the old Tribune Building.

In 1792, the Tontine, later known as the Merchants' Coffee House, was built on the northwest corner of Wall and Water Streets, by merchants, shipmasters and captains, who used it as a meeting place. It existed until 1816. This house, with its "piazza stretching over a six foot strip of sidewalk, was valued at $7,000 in 1799—the highest figure on the list of Manhattan houses, and exceeded only by Peter Stuyvesant's 'suburban residence,' which was estimated as worth $13,000." [6]

A famous old tavern, the City Hall, at No. 4 Wall Street, and the Bunker Hotel at No. 41 in the same street, appear on a map of 1822. The Golden Hill, another old-timer, at 122 William Street, was open until 1895, when it closed under the Raines law.

The Broadway Hotel, at 721 Broadway, stood on the site of an older house of the same name, which was in existence in 1810. The Astor House, built about 1830, stood until comparatively recently on Broadway, occupying the site of the old Drovers' Inn, frequented by the sporting element, for there was a race-course close by, on Church Farm. Later, these gentlemen took themselves to the Bull's Head, on the Bowery, and on the site of this tavern was later built the old Bowery Theatre.

This Bull's Head was also much patronized by drovers. A biography of Daniel Drew, born in 1797, quotes him on his early days as a drover, shortly after the War of 1812.

New York's population was now "growing like sixty. City Hall Park had formerly been way up town. Now it was getting to be in the centre, with houses all around.

---

6 *A Century of Banking in New York,* Henry W. Lanier.

. . . The city was growing so fast that our little section up in the Harlem valley couldn't raise cattle fast enough to supply her butchers. . . . So I got to going 'out West,' as we called it, up into the Mohawk Valley. There I would get a drove of cattle and start with them back towards New York City. The taking of live stock to the New York market had got to be an established business by this time, with regular stopping places. There were tavern keepers here and there along the route who catered to drovers. They would have a big pasture lot alongside the tavern, divided into several pastures to take care of several herds at once.

"Formerly drovers into New York City had to take their droves to the old Bull's Head, which was on Bowery Lane, not far from where the Bowery Theatre stands. There the butchers from the stalls down on Fulton Street would meet the drovers coming into town, and buy their stock.

"But there was a butcher by the name of Astor—Henry Astor his name was—who got into the habit, whenever a drover would be reported as coming into town, of leaving his brother butchers tippling at the Bowery Bull's Head, skip out through the back door of the tavern, mount his horse, ride up the Bowery Road, and meet the drove before it got down to where the other butchers were waiting. Astor would stop the drove and pick out the prime beeves before any one else had a chance at them. By and by the other butchers got on to his trick, and also began to ride up the Bowery to meet the herds. In this way a new Bull's Head was established, way out on the Boston Road, where Twenty-sixth Street now is. By my time, this new Bull's Head had got to be the cattle market, the drovers' headquarters for the city." [7]

Some years later, Drew became the landlord of this second Bull's Head, around which "were cattle pens for the care of fifteen hundred head of cattle at once."

[7] *The Book of Daniel Drew,* Bouck White.

# Inns from New York to Springfield

This second tavern was owned by the Lorillards, and stood on what in Revolutionary times had been their farm. General Washington once stopped for a meal at their house, Drew tells, and "when the tavern was built, the mahogany table from the Lorillard house was put into the tavern as part of the furniture. When I had any guests that I wanted to honor, I would set them at that table for dinner, and tell them how General George Washington had eaten from it.

"The taproom of the tavern was on the corner. This was also the office and all-around room. The dining room was across the hall, and looked out onto the post road, which is now Third Avenue. People eating in the dining room could peer out through the windows and see riders and vehicles passing well-nigh all the time, because this was the . . . high road to Boston. In that day all the through travel to New York City went by my tavern. Back in my time, the tavern was seated on a hill, and you had to go down in order to reach the road. When the city streets were put through, this hill was cut down, and a ground floor put in underneath.

"There was a big wheat field behind the tavern, and not far beyond that a grove of trees. Being on the post road, picnic parties used to drive out from the city, and spend the day in the grove. Cato's tavern, further up by Yorkville, was more of a resort for society people of the city . . . but for turtle feasts, turkey shoots, and such like affairs, the Bull's Head was the leading resort. . . . These shoots and like affairs were held back of the tavern towards the 'Winding Green,' as we called it—Crumassie Vly, in Dutch. (That's where Gramercy Park got its name.)" At this time, "Bleecker Street was a lane lined with blackberry bushes." [8] Mr. Drew also mentions Stone Bridge Tavern, beyond the Canal Street Brook, and the Buck's Horn, "a pretty good place," but "more for fashionable sports."

This Buck's Horn, at Twenty-second Street and Broad-

8 *The Book of Daniel Drew,* Bouck White.

[35]

way, on the direct post route, was spoken of in 1816 as "an old and well-known tavern." A two-storied house, with stables and sheds, it was a favorite roadhouse with drivers on the Post or Bloomingdale Roads. That part of the former road turning east on Twenty-third Street, was closed in 1839.

Cato's roadhouse, which Drew styled "more fashionable" than his own Bull's Head, stood on the Post Road between Fifty-first and Fifty-second Streets, and was famous for its egg-nogs.

The Reverend William Burnaby, a visitor in colonial times, mentions another popular resort, Brannan's roadhouse, on the Greenwich road, and here, too, turtle feasts were held. He wrote:

"There are several houses pleasantly situated up the East River, where it is common to have turtle feasts. These happen once or twice a week. Thirty or forty ladies and gentlemen meet and dine together, drink tea in the afternoon, fish, and amuse themselves until evening, then return home in Italian chaises, a gentleman and a lady in each chaise." [9]

Meanwhile, in Greenwich Village, that "quiet dreamy village, where the magnates of the city loved to come for rural retirement and repose," the Greenwich Hotel advertised in 1811 that "a few gentlemen may be accommodated with board and lodging at this pleasant and healthy location, a few doors from the State Prison. The Greenwich stage passes this to the Federal Hall, and returns five times a day." [10]

New Yorkers remembered Greenwich Village during the yellow fever fright of 1822, when the city was almost deserted, its inhabitants having fled to quiet Greenwich in such numbers, one writer states, that Messrs. Sykes and Niblo built in two days "a house capable of holding three hundred

9 *New York Old and New*, Rufus Rockwell Wilson.
10 *Stage Coach and Tavern Days*, Alice Moore Earle.

boarders," while "even the Brooklyn ferryboats ran up there daily." [11]  He adds that, strangely enough, the yellow fever actually never crossed the swamps and meadows between the city and the village of Greenwich.

Of all the old New York taverns but two remain: Fraunces' and Ye Olde Chop House.  In 1700, Colonel Cortlandt gave the lot on which the former stands to his son-in-law, Etienne de Lancey, a French Huguenot.  Mr. de Lancey built a house here for himself and his wife, Anne, in 1719, and they probably lived in it until 1730, when de Lancey built a new house on Broadway, north of Trinity Church.  By 1854, this second residence had become a tavern, the Province Arms already mentioned.  (If a tavern by this name did actually stand, as has been stated, at the time the Dutch left New Amsterdam, in 1674, this Province Arms must have been the second of that name.  There is much confusion as to the exact sites of some of these early taverns, and authorities differ.)

In 1737, a ball was given by Henry Holt, a dancing master, in the first de Lancey house, and for many years afterwards, balls, concerts, and other entertainments were held there.  For a time the building was used as offices, but in 1762 the property was bought by Samuel Fraunces, a man of French extraction who came from the West Indies, and who had already kept a tavern in New York for seven years.  He opened the newly purchased house as a tavern in 1763, calling it the Queen's Head, and it has been open as a tavern ever since.  Patronized from the first by the best people of New York, it became famous for its Madeira wine, while the "Long Room" continued to be used for concerts and other entertainments.

Fraunces did not long run this tavern, but leased it, and turned his attention to the Vauxhall Gardens, on Trinity Church farm property.  The tavern was meanwhile known

11 *A Century of Banking in New York,* Henry W. Lanier.

as the Free Masons' Arms, and in stormy days before the Revolution many meetings of protest were held within its walls.

In 1775, after unsuccessfully advertising the tavern for sale, Fraunces again ran it himself, and continued doing so all through the Revolution, at the same time rendering such services to the American cause, such aid to American prisoners, that, after the war was over, Congress gave him a vote of thanks and a gratuity of £200, at that time a considerable sum. In 1783, the house was first called Fraunces' Tavern, and although it had other names afterwards, this one has persisted.

Samuel Fraunces sold the property and retired to his farm in New Jersey, but whether because he found country life not to his taste, or for financial reasons, he opened another tavern at 16 Nassau Street. Then he became steward for Washington, later again kept a tavern at 40 Cortlandt Street, and still another on Broad Street. After his death, about 1797, his widow and a partner opened a "House of Entertainment," at 12 Water Street.

Many have been the stirring and interesting happenings in Fraunces' Tavern and its Long Room. Here the Sons of Liberty and the Vigilance Committee met in 1774, and arranged to attack the ship *London,* then at the East India Company's wharf, where they broke open her cargo of teachests, emptying their contents in the waters of the bay, thus celebrating New York's own tea-party. Here at the tavern merchants met to consider uniting with the other colonies in calling a congress. In the same year, the Massachusetts delegates to this Continental Congress were entertained in the Long Room, at a banquet given them by the New York delegates. Washington and his suite were given a dinner here in 1776, and it was in this room that, in 1783, Washington bade his memorable farewell to his officers.

One innkeeper succeeded another; many changes of name

and of structure were made in the old house, and finally, when it seemed probable that it would be razed, the Sons of the Revolution purchased it, and began a very careful and accurate restoration. To aid in this work they had only a picture of the tavern, apparently showing it as it stood in the 1830's, which picture appeared in *Valentine's Manual* for 1854, and Fraunces' own description, when he advertised it for sale in 1775. "The Queen's Head Tavern, near the Exchange, is three stories high"—in a later advertisement he described it as three and a half stories—"with tile and lead roof, has 14 fireplaces, a most excellent large kitchen, fine dry cellars," etc.

Several fires had done much damage within and without, and it was necessary to replace the woodwork. This was done with great care, patterning after old colonial specimens. The committee even sent to Holland to match the old greenish bricks originally used, which could be found nowhere else, and brought red bricks from old houses in Baltimore of about the same period of building. The old hewn timbers had survived, and the present Fraunces' Tavern is as nearly as possible within and without what it was before alterations defaced it. The historic Long Room is now a museum, where are preserved many interesting relics, the lower floor is leased as a restaurant, and the upper floors are clubrooms for the society.

The other tavern surviving in New York is Ye Olde Chop House, at 118 Cedar Street. These premises have, it is claimed, been in use for restaurant purposes since 1800, when they were first known as Old Tom's. The first Olde Chop House stood on Duane Street, but seventy-five years ago the proprietor moved to the present address, and brought the old name with him. The building is evidently very old; ancient rafters support its ceilings, and the lower rooms are filled with pews or benches and tables such as characterize old London chop houses, notably the Cheshire Cheese. A

[39]

narrow staircase close to the front door, and within, leads
to two rooms upstairs, also used for serving meals, and there
is a grill room in the rear, where prominent business men
of the city still meet for luncheon. At this hour, ladies are
excluded from the grill, but are served upstairs.

Many are the interesting objects here assembled. Toby
jugs, old ship models, a quaint windmill clock, whose six
wings, now broken off, used to proclaim the time in six
leading European cities, while the main body ticked off

New York time. Old prints and documents almost entirely
cover the walls, among the latter a certificate of the in-
corporation in 1731 of an Irish Free Masons' lodge, and on
the margin are scrawled the initials: "G.W."

Here one may enjoy all kinds of game in season, and
even, it is said, reindeer steak.

It is hard to picture the New York of even the early
19th century. James Gallatin's diary, quoted by Mr. Lanier
in his book already mentioned, states that as late as 1823
there were "only about three private coaches in New York
—no means of getting about. The streets absolutely filthy
and the heat horrible." (This was in July.) "I have been

nearly every night for a long walk. No roads—no paths. I never realized the absolutely unfinished state of American cities until I returned." Mr. Lanier mentions that in 1822, Manhattan was merely "an overgrown country village," which "disposed of its garbage and ashes by the nonchalant method of providing that every householder should, twice a week, from April to December, shovel and sweep the refuse, garbage and ashes to the middle of the street . . . where it fattened the pigs until it pleased the city officials to remove it. There were no sewers, but each house had a pit. . . . It had practically no water supply, drinking-water coming from numerous wells with pumps in all parts of the city. One of these pumps stood right opposite St. Paul's; it tapped a well sunk in 1754. . . . Not till 1808 were all the pumps removed from the middle of Broadway, and others established at the sidewalks. There were some two thousand buildings south of Spring Street, half of them dwellings, but there were no lodgings or apartments, and the eight small hotels (two on Wall Street, one on Nassau, one on Pine and one on Pearl) provided quite inadequate accommodations.

"Broadway ended at 10th Street, where it ran into the Bloomingdale Road. The whole city was about four miles long nominally, extending to about 31st Street, but above Union Square it resembled one of the 'developments' in the interior scrub-oak flats of Long Island.

"There were no police in the ill-lighted streets, but a few ununiformed watchmen, each carrying a lantern on a pole, and crying out the hours of the night.

"The coach line to Albany started at four in the morning; another took twenty hours for the trip to Newburgh, where it connected with the line for Ithaca. There were a few steamboat ferries, tri-weekly service to Albany; the *Connecticut* and the *Fulton* ran to Providence, and a new service took passengers by steamer *Bristol* to Elizabethtownport, thence by coach (via New Brunswick, Princeton, Trenton and

Bristol) to Philadelphia, at a cost of four dollars. When in January, the Citizens' Post Coach made a trip from Philadelphia in eleven and a half hours, the *Commercial Advertiser* chronicled the fact under the heading: 'Rapid travelling.' " [12]

John M. Duncan, a Glasgow visitor in 1820, is quoted by Mr. Lanier as follows:

"The streets in the lower and older portion of the city are very narrow and crooked, and what is more immediately inexcusable, kept in very bad order. Garbage and litter of almost every kind are thrown out upon the pavement, where a multitude of hogs of all ages riot in abundance. The foot walks are encumbered with projecting steps and cellar doors, lamp posts, pump wells, and occasionally poplar trees, and where any open space occurs, barrels, packing boxes and wheelbarrows are not infrequently piled up.

"Broadway, the Irongate of New York, passes longitudinally through the center of the city, and occupies in general the highest part of the ground; it is wide and straight, and pretty compactly built for nearly two miles. It contains a great many well built houses of brick, but there is still a considerable admixture of paltry wooden ones; a few scattered poplars skirt each side.

"On a summer evening, the Battery is a deservedly favorite promenade, and the prospect which it affords is very rarely to be equalled."

Duncan paid $8 a week for a room in New York on his visit, and if he wished a fire in his bedroom, was obliged "to lay in my own wood, which is three times as expensive as in Glasgow." He also tells of dining at Tammany Hall, a public hotel, "noted for the public meetings of the Democratic Party, or Bucktails." The dinner hour was 3 P.M., and "covers are set every day for from 30 to 80. They take their seats at the sound of the dinner bell, and in little

[12] *A Century of Banking in New York,* Henry W. Lanier.

more than a quarter of an hour, most of them are ready to leave the table. Rum and water is the usual beverage; few take wine unless they are entertaining a friend." [13]

Mr. Lanier quotes an English visitor of about the same period as writing that:

"Broadway, the chosen resort of the young and gay, in these cold bright mornings seems one moving crowd of painted butterflies. I sometimes tremble for the pretty creatures (and very pretty they are), as they flutter along through the biting air in dress more suited to an Italian winter than to one which approaches nearer to that of Norway."

"All the road from the city to the extremity of and beyond the isle (Manhattan)," another visitor testifies, "is adorned on both sides with the country seats and pleasure grounds of rich citizens, who, like those of London every morning and evening drive to and fro in great numbers. The houses on the roads thus leading through the isle to the city, have each from five to ten acres of green pasture, park or pleasure gardens.

"Chatham Garden, a pleasant retreat on the north side of Chatham Street, between Duane and Pearl . . . was run by a French gentleman, Henry Barriere, and the city's beauty and fashion flocked here to concerts and light dramatic entertainments."

By 1829, there were complaints of the new "tall, massive buildings" on Pine Street, which "overshadow the narrow passage between, and make it one of the gloomiest streets in the city. The very bricks look of a darker hue than elsewhere," for "formerly the shops were low, cheerful two-story buildings, or light colored brick or wood painted white or yellow, and which scarcely seemed a hindrance to the air and sunshine. These new buildings were four or five stories high," adds Mr. Lanier.

[13] *A Century of Banking in New York,* Henry W. Lanier.

# Early American Inns and Taverns

In this same interesting book are noted the experiences of James Stuart, "a very intelligent Scotchman, who visited New York in 1826." He paid $1.50 a day for board and lodging, and had "turtle soup twice without extra charge; beef, good; poultry, excellent; beef, fish, melons, tea and coffee for dinner; fish, steak, chicken and eggs in large quantities for breakfast; but beds without curtains; not a bit of carpet in the bedrooms; and water not as plentiful as requisite, most of all in a warm climate; neither hot nor cold baths, in this one of the two greatest (hotels) in New York." There was a water supply at this time, to be sure, "supplying a limited amount of muddy water to 2,000 houses, but rain caught in cisterns was in most homes depended upon." [14]

Mr. Lanier further tells a curious story. The new Museum was finished in 1824, the second marble-fronted building in the city, but such was the prejudice of workmen against working with this material that it was found necessary to pardon a convict from Sing Sing that he might do it. (One assumes this meant marble-cutting.)

Resuming our trip over the Post Road, on the west side of Madison Square there stood until 1853 the Madison Cottage, a roadhouse. Although Broadway between 45th and 71st Streets was not laid out as such until 1845, there stood at Eighth Avenue, Broadway and 59th Streets, as we now know them, the old Half Way House, a tavern. Later, the Boulevard Hotel occupied this site, and the building, but little altered into stores and offices, stands to-day. What was known as the New Boulevard did not become Broadway until 1868.

At 74th Street and the Bloomingdale Road, now Broadway, a famous roadhouse, Burnham's, existed before 1820, and until its proprietor opened the Mansion House in what had been the old Vanderheuvel home, at 77th Street and

[14] *A Century of Banking in New York,* Henry W. Lanier.

the present West End Avenue. This was a house to which men took their families.

At 85th Street, the old Bloomingdale Road turned east, then west again at 97th Street, became Riverside Avenue, curved uphill, and joined Kingsbridge Road from Harlem near 147th Street. The curious little winding street to-day called Old Broadway, beginning at 125th Street and only a few blocks long, is part of the old Bloomingdale Road.

At low tide, there was a ford across Spuyten Duyvil Creek; later a ferry, and in 1693, King's Bridge was opened by Frederick Philipse, in fulfillment of one of the conditions under which he received the patent for his manor. Another directed him to open an inn on the Manhattan side of this bridge, over which farmers and others should have free passage on the day preceding a fair, during the fair, and on the day following. This inn was known as Cook's.

Over near McGown's Pass, a Dutchman, Jacobus Dyckman, had a tavern, the Black Horse No. 2. There was a "wading place" near what is now East 121st Street, about three hundred feet from First Avenue. Johannes Verveelen received a concession to operate a ferry here, with the usual stipulation that he also open a tavern. He built one on the Manhattan side, and there was another on the Bronx side, but the ferry was not very profitable, so three years later it and the Bronx tavern were abandoned. However, another tavern at 230th Street and Broadway is mentioned as kept by the same Verveelen.

When in 1758 a free bridge was built for farmers and others, Jacobus Dyckman sold his tavern at McGown's Pass, which tavern was later known as the Red or McGown house, and has long since disappeared. Dyckman opened a new one at the foot of Marble Hill, opposite the free bridge, which he sold before the Revolution to Caleb Hyatt. This was patronized in the days when Third Avenue was a fine, well-paved street, much used as a drive by gentlemen with fast horses, and was known as Hyatt's or Hoyatt's. Here Washington stopped. Its successor, on the opposite side of Broadway, the Kingsbridge Hotel, stood until 1917, when it was torn down.

The Farmers' Free Bridge, Mr. Bolton mentions in his book on Washington Heights, is now *under* the re-graded 225th Street.

Another Black Horse Tavern stood on the south side of Dyckman and 204th Streets, and was later a roadhouse for drovers. It was two stories high in front, and one in the rear, the roof sloping down over this from the ridgepole, of the type known as "salt-box," and was a halfway house and stop for Albany coaches between New York and Yonkers. On its signboard was painted a black horse.

On the site of the second Verveelen tavern at 230th Street, another building was erected in 1775, known as Cox's Tavern, and here John Adams lodged the following year. It, with adjoining property, was purchased in 1850 by Mr. Macomb, and a fine residence erected. It is said that this house surrounded the old tavern, but in 1918 it all was removed to make room for modern buildings.

Another famous old tavern on the Post Road was the Cross Keys, at 165th Street, its signboard showing two crossed keys. This was used until 1881, and the New York Historical Society has a drawing of the old inn. Another at 126th Street was opened in 1770 by a blacksmith, and still another, at 141st Street, was kept by John Myer. The Post Inn, at 177th Street, opposite Depot Lane, survived until the middle of the last century.

In 1758, the Blue Bell was opened at 181st Street, on Washington Heights. This sheltered wounded soldiers during the Revolution, but disappeared early in the 19th century. Another Blue Bell was then opened on the opposite side of the road by Blaze Moore, who used the old sign, and it stood until the Kingsbridge Road was widened. *Valentine's Manual* for 1857 has a picture of this old tavern.

Morris' Tavern or White House existed in the early part of the 18th century, and was bought by Morris in 1765.

Claremont, with its broad piazzas overlooking the Hudson, was built before 1776 for a private residence, by Doctor Post. Near here was fought the Battle of Harlem Heights, while the low ground now crossed by the Riverside Drive viaduct was referred to by Washington in his dispatches at that time as "Hollow Way." From 1803-6, Claremont was owned by Governor Joseph Alston and his wife, daughter of Aaron Burr.

In 1807, the first British Minister to the United States, Lord Courtenay, watched from Claremont the first trip on the Hudson of Robert Fulton's first steamboat, the *Clermont*. When war broke out, Lord Courtenay returned in haste to England, leaving behind his furniture and plate to be sold at auction. In 1815-16 it was the residence of Joseph Bonaparte, ex-King of Spain. Opened as a roadhouse more than seventy-five years ago, it was acquired by the City of New York in 1872, and has been leased ever since as a restaurant. Many are the distinguished persons who in both early and recent years have lunched and dined here.

After crossing Spuyten Duyvil Creek, the Post Road turned east through a marsh, then divided; one fork going over a hill to Williamsbridge, and on to Boston; the other turning north and east, becoming part of the Albany Post Road, opened as far as Sawkill in 1669. We shall return to this road in another chapter.

Diverging from the present Boston Post Road, in Eastchester, now part of Mount Vernon, stands a house that was once an inn, although it is many years since it has been so used. Opposite St. Paul's Church, it was known in Revolutionary days as Crawford's Inn, kept by a man of that name, and frequented by British troops. Tradition says that a British deserter was once hanged from its sign-post. It is a two-story, square house, with a single and modern front door, but a few old hinges remain on old shutters. The church opposite, old as it is, replaced a still older one, and many American Revolutionary soldiers lie buried in its churchyard. Another old tavern in the village of East-chester, known as "Romy Guion's," has vanished.

At the corner of Huguenot Street and North Avenue, New Rochelle,—Huguenot Street was formerly the old Post Road,—is an old inn where horses were changed and travelers refreshed themselves. Of several old taverns in New Rochelle, this one, Besley's, alone survives, nor will it be long before this too disappears. Probably built about 1760, it is sadly dilapidated. One corner is occupied by a store, but the main portion and wing have been empty for several years now, and were last used as a cheap lodging-house.

Early records show that James Besley, descended from a Huguenot family, kept this inn from 1773 to 1776, but it was owned in 1768, and probably much earlier, by Peter Badeau, a cordwinder. The house was an inn as late as 1820, and at one time was used as the court house. When Madame Knight made her famous journey on horseback from Boston to New York, in 1704, there were three taverns within sight of each other in New Rochelle, but there is nothing to prove that the Besley Tavern then existed, nor does a map of the town drawn in 1711 show it.

Beyond the old mile-post in Mamaroneck, carefully guarded now by an iron railing, the road turns sharply to the right. For a short stretch here a new road, parallel but higher, has been built, but on the old one stands the Lawrence Inn. This has been open as an inn ever since the present owners bought the property thirty-nine years ago, when it was known as the Guion farm, from the Huguenot family which had owned it for many years. The old part

COLLINS TAVERN, STRAITSVILLE, CONNECTICUT

[*See page* 56.

CURTIS HOUSE, WOODBURY, CONNECTICUT

[See page 59.

of the inn is believed to be one hundred and seventy-five years old, and it seems highly probable that it was an inn during stage-coach days, for it was on the Post Road, and contained sixteen rooms, more than the usual farmhouse of the period.

In spite of the broad piazzas which replace a much narrower porch, in spite of a large dancing and dining hall added, it is not difficult, once the threshold of the main entrance is crossed, to distinguish the old portion.

There are the low-ceiled rooms, several now thrown together, a narrow hall at the right, leading to the bar-room, and narrow stairs mounting to the second story. From the second story, a still narrower flight beside a large old chimney, mounts to the attic, where hand-hewn timbers of the early days may be seen.

Behind the old barroom downstairs is a small room which may have been the old kitchen, for there is a large chimney which must once have had a great open fireplace, although now entirely filled with metal-lined cupboards. At some period of its tavern existence, some wag painted an owl on one of the panels, adding his initials to show that he was a wise old owl, or perhaps merely a night owl.

The village of Rye is to be congratulated, for it has preserved its old inn and is using it as a Municipal Building.

Close to the highroad stands this Square House, as it was first known. With two stories and an attic, its outer covering of shingles with rounded ends pointing downward makes it unusual looking.

The village of Rye goes back to Dutch days, but this inn was built in 1731 by Peter Brown, who may or may not have kept a tavern in it. In 1770 it was Haviland's Tavern, after its proprietor, Dr. Ebenezer Haviland, a surgeon in the Revolutionary Army, who was killed in that war. After his death the house was kept by his widow.

John Adams stopped here in 1774, and Washington notes

in his diary: "October 15, 1789. After dinner, through frequent light showers, we proceeded to the tavern of a Mrs. Haviland in Rye, who kept a very neat and decent inn." He stayed here again in November of the same year. Later, as Penfield's Hotel, it was a well-known stage-coach halt, and continued as a hotel until about 1830.

The interior of the house has not been greatly changed. Old doors, and a few old hinges remain. A broad stairway

with a landing leads to the second floor, where at the right is a large room with two fireplaces. This was quite probably a ballroom.

There was an earlier tavern in Rye, kept in 1704 by Daniel Straing, a Frenchman. Here justices and the church vestry met as early as 1734. This tavern survived until about 1850, but only one of the outbuildings, now a garage, stands, and even its authenticity is doubtful. Van Sicklen's Tavern, built of stone and clay, with walls thirty inches thick, stood in Rye, facing south, with one gable on the turnpike. This was sometimes called the Old Stone Fort, and remained until 1868.

Early records fix "horses hyer from Rye to Hartford at 12 shillings; man and expences, 20 shillings." The first coach between Rye and New York ran in 1772, and fifteen years later these were running three times a week, but for a long time the favorite mode of travel was by boat. In 1739, a ferry was run between Rye and Oyster Bay, and old records show that Mr. Isaac Brown bought the ferry owned by a German, Frederick de Weisenfeld, in 1786. There was another tavern close to Byam River, here the dividing line between New York and Connecticut.

The road east of Rye had probably already been laid out in 1676, and followed about the same course as the present Post Road.

Greenwich presumably had its old inns, but although seventeen stage-lines used to stop here, town historians have found no inn older than ninety years, the Silleck House, now apartments. The "Putnam Cottage" was not, according to them, an inn, but Knapp's residence. Stamford, too, is said to have had an inn at which Washington breakfasted, and Norwalk had until a year ago an inn dating from 1775, but this has been torn down.

Fairfield has two old taverns, although both are now private residences. The Benson House, on Main Street, built shortly after the Revolution and occupied by General Abel, was later turned into a tavern and run by Captain Benson. His descendants still occupy it. Stages changed horses at Stamford, arriving in Fairfield in time for supper. Macready, Fanny Kemble, Edwin Booth, Aaron Burr, Daniel Webster and General Jackson have all stayed here.

The inn was headquarters for the first American circus, Van Amburgh's, which brought the first show elephants to this country. (Not the very first elephant, which distinction belongs to a resident of New York State.) These elephants were kept with the circus horses in the great stables of the Benson Tavern.

On the south side of the village green stands the old Sun Tavern, at which, in 1789, Washington spent the night, while on his Grand Tour, going on to New Haven the next day. The innkeeper was a Mr. Penfield. In 1818 the tavern became a private residence, and, except for a period when it was a school, has been one ever since.

The next old inn on the road, which here becomes Broad Street, is at Milford. To see Clark's Tavern, a slight detour to the left is necessary, toward the old churches at the head of what resembles a placid pond, framed in sloping, grassy banks, but which is in reality part of the river, later becoming a swifter stream which turned the old grist mill once standing in the town.

Washington mentions Milford in his diary: "In this place there is but one Church, or in other words, one steeple, and there are Grist and Saw Mills, and a handsome cascade over the Tumbling dam."

There are several "steeples" now, and two churches stand where the old highroad once lay, now a street turning almost at a right angle into the present Post Road. East of these churches was a tavern, now gone, but a few doors from the fine modern schoolhouse is the old Clark Tavern, greatly modernized, and for many years a private residence. The original part of the house is believed to have been built between 1644-50. The original Dutch door with its old hinges is still hanging, although no longer in the front; one old fireplace and some of the old flooring remains, and upstairs, in what is now a closet, may be seen hand-hewn beams.

The tavern, a salt-box house, probably contained five or six rooms on each of the two floors. An enormous stone chimney, in the memory of the present occupant, almost filled the hall, and around this chimney, the stone of which came from the Milford quarry, a spiral staircase led to the rooms above. When the chimney was removed, there was enough stone not only to build foundations for an addition to the house, but sixteen ox-team loads were taken away for other building purposes. Every room had its own fireplace. Washington stayed here, not once but several times, and the house was saved only by accident from being demolished.

After a long life as Clark's Tavern, it was bought by a sea captain. He intended to raze it and build a new house on the site, but before he could do this, he was lost at sea. The house belonged to his widow for her lifetime, but she could not tear it down, and eventually it came to the present owner, another Mrs. Clark, though not related to the original owners. She remembers, however, that when as a little girl she stayed in the house, she was often sent to show visitors which of the stone steps outside were there at the time that General Washington came to the tavern, and very tired of showing them she became. The lower two steps of the flight leading from the sidewalk to the road are the old ones.

The south parlor is thought to be the room in which Washington ate his breakfast porridge, although the old room was smaller than the present one.

Returning to Broad Street, the road crosses a bridge with a tower at one side in honor of Governor Robert Treat, who "was for 30 years Governor of the Connecticut Colony, and died in 1710." Close beside it is an old millstone belonging to the first mill in this colony, whose owner died in 1660.

Old as New Haven is, no tavern of the early days remains. From here at least four roads may be taken in search of old inns, but continuing along the main highroad, Hartford is soon reached. Nothing remains of the Bull's Tavern, where Washington lodged, having been met at Weathersfield and escorted to Hartford by a party of the Hartford Light Horse, and other gentlemen, with Colonel Wadsworth at their head. Nor could one find the Free

Masons' Arms on Front Street, operated in 1771 by James Tilley, a member of the Governor's Guard.

Charter Oak Avenue commemorates the famous oak tree in which the Charter was hidden, and some will tell you that the Wadsworth Tavern in which the famous meeting was held, stood on this avenue, where now there is a business building. Others assure one that there never was a Wadsworth Tavern, but that Colonel Wadsworth's residence stood here, and that the Charter incident occurred in a room in the second story of the old meeting house. Alice Morse Earle describes a Wadsworth Tavern three miles from Hartford.

At all events, the colonial governors met in 1687 here in Hartford, to decide whether or not to return the Charter to the new English Governor. The lights were suddenly extinguished, Captain Wadsworth stole the Charter, and hid it in the hollow of the tree known thereafter as the Charter Oak, and thus settled the dilemma. The tree stood until 1856, on the spot now marked by a marble tablet. Part of its wood was made into a chair for the presiding officer of the Connecticut Senate.

The condition of Hartford's streets in olden days was such that in the early 1700's, when on Thanksgiving Day Mrs. Daniel Wadsworth wished to cross Main Street from her home near the City Hall, she could do so on horseback only.

From Hartford it is but a short run to Manchester, Connecticut, where is the old Woodbridge Tavern, at which, in 1817, President Madison stopped. Until 1823 the town was known as the Parish of Orford, in the town of East Hartford. Stages on the Boston Turnpike stopped here to change horses, and there were several taverns: the Green, Buckland's, Olcott's, Richard Pitkin's and the Woodbridge. As always, stage-drivers announced their arrival by blowing

[54]

their horns, so that dinner should be ready to serve as soon as the coach drew up at the tavern door.

In 1781, Rochambeau and his army were expected to pass through here, and Mistress Pitkin and her daughter were busy indeed. "Bread was baked in the brick oven, and great kettles of beef, pork and vegetables were hung on to boil. Tables were laid out of doors, and a bounteous meal made ready."

All of these taverns save Woodbridge's on the Green have gone, and for thirty-five years the survivor has not been a tavern. The ballroom on the second floor and the huge old kitchen have been divided into smaller rooms, the large front porch has disappeared, and the building is now a residence for several families.

Not far from Hartford are three Windsors, originally one town. In what became South Windsor stood Bissell's Tavern, now gone, near the ferry established in 1648 by John Bissell, the first ferry in Connecticut, and still in use, although now about a mile from the old location. Stoughton's, another old inn here, has been greatly remodeled, as has a tavern in Windsor Centre, and both are now private residences.

On the other side of the Connecticut River, the Fyler homestead, now the Betsy Kob Tea-room and a species of museum, owned by the Windsor Historical Society, merits a visit.

For services in the Pequot War, Sergeant Walter Fyler was granted an acre and a half in the Palisado, and built this house, consisting originally of "a parlor, parlor chamber, hall chamber, kitchen and lean-to." Fyler's grandson sold it out of the family, and it was at one time the post-office.

Palisado Green, on which the house faces, was at the beginning of the Pequot War enclosed by a palisade of high stakes, with a ditch outside. Here guard was constantly kept, but the Indians never attacked Windsor, it is believed because of kindness shown them by the first white settlers.

The little old house, set in an old-fashioned garden, shaded by venerable trees, is charming. Papered throughout with reproductions of old wall papers, it has many old fireplaces and wall cupboards; steep stairs lead to the half story above, and the entire house is filled with interesting old furniture.

Suffield is said to have had twelve thriving taverns. Only the Suffield House, now owned by the Suffield School, remains.

At Durham, north of New Haven by another route, is the Swathel Inn (1730), and at Middletown was an inn at which Washington is said to have stopped. The latter is now the property of the Berkeley Divinity School. Near Middletown, before 1792, a band of robbers had their retreat in caves in the mountains, and brought with them their wives and children, but "apparently committed no act of extraordinary ferocity."

Another road from New Haven, practically following an old one, passes through Naugatuck. In that section known as Union City, a short distance from the road, stands a very old house, dilapidated, only part of it occupied. At this, the Porter House, some say that Washington stopped, but there is no proof of it, although it may have harbored some Revolutionary Army officers. It is not certain that the house was ever an inn; it may have been what was known in colonial days as a "racon" tavern, meaning that, although a private residence, travelers might be accommodated, and on leaving, these paid "a reasonable reckoning."

Not far from Naugatuck, at Straitsville, stands the old tavern built in 1811 by Ahira Collins. Three doors across the front opened into the barroom, the "ladies' sitting-room," and two additional connecting parlors.

The old sign, with the name in gold letters on a blue

ELM STREET, AND HOME OF ISAAC LAWRENCE, CANAAN, CONNECTICUT

[*See page 62.*]

ground, used to hang across the street suspended from long poles by chains. Opposite the tavern, Collins kept a general store, with a bowling alley in the basement. The store is gone; the inn sign, bar and racks have been sold and removed. The tavern was not used as such after 1846, but although several times remodeled, the exterior is little changed.

The modern city of Waterbury has an old tavern not greatly changed externally, but long since divided into stores and offices. On the corner of Main and South Streets, this was a stage-stop. Some say that the building is more than one hundred years old, others that it is not more than seventy-five. On the second floor may be seen what was once a fine ballroom, with barreled ceiling, but now divided into small offices.

From Waterbury a side trip may be made to Litchfield, a charming old town, with many old houses modernized into summer homes. The road runs through Bethlehem, where in 1770, the diary of Miss Bethia Baldwin mentions "a very good racon tavern at Dr. Bellamy's." This gentleman was a leading theologian of his day, and regarded as wealthy, for he was said to be worth £1800.

Litchfield had many taverns, for it was an important stage stop, and to-day, off the railroad, is connected by buses with Torrington and Waterbury.

The original Phelps Tavern was the second house west of the present hotel. Built in 1782 by Joseph, son of Timothy Collins, a clergyman, it is now occupied by members of the Phelps family. The old portion of the present hotel was built in 1788 by David Buell. Its entire third floor was occupied by the ballroom where Lafayette was given a ball in 1824, and here dances used to be held by the students of Litchfield's famous early law school, attended by the girls from Miss Pierce's school. This room was very lofty, with a musicians' gallery. A bit of the barrel ceiling may still

[57]

be seen in some of the present bedrooms into which the ball-room has been divided.

This second tavern was originally three stories high, with an attic and flat roof, and the attic stairs are doubtless the old flight. Until one inspects these and some of the fireplaces, or goes into the cellar, there is little to suggest the house's age. But in the cellar is a huge fireplace with a Dutch oven, in what was evidently the old kitchen, and some of the beams and planks are so large that they indicate age.

The present kitchen and some small rear rooms look old, as does a fireplace with arched recesses on either side. In one recess a closet has been built, but hardly recently, for walls and ceiling are of very wide planks. A few of the doors still have their HL hinges. As this name for a hinge will appear frequently in these pages, those unfamiliar with its derivation may be interested to learn that the hinges take their name from Holy Lord, and were supposed to afford great protection against witches.

On North Street, built in 1760 for a residence by Elisha Sheldon, is a beautiful old house which his son converted into a tavern. It is now a fine summer home, but modernized so as to keep its old-time charm. During its tavern days, Washington was entertained here.

A house on the east side of South Street, built in 1780 by Benjamin Hanks, was a tavern until about 1820, and is now a residence; another, Grove Catlin's, later known as the Mansion House, on the corner of Main and South Streets, where now stands a drug store, was burned.

In 1791, a post once a week to Hartford was established from Litchfield, "a link on the Post Road from New York." Along this route are interesting old inns which will be mentioned later. A turnpike company was formed in 1797 to connect Litchfield and New Milford, and other companies followed, so that soon afterwards it was complained that one could not get out of Litchfield in any direction without passing through a toll-gate. (It seems to have been a popular game in those days to dodge toll-gates. Often by taking a detour over an unimproved road or private lane, this could be accomplished.)

Litchfield's very broad streets were, according to White's history of the town, for the convenience of cattle rather than for beauty, and originally were probably even wider. However, North, then Town Street, is not in direct line with South Street on the opposite side of the Green, because a fine old elm tree stood on the line and the townspeople preferred a jog to sacrificing the tree.

A tavern in Washington, south of Litchfield, the Coggs-well, although undoutedly old, has not been used as such for between seventy-five and one hundred years.

Halfway between Torrington and Litchfield, on the left, is a red house, once a tavern. Now a private residence, its purchaser had it carefully moved from the original site in Chestnut Hill, Connecticut, reassembled here, and painted its original color. He has a large collection of antiques, and it was this gentleman who bought the old sign and tap-room fittings of the Collins Tavern, Straitsville.

Returning to Waterbury, and turning west through Middlebury, Woodbury is near, on the main route from New Haven to Pittsfield. A broad, shady street widens at one side into a Village Green. Shortly before reaching this there stands on the left the Curtis House, three-storied, with an attic, broad verandas, and hardly suggesting an old tavern. But the southern end was built in 1754 by Anthony Stoddart, another preacher's son turned tavern-keeper. Its northern end was added fifty years later, according to a date inscribed in the chimney. On the second floor was a a ballroom, now altered into bedrooms; the third story was added by the present proprietor's father, and a large addition has been made on the north end. The office, one of the parlors on the north, and some of the upper rooms are old.

[59]

The fifth proprietor, a man named Hatch, was up on the roof mending it one day, when a neighbor, Beers, came by, and called out:

"There was a man whose name was Hatch, and he was very good to patch." Whereupon the other responded:

"There was a man whose name was Beers, and he deserved to lose his ears."

After these neighborly greetings, mending was resumed.

The Curtis House has had several names. When the present owner's father bought it in 1882, it was known as the Woodbury House. He restored the earlier name. Among articles of old furniture cherished here is a unique four-post bedstead, with a large eagle carved on its headboard.

Farther down the street there stood another old tavern, which was purchased a few years ago and removed, with each piece marked, to be set up on Long Island.

Danbury had its old inn, the Taylor Tavern, built in 1777, at the foot of what is now Main Street. It is gone, and only an old milestone remains, with the inscription:

67 miles to H. [Hartford]
69 to N. Y.
This Stone erected by H. M. Taylor
1787

Danbury has, however, a most interesting old tavern brought from Brookfield, Connecticut, where it had stood for some two hundred years on the old Post Road between New York and Hartford. This road later was little used, the tavern deserted and falling to ruin, when it was purchased and moved to its present site on Wooster Heights, Danbury.

Of the salt-box type, it has been rebuilt with its old fireplaces, stone chimneys, old floors and stairways. The old tap-room, an eighteen-inch rafter supporting its ceiling; the

[60]

# Inns from New York to Springfield

built-in bar, original money-till, etc., are all in place. The house was quite evidently originally built for a tavern, and an article in the Danbury *News* at the time it was brought there, pronounced it unique in the possession of "an eight-window front of twenty-four light windows," six-window fronts being the usual New England colonial type.

It contained ten rooms, including a large ballroom on the second floor, connected with the lower hall by a staircase with two landings. The old kitchen extends almost the entire length of the house in the rear, and many choice specimens of old furniture and ornaments may be admired. It is now a residence.

From Danbury, through charming country, one may motor to Ridgefield, with its old Cannon Ball Inn, now a summer residence with few exterior changes.

S. G. Goodrich (Peter Parley), whose father was pastor of the Ridgefield Congregational Church, in his *Recollections of a Lifetime,* says: "A few rods south of the meeting house there was a tavern, kept in my day by Squire Keeler. This institution ranked second only to the meeting house, for the tavern of those days was generally the center of news, and the gathering place for balls, musical entertainments, public shows, etc., and this particular tavern had special claims to notice. It was, in the first place, on the great thoroughfare of that day between Boston and New York"—Ridgefield and Danbury may be visted now on this other road—"and had become a general and favorite stopping place for travelers. It was, moreover, kept by a hearty old gentleman, who united in his single person the various functions of publican, postmaster, representative, justice of the peace, and I know not what else. He besides had a thrifty wife. . . .

"She loved her customers, especially members of Congress, governors and others in authority, who wore powder, and white-top boots, and who migrated to and fro in the lofty leisure of their own coaches. She was indeed a woman of mark, and her life has its moral. She scoured and scrubbed, and kept things going until she was seventy years old, at which time, during an epidemic, she was threatened with an attack. She, however, declared that she had not time to be sick, and so the disease passed her by.

"Besides all this, there was a historical interest attached to Keeler's Tavern, for deeply imbedded in the northeastern corner post there was a cannon ball, planted there during the famous fight with the British in 1777. It was one of the chief historical monuments of the town, and was visited by all curious travelers. . . . In the summer of 1804, I remember Jerome Bonaparte coming up to Keeler's Tavern with a coach and four, attended by his young wife, Miss Patterson of Baltimore. It was a gay establishment, and the honeymoon sat happily on the tall, sallow stripling and his young bride. The arrival of the brother of Napoleon . . . made a sensation."

The tavern is described by another author as "one of those quaint, old-fashioned shingle hostelries, many of which dotted the country." It faces south, has a hipped roof, and originally ended in a one-story extension at the rear, with a shed at right angles to the main building, for horses and vehicles.

From Hartford again, before continuing to Springfield, one may go to Canaan, almost in the extreme northwestern corner of the state, or this may be reached by a good road from Poughkeepsie, New York. Here is the Capt. I. Lawrence Tavern, now a private residence. On Canaan's broad, shady Elm Street, this old house is believed by its present owner, the great-great-granddaughter of the Captain, not to have been an inn for about seventy-five years. Captain Lawrence came to Canaan in 1738, and built the inn ten years later. The doorstone is the original one, and bears the following inscription:

[62]

# Inns from New York to Springfield

Isaac Lawrence came here June 2, 1738
Lydia Hewitt, his wife, November 1767, aged 60 **years**

| Sons | Daughters |
|---|---|
| Jonas | Azubah |
| Stephen | Ama |
| Isaac | Lydia |
| Asa | Hannah |
| William | |
| Elijah | |
| Solomon | |

This house, too, has a ballroom. Hawthorne wrote of the old tavern:

"It is odd to put a family record on a spot where it is sure to be trampled under foot."

On still another highway from New Haven is Meriden, with a fascinating old house now known as "Ye 1711 Club Inn." Its hipped roof will attract attention.

Samuel Goffe built it in 1711 for his residence, but the gentleman who bought it fifteen years ago accomplished a miracle of restoration. It had been used as a tenement for several families; its walls painted repeatedly, but everything then grimy and defaced, while cattle had been stabled in the old basement.

Now the walls are covered with reproductions of old wallpapers, one patterned from a paper at least one hundred years old, found in the Morse house at Cherry Valley, New York. Entering what is now one of the dining-rooms, one faces an old fireplace with cupboards filled with old china on either side. Several old strap-hinges, one HL, and a few hand-made nails have survived the tenants' rough usage.

The old cellars of the house are as when built; it would be almost impossible to change these massive walls. The basement kitchen, with great open fireplace and Dutch oven,

[63]

is now a grill room. On the second floor the rooms are little changed, save that two small ones have been thrown together to make a charming sitting-room. From this, a door opens on stairs, narrow, steep and worn, mounting beside the big original brick chimney to the old attic.

During the recent war, the house was used as a club by soldiers, and their names, starred with gold in the case of those afterwards killed, remain on the original rear outer wall, now within an added dining-room. The inn is at present open for the serving of meals only.

The Daughters of the American Revolution have established conclusively Washington's visit to this house in 1776.

CAPTAIN SAMUEL FORBUSH'S TAVERN, WESTBOROUGH, MASSACHUSETTS

[*See page* 71.

GARDEN, WAYSIDE INN, SUDBURY, MASSACHUSETTS

[*See page* 75.

BROOKFIELD INN, BROOKFIELD, MASSACHUSETTS

[See page 69.

## CHAPTER II

*From Springfield to Boston. Deerfield and Hadley*

ALTHOUGH there was no opposition to the opening of taverns in New England towns—in fact, the local authorities sometimes went to considerable trouble to find men able and willing to conduct them—landlords were none the less often bound by restriction which varied in severity with the location.

In Andover, for instance, tavern regulations in the year 1692 forbade the landlords to permit "playing at Dice, Cards, Tables, Quoits, Loggets, Bowls, Ninepins, Billiards, or any other unlawful Game or Games in his House, Yard, Garden or Backside, nor shall [he] suffer to be or remain in his House any person or persons not being of his own family upon Saturday night, after it is Dark, nor any time on the Sabbath Day or evening after the Sabbath."

When stage-coaches became plentiful and travel increased, there developed great rivalry between the different stage lines. Miss Crawford tells of two rival lines between Boston and Providence which carried on a cut-rate warfare quite like those of more recent railroad days.

The older line advertised that it would carry the first applicants for nothing, whereupon the newer line announced that it would not only carry passengers for nothing, but would furnish them with a dinner free. The older one then added a free bottle of wine with the dinner to its inducements, and before the two companies had made terms with each other, a party of gay youths spent the time between a

[65]

certain Tuesday and Saturday traveling back and forth between the two towns, eating dinners with free bottles of wine at the companies' expense.

The New England stage drivers were important persons in their day. Of one who had driven for years, and finally retired to the farm he owned, planning to live there quietly for the rest of his days, they tell the story that on his third day as a farmer, he saw the stage which he had so often driven pass his farm. He waved to it, and driver and passengers waved back. Hardly had the stage disappeared than he hurried back to the farm-house, packed his bag, and departed. By the end of the week he was once more at his old post, driving his old stage, and continued to do so for the rest of his life. When he died, it was said that he had driven *one hundred and thirty-five thousand miles.*[1]

The most frequently traveled route from Springfield to Boston follows, in part, three former roads: the Old Connecticut, the New Connecticut, and the Old Bay Path. The first ran from Boston, through Marlboro, Grafton, Oxford, and Springfield; the second turned west from the Old Road at Grafton, and continued through Worcester and Brookfield; the third left the Old Road at Wayland, running through Marlboro, Worcester, Oxford, and Brookfield to Ware, where another road, known as the Hadley Trail, led through Belchertown to Hadley.

Although the Old Connecticut road was established in 1639, for nearly one hundred years trade between Boston and western Massachusetts was largely by water, around Cape Cod, passing Saybrook Fort, "where it was wont to evade toll," and then by river to Windsor and Hartford.

In Springfield no old taverns survive. Parsons', which stood at the west end of Court Street, has come down to us by name only. A few miles west of Springfield is Westfield, where once were several taverns, three of which are now residences.

[1] *Old New England Inns,* Mary Caroline Crawford.

## From Springfield to Boston

Approaching the town from Springfield, the old Fowler Tavern, built about 1760, stands on the left, at the corner of Main and Noble Streets. Little of it save the outer walls remains, for it has been altered into apartments, its front porch and beautiful old doorway removed, the latter sold to the Metropolitan Museum of Art in New York City. The Museum, it is said, also wished to buy the fittings, panelings and so forth, of one of the lower rooms, but for some reason the offer was refused. General Rezique, a Hessian, was lodged as a prisoner of war in this old tavern in 1777.

Westfield's first tavern was opened in 1688 by Captain Aaron Cook, in the Little River District. On the north side of Court Street, about two miles from the center of the town, was Washington Tavern, now much altered into a private residence. On the south side of the same street, Holcomb House, now a residence for several families, was in olden days "a kind of tavern," where men used to gather for card games, being solemnly warned by the landlord that he would not tolerate gambling.

A tavern on the Green first kept by Mr. Goodenough, later by Joseph Morgan, was burned in 1833 at the time the Post Office also was destroyed. It stood on the old Boston and Albany Post Road. Gad Palmer's, replaced by a business block, was a favorite stopping place for Judges of the Supreme Court and their families.

Still farther west, on the Post Road, is the old town of Blandford, originally known as Glasgow. Sumner Gilbert Wood has written a book on the taverns of this township alone, and he describes an amazing number, beginning with Pixley's (1733) "on the great road leading to Housatunock." Levi Pease, who will be mentioned again in Shrewsbury, had a corner tavern in Blandford.

By 1784, Mr. Wood tells, there were "at least seventeen licensed inns" here, while Springfield in the same year had thirty. Although none survive in Blandford as inns, a few remain, altered into private residences. For reference, the taverns mentioned by Mr. Wood are included in the index.

Traveling from Springfield to Boston, the sleepy little village of Wilbraham is soon reached, but the Washington tavern here has long been a private residence.

The old inn fronting directly on the highroad at West Brookfield will tempt one to linger. Built in 1760 by David Hitchcock, he was its landlord for fifteen years. The old tap-room, now a dining-room, has a large fireplace, around which it is not difficult to imagine jolly souls gathered, with pipe and bowl, before a cheerful fire. Over the fireplace is the following inscription, also found in the Elm Tree Inn at Farmington, Connecticut:

"Whoe'er has traveled life's dull round,
　Where'er his stages may have been
　May sigh to think he still has found
　His warmest welcome at an inn."

The original, with additional verses, was written by William Shenstone, who lived near the White Swan at Henley-in-Arden, and this stanza is scratched with a diamond on a window-pane in the English inn.

Large beams in the tap-room ceiling offer additional testimony to the age of the house. Curious five-paned transoms are set above shelves forming the tops of the double doors opening from this room into the hall, with a second front door. Opposite the tap-room is the old parlor, whose fireplace has another inscription:

"There is no private house in which people can enjoy themselves so well as at a capital tavern."

Beside the fireplace are two old wall-cupboards.

In the hall are the stairs to the second story, and here is the bedroom where Washington slept, when in 1789 he visited the inn. An engraving of our First President hangs above a writing desk almost old enough to have been used by him, and close by is a silhouette of Martha Washington. She has a severe expression, while her husband's pose, with hand slightly extended, drolly suggests that he might be making a conciliatory explanation to the lady. Could he have been giving reasons why he spent so many nights away from home, in taverns all over the country?

In the adjoining bedroom to the south, Lafayette is believed to have slept, when he came here in 1824. Downstairs, in what is now the office, across the entry from the tap-room, Washington dined.

The Constitution of Massachusetts is said to have been signed in this West Brookfield Inn. President John Adams visited it in 1799, Jerome Bonaparte and his bride were guests, while a Minister from the Netherlands was taken ill here, died, and was buried in the West Brookfield graveyard. On West Brookfield Plain was held in 1784 the first celebration of independence in this section, when an ox was roasted whole, with hoofs and horns, and served to those celebrating, with "plenty of rum and water."

Farther east, on the opposite side of the road, is the Brookfield Inn, the oldest part of which dates from 1771. Although numerous additions have been made, much of the old-time charm remains, and the present proprietor has filled it with antiques of great beauty and value, many of them having been brought from England.

On the present site of the old inn there may have stood an older tavern, visited, as told in a local history, by the unfortunate Spooner on the night that his wife, with the aid of three ex-soldiers, murdered him when he returned to the farmhouse about a quarter of a mile away. The four threw his body into a well, but it was discovered, all of the murderers arrested and hanged, with none of the delays of modern murder trials. Rice's is also mentioned as an early Brookfield stage inn.

East Brookfield was, until comparatively recently, part of the old settlement from which North and West Brookfield are also offshoots. Here in 1800 were Wait's and Thomas Ball's Taverns, but nothing of them now remains.

Worcester had its old inn, the Exchange, office of Pease's stage line, and here Washington stopped on his tour of New England, but this inn too has disappeared.

Shrewsbury once had several inns. The present highroad is about a mile north of the old one. At the corner of Grafton Street and the old highroad, just beyond the Post Office, stands what was the Harrington Tavern. In spite of alterations, traces of the old building remain, although the old porch and doorway were removed when the driveway in front, where stages used to dash up, was leveled into a lawn. The chimney with fireplaces on all four sides, once occupying the center of the hall, has been removed; what was a ballroom is now a storeroom; but the old stable, with its double row of stalls, is as it was in tavern days.

Shrewsbury was settled in 1727, and the first landlord of Harrington's was one of the earliest settlers. His home down the road and one other house near by were the oldest in the settlement. Opposite the tavern used to stand the old Universalist Meeting House, to which people drove from twenty miles away to attend the service.

# From Springfield to Boston

In time another tavern, the Old Arcade, was opened half a mile from Harrington's, but the landlord of the older one did not care for competition, so he bought out his rival, and after but a short life as an inn, the Old Arcade became a residence, as it is to-day.

Farrar's Tavern, kept by Major John Farrar and later by Captain Pease, who opened the first regular stage line between Boston and Hartford, and Baldwin's, in which house Artemas Ward was born, have long since disappeared.

Off the direct route to Boston, but not far from Shrewsbury, is the old town of Westborough. Here the buildings of several old taverns survive, although they are no longer open for entertainment purposes.

At 1108 Main Street stands what was the Blue Anchor, built in 1681 for his second wife by Thomas Rice, head of a little group of wealthy, titled Englishmen who in 1638 had settled Sudbury. In this house, the settlers took refuge when danger threatened. To the original one-story building Rice added a second story, making the house, according to Dr. Charles E. Reed, a Westborough resident who has made an extensive study of his town and its vicinity, one of the earliest two-story houses in America. In 1820 the Blue Anchor was removed or rebuilt on its present site, when Rice built himself a new house.

Indian trails north of Cape Cod centered in Westborough, and either the Old Connecticut or the Bay Path was probably blazed by John Oldham, when, soon after the landing of the Pilgrims, he journeyed from the Massachusetts Bay settlement into Connecticut. This trail passed through Westborough.

The Amsden Gale Tavern on East Main Street, near the Southborough line, was a noted Westborough house, now a residence. Jacob Amsden's mother was the daughter of one of Sudbury's settlers. When Jacob married, in 1719, he was given a tract of land, and built the house on the trail from Wayland, Massachusetts into Connecticut. It has been written of him that "Jacob was an aristocrat," and his tavern became the meeting place of the neighborhood gentry; all the noted men of the day being entertained here. "His cellar was specially built to maintain an even temperature for the imported viands reserved for the entertainment of the King's officials."

He had two daughters, whom Judge Samuel Sewall, a frequent visitor at the house, declared to be "among the most beautiful women in America." The younger married Abijah Gale, and at her parents' death, inherited the tavern.

The Westborough Minute Men made the Gale Tavern their rendezvous when the Revolution broke out, and there the captain trained his company. At the Powder Alarm, in September, 1774, the men were ready, and before daybreak seventy-two of them left the tavern and went down the old trail to meet the British at Concord. Even the aged landlord would not be left behind, but shouldered his musket and went along.

When Samuel Forbush married, in 1699, he at once opened a tavern at the corner of the present Lyman Street and the turnpike. For many years stages stopped at this house, and it was especially prosperous after the Boston and Worcester turnpike was opened, and until the railroad was built. In 1832, it passed to a descendant of the Howe family, famous tavern-keepers, and is now a residence, its old ballroom having been made into bedrooms. Externally, however, the appearance is that of the taverns of its day; a long, low building with a veranda across the front, set sufficiently back from the road to permit a sweeping driveway up to the entrance. The eastern part of the house is the oldest, and between 1702 and 1713 it was a garrison house. It is built on the same general plan as that of the Blue Anchor.

South of Westborough, in Woodville, was another Revo-

WAYSIDE INN, SUDBURY, MASSACHUSETTS

[See page 75.

KITCHEN, WAYSIDE INN

[*See page* 75.

THE TAP-ROOM, WAYSIDE INN

[*See page* 75.

THE LAFAYETTE ROOM, WAYSIDE INN

[*See page* 75.

lutionary tavern. Abner Newton of Southborough, whose father kept the Blue Anchor, married Vashti Eager, daughter of the Northboro tavern-keeper. Abner succeeded his father, and in 1732 built a two-story tavern in Woodville, which he and his wife ran successfully until his death. His widow and sons continued the business, and then Vashti married Benjamin Wood of Woodville, son of another tavern-keeper. The house kept by her and her second husband soon became famous, and during the Revolution was a center of anti-royalist feeling. Patriotic leaders frequently met here, and Benjamin Wood used to surround the house with his men, that no Whig might pass through. Later, the tavern was known as the Coolidge, and although it had not been used as an inn for years, it stood until 1909.

From Shrewsbury the direct route runs to Northboro. Martin's Tavern is mentioned as a stage stop in Northboro at an early date.

Captain James Eager married in 1713 Tabitha, daughter of Thomas Howe, tavern-keeper of Marlboro. Her sister married the second Abraham Williams of the latter place. Captain Eager built the first house between Marlboro and Worcester on the old Post Road, and near the center of Northboro. Here he and his wife opened a tavern. The captain became prominent in town affairs, was chosen first representative from Westborough to the General Court, and when Westborough and Northboro were divided, he gave land for the meeting-house. His house no longer stands.

In Marlboro is the very old Williams Tavern, now open during the summer season only. Although there have been many additions, something of an old structure remains, but it can not justify the claim of being the "oldest in the United States."

There was a tavern where the present Williams House now stands, as early as 1662, built by Lieutenant Abraham Williams, and licensed in 1663, the first tavern in the neigh-

[73]

borhood for "feeding man and beast." It was well patronized until 1676, when it was destroyed by fire during an Indian raid. The proprietor built another house on the same
site, and called it the Williams Tavern, but Dr. Reed believes
that nothing of the present building existed earlier than
1820.

Abraham's son died before his father, but the grandson
took over the tavern management as soon as he was of age,
and, as Colonel Abraham Williams, was a distinguished citizen of Marlboro. He was a Royal Magistrate, held many
town offices, and was Colonel of the Third Regiment, the
First and Second being commanded by his son-in-law,
Cyprian Howe, of the Black Horse Tavern, and Artemas
Ward of Shrewsbury.

The Howe family has been mentioned as one of noted
landlords. Colonel Abraham's wife, Prudence Howe,
daughter of a famous landlord and soldier of Marlboro, was
a cousin of David Howe, landlord of the Red Horse in Sudbury. Prudence's sister, Tabitha, married the Northboro
tavern-keeper, and her niece was the Vashti Eager already
mentioned.

Colonel Abraham was succeeded by his son, George, who
kept the tavern until 1803. After that it was known as the
Gates House, but the old name was restored a few years
ago, and the present proprietor is a Williams.

When, in 1772, stages began running between New York
and Boston, the second stage line in America, the Williams
Tavern was one of the three stage stops between Boston and
Worcester. In its early days, the large front room was used
as a court. Of course Washington dined here, on October
23, 1789, and de la Rochefoucauld was another distinguished
guest.

The present building, with three stories and an attic, has
a few of the old doors and fireplaces. The old stable in the

rear has been made into a large ballroom, with great rafters across its ceiling.

So much has been written about the Wayside Inn, Sudbury, that most of my readers are familiar with its general appearance. Before Mr. Ford bought it, it had been a kind of show place, with an admission charge, but it has now returned to its early function, and the owner delights in filling it with the furniture and fittings of its original period. Once more the inn has an old-fashioned flower garden.

The present house, with its many old fireplaces, is believed to be not older than one hundred and six years, but an inn stood here earlier than 1820, for Sudbury is one of the oldest towns in Massachusetts. In 1661, John Howe bought the Red Horse Inn, which was kept by his grandson, David. John Howe kept the Black Horse at Marlboro, which no longer stands. Longfellow speaks in his diary of driving with Fields to the old Red Horse Tavern in Sudbury, "alas, no longer an inn." The name Wayside was, of course, given it after the appearance of Longfellow's poem.

Wayland, with broad, shady streets, was once an important stage halt, but few people linger here now. On a branch railroad, with infrequent trains, its old inn, first known as the Pequod, later the Wayland, stands at the crossroads in the heart of the village. It was open in the summer of 1925, but by October had been given up, and stood vacant.

Continuing to Boston by way of Arlington, here stands, remodeled, the oldest portion torn down, what was the venerable Tuffts' Tavern, or more recently, Russell Hotel. Its exact age is not known, but Mr. Charles S. Parker, in his *Arlington Past and Present*, states that James Cutler was innkeeper here in 1734, and was succeeded by his son William. William's daughter, Rebecca, married John Tuffts, and on the memorable April 19th, 1775, he was landlord of

[75]

the house known as Tuffts' Tavern. It stood on Massachusetts Avenue, in the path of the British march to Concord, and the present house is on the original site.

At Ware, between North Wilbraham and West Brookfield, an automobile road practically follows the old Hadley Trail, through Amherst, where a hotel, the Amherst Inn, was built in 1857 on the site of an old inn. During stage-coach days, an inn or tavern could be found every ten or fifteen miles in this part of the country. About 1745, Ebenezer Pomeroy built a house in that part of Hadley known as Hochanum. A few years later this became the White Horse Inn, and is now a farmhouse, with the original low-ceiled rooms, and some of the old inn furniture.

In Florence, on this same road, Solomon, second son of Joseph Warner, the town's first settler, and his wife, Florence, built a house in 1812, near the town limits. He kept this as a tavern for nearly forty years, until the railroad practically abolished stage travel. After his death it became a farmhouse, and is now rented to tenants employed on the farm, which is now owned by the Federal Government. Veterans' Hospital No. 95 is located in the woods on the place.

From Amherst, another route takes one to Deerfield, where Frary's Tavern, now a residence, still stands. The oldest part of the house dates from 1669, the rest was added in 1748, when it was opened as a tavern. Benedict Arnold halted here on his way to Ticonderoga, in the early days of the Revolution, *but there is no record that Washington ever stopped here!* This fact deserves mention as being unique in the history of our old taverns. It is now occupied by a descendant of the Frary family.

## Chapter III

### *Taverns In and Near Boston*

ONE IS SORELY TEMPTED to dwell at length on the old Massachusetts taverns, and the many quaint restrictions and orders issued by the selectmen when they agreed that such taverns might be opened. Since, as has been said, these taverns were usually located near the meeting-houses, that the weary worshipers, chilled during long winter services and perhaps almost equally dis-comforted during hot summer days, might later seek rest and refreshment in the tavern bar or parlor, one notes with interest the subjects of some of the sermons which the con-gregations heard before leaving the meeting-house.

What shall be said to such sermons as "An Arrow against Profane and Promiscuous Dancing. Drawn out of the Quiver of the Scriptures," delivered in Hingham's noted Old Ship Church? Or, "The Unloveliness of Love-Locks, or a summarie Discourse proving the wearing and nourishing of a Love Lock to be altogether unseemly and unlawful unto Christians, with some passages out of the Fathers against Face Painting"?

Miss Elizabeth H. Russell, who quotes these titles in her interesting brochure on the Old Ordinary at Hingham, which will be described later, is also responsible for the following directions as to the conduct of this old inn, taken from an old document. This document, made out in 1702 by the select-men of Hingham, "gave Landlord Andrews permission to sell 'Strong Waters on Broad Cove Lane,' provided he sent

[77]

his customers home at reasonable hours, with ability to keep their legs."

As to the "strong waters" which Mr. Andrews sold, Miss Russell cites some of these: "Metheglin, Calibogris, Canstantia, Kill-Devil, Rumbullion, Alicanti, Spiced Syder, Switchel, Mumbo and Ebulum."

None of Boston's many old taverns survive, although the present Adams House is on the site of one, the Lamb; and a tablet commemorates another, the Green Dragon, a famous meeting place of the patriots.

Boston's inns have been described in several books and many magazine articles, from the earliest, Cole's, later known as Hancock's, probably opened in 1634, and Hudson's (1640), down through many with picturesque names such as the Blue Anchor, Liberty Tree, Oliver Cromwell's Head, the Royal Exchange, popular with British soldiers, and so forth, to what must be called the newest of her old inns, the Lafayette Hotel, finished in 1824, just in time to do honor to the great Frenchman. Later, this was known as the Brigham Hotel.

From Boston, one may take short trips to a number of interesting old inns or taverns. Particularly famous are those of Lexington and Concord.

Were it not for the charming colonial houses still lining its beautifully shaded streets, and its historic Green, Lexington would be a truly modern town. Before reaching the Green, where the Colonials gathered to harass the British retreating from Concord, there stands on the left of the old stage road, now the motor road from Cambridge, the historic Munroe Tavern.

Built in 1695, it was open as a tavern until 1858, and except between 1730 and 1770, remained in the family of the original owners until 1911, when its owner generously deeded it to the Historical Society of Lexington, in the name of his deceased brother and himself. It is now a museum.

## Taverns In and Near Boston

Owing to years of use as a private residence, the original building has been somewhat changed, but the main part is intact.  A long addition was built before the Revolution, with a store on the ground floor, kept by the landlord; above this was a dance hall, with one of those partitions often found in old inns, which could be raised or lowered according to the size of room desired.  In this dance hall, rows of beds used to be set up when a large number of drovers

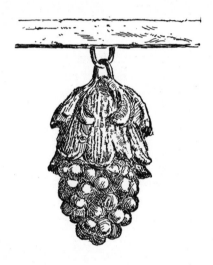

visited the tavern, for this was a drovers' inn, and they were its chief patrons, coming from New Hampshire, Vermont, and even the Canadian boundary.  When the inn became a private residence, this wing was torn down.

The first Munro (as the name was then written) to come to this country, had been taken prisoner by Cromwell's men at the Battle of Worcester.  He was deported to Boston, and in about 1660 settled in Lexington, then known as Cambridge Farms, built himself a house, and is first mentioned in the town chronicles as having been fined for failing to put rings in the noses of his swine.  His son William built the tavern, and obtained his license in 1696.  It is listed in old

[79]

almanacs as being on the stage route from Charlestown to New Hampshire. William's great-grandson, who deeded the tavern to the Society, remembered seeing the long lines of drovers' pungs, coming in on winter nights, and in summer, the progress of herds going toward Boston which might be followed by the clouds of dust they stirred up. In his boyhood, a night's lodging, with supper and breakfast, cost twenty-five cents.

"One hundred horses could be stabled in the barns, and two or three hundred cattle could graze around the tavern," the custodian's narrative informs one, and she got her information from a granddaughter of the tavern's builder and first landlord, who lived to be a very old lady. "There were pens for the sheep, and turkeys, driven in flocks through the roads to the Boston markets just before Thanksgiving, would roost in the trees, and on the tavern and its outbuildings—if the farmers were fortunate enough to make the tavern before sunset—if not, they roosted somewhere up the road, compelling the drivers to go back for them in the morning."

The old sign which hung outside in 1775, and on the day when Washington visited the tavern, is now preserved inside the house.

The old dining-room is now known as the Earl Percy Room, from the portrait of that nobleman, a copy of the one presented to the city of Lexington in 1878 by the Duke of Northumberland. The hand-made bricks in the fireplace are the originals, although relaid when a furnace was installed in the house. All of the rooms are furnished either with pieces belonging here, or with others of colonial and Revolutionary days. There are tables, chairs, a four-post bed belonging to the first Mrs. Munro to live here; a Sheraton desk belonging to Colonel Munroe, grandson of the builder, and the uniform which he wore as a colonel of the militia, after the Revolution; chests, china, pictures and mirrors, all meriting close inspection. The Colonel was first

MUNROE TAVERN, LEXINGTON, MASSACHUSETTS

[*See page* 78.

INTERIOR, MUNROE TAVERN

[*See page* 78.

BUCKMAN TAVERN, LEXINGTON, MASSACHUSETTS

[See page 83.

OLD TAP-ROOM, WRIGHT HOUSE, CONCORD, MASSACHUSETTS

[See page 84.

THE OLD ORDINARY (1650), HINGHAM, MASSACHUSETTS

[*See page* 86.

THE KITCHEN, THE OLD ORDINARY, HINGHAM, MASSACHUSETTS

[*See page* 86.

YE OLDE BURNHAM INN, IPSWICH, MASSACHUSETTS

*[See page* 87.

FIREPLACE, YE OLDE BURNHAM INN

*[See page* 87.

Master of the Hiram Masonic Lodge, organized in this dining-room. When the floor was taken up, the top boards were found to measure twenty-two inches, and the sub-floor was as well matched as the upper. Behind the dining-room is "the Munros' little new sitting room," its woodwork almost all hand-tooled, probably added about 1770.

In the old barroom is the original fireplace; the center beam of the ceiling is the original, with adze marks along its entire length. Behind the barroom was the first kitchen, made into a dining-room after the house ceased to be a tavern. The old fireplace and brick oven were then walled up, a shed converted into the present kitchen, and the old front door then or later moved to the rear.

The front entry and staircase, and all of the upstairs floors are the originals.

After the death of the first owner, the inn passed to his daughter, and her son sold it out of the family. In 1770, Colonel William Munroe (the name was then written with the e) bought it back, and was landlord until 1820, when his son Josias succeeded him, continuing until 1858. Then the house ceased to be a tavern, for William Munroe rented it, reserving one or two rooms for himself. Nine years after his death, his brother, James S. Munroe, deeded the property to the Historical Society.

Stirring days has the old house witnessed. After the skirmish at Concord, Earl Percy, arriving with reënforcements for the British, met them retreating. Forming a hollow square, and posting two cannon, he held back the Minute Men long enough to bring his wounded into the tavern, where he remained for an hour or so.

Tradition in the family says that Mrs. Munroe buried the family silver under an old oak tree on the hill behind the tavern, then with her three children left the house, and hid until the British had gone. She had baked bread that morning, which the soldiers ate, but fortunately she arrived home

[81]

again in time to extinguish the fire they had started in the old barroom, after using it as a dressing station. Of the seventy-seven Minute Men who faced the British in Lexington on that memorable day, sixteen were Munroes.

In the bedroom upstairs now known as the Washington Room, the General dined. Washington came in his own coach, with two secretaries and six servants, on November 5th, 1789, returning from New Hampshire. The very chair in which he sat, the hatrack on which he hung his hat, are shown. Colonel Munroe stood behind Washington's chair, and served the guests, his daughters carrying away the dishes and washing them.

Those wishing to inspect the house carefully may see in the cellar the foundation arch of hand-made bricks and stone, and an old closet door with hinges attached by hand-made nails. In the attic is another of these HL hinges; the chimney is of bricks made in the town in 1694, originally joined with mud mortar. The floors and most of the roof timbers are the original white pine, and some of the old wooden pins with which they were put together still remain.

Mrs. Mary Munroe Sanderson, during the thrilling days of April, 1775, lived next door in a house which was five or six years older than the tavern. She was probably a sister to the tavern-keeper. Miss Batcheller tells that "when her husband heard that the British were coming, he took her across the marshes to her father's on Woburn road. When he brought her back at night they found a British soldier left in the house, who was too sick for the British to take with them. She also found that they had killed her cow. She said she would not feed the soldier. They told her she must. So she did. She said 'I gae him enough to eat, but gae him a deevilish honing with it.' He would not eat anything until some of the family had tasted it; he was afraid she would poison him." Mrs. Sanderson lived to be one hundred and four years old, and Miss Batcheller further relates that "as late as when 103, she would tell this in her Scotch dialect to visitors who called on her at her home in East Lexington, to hear her tell her story of April 19th."

A little farther along the road, on the opposite side, stands the old Buckman, Lexington's "aristocratic" tavern. There was a house on this site as early as 1690, for it was mentioned when the lot was bought then by Benjamin Muzzy. In 1794, Rufus Merriam opened a tavern here, which continued as such until between 1815 and 1820. After that, although Merriam's descendants lived in the house for four generations, it was not again a tavern.

The old tap-room of the Buckman is just as it was in the old days. Above a huge fireplace is a small square opening, accidentally discovered, for it had been bricked up, and in it was found an old pipe, so it is thought that the niche served as a receptacle for the pipes of the Minute Men, who frequented this tavern also. In this fireplace, chains attached to green wood staples held pots and kettles. The staples must sometimes have burned through, letting the utensils fall, with unpleasant consequences to those near the fire.

Behind the tap-room, with its original bar, is the kitchen. These two rooms, with an entry, formed the first floor of the original house. The old front door is now kept inside. Despite its two thicknesses of wood, one of oak, the other of pine, a British bullet pierced it, and the hole can be seen. The kitchen has the huge rafters and solid flooring of its day, and the ceiling is quite unique; whitewashed, then covered with a herring-bone pattern in dark brown paint or stain.

From the kitchen, a flight of stairs, now closed, used to descend to the cellar. A small door opened into the tap-room, behind the bar, so that fresh supplies of liquor brought up from the cellar might be pushed through without extra effort.

In the small entry hangs a framed fragment of the paper

[83]

which in 1819 covered its walls; a curious and rare French design in black and white. The Historical Society now owning the tavern hopes some day to rehang the walls with a reproduction of the old paper.

Upstairs are the original large bedroom, and small connecting one. Later, two parlors were added downstairs, with two rooms above, which could be thrown into one for a ballroom. Partition and folding doors have now been removed. A third story also was added by raising the roof, and this is reached by a curious hanging stairway.

Interesting old furniture, a collection of gay, paper-covered bandboxes, a musket used in the Indian wars, and another which belonged to a British soldier at Lexington; a British red coat of homespun, the color still brilliant, are some of the articles preserved here. There is also a curious old powder horn, with the date, 1774, the initials of the original Yankee soldier owner, and: "Horn, we will strike together," in raised letters on it. Falling into the hands of a British soldier, he added: "Ye d——d Rebel did."

A ground-floor room here served as Lexington's first Post Office, but partitions and boxes have long since been removed. It was in the Buckman Tavern that the following recipe for flip was given:

"Fill a quart mug or cup three quarters full of bitter beer; add 4 tablespoons of cream and sugar mixed; 1 gill of rum or gin, and into this mixture plunge a hot iron to warm it." Other similar recipes for this strange drink are given, and one informant added that the iron gave it a slightly scorched taste.

The oldest existing tavern in Concord, the Wright House, was opened by Ephraim Jones, captain in the militia, in 1747. In 1751, Thomas Munroe became landlord.

Tap-room, dining-room, parlor and some of the other rooms are much as they were in olden days, their walls covered with reproductions of the old papers. The very bar that Major Pitcairn thumped, as he drank his brandy—or stirred his punch with bloody finger; whichever version is preferred—and vowed that he would "stir the Yankee blood this day" has been preserved. The tavern was headquarters for the British on April 19th, 1775, when the *skirmish* occurred. (Old residents of Concord and Lexington consider the word battle too pretentious.)

In the old parlor is one of the first pianos made by Chickering, and two pairs of andirons with the date, 1741. The rooms have the low ceilings, heavy beams and wall-cupboards of the early days when the house was built. The floors in the present office, dining-room and tap-room are all the original broad planks, fastened to the supporting beams beneath with hand-made nails. From the narrow hallway, a narrow staircase leads to the second story, where are large, low rooms which modern improvements can not rob of their old-time charm. *Of course*, Lafayette slept here, when he visited Concord in 1820. In the old dining-room Washington was entertained on his farewell tour of New England.

Quaint framed sentiments hang on the walls.

"The legend says that in this house the silver of the church
Was hidden in a keg of soap away from British search.
Certain it is her ancient creed so guarded sacred things
That to her solemn verity, no soft soap ever slings."

and:

"One John Brown once kept the Tavern Wright, and a brave man
was he,
For in the Boston tea party he helped to pour the tea.
This fact is chiseled on his grave, and gravestones never lie,
But always speak the living truth, just as do you and I."

The Colonial Inn in Concord, although modern in ap-
[85]

pearance, is really composed of three old houses grouped into one. In 1775, arms were hidden in one of the three.

Billerica, visited by Washington on his way to the Munroe Tavern, had four old inns during stage-coach days. The buildings are standing, but they have not in years been inns. Woburn, too, had its Winn House, where Washington stopped, and on this same trip he visited Andover, stopping at Abbott's Tavern. From Woburn, it is not far to Winchester, but the Black Horse there was torn down in the early part of this century. The oldest house in Easton, not far from Brockton, is still standing, and was once an inn. Bedford had the David Reed Tavern, burned several years ago, and replaced by a modern residence.

South from Boston, the Arnold Tavern stood in Weymouth until about three years ago, when it was torn down and the Post Office built on the site. Turning east, one may visit the Old Ordinary at Hingham.

The land on which it stands was granted to Joseph Andrews when the town was settled in 1635, and the main part of the building was put up by either him or his son. The old sign which again hangs outside, since the Hingham Historical Society acquired the property, bears the date, 1650, and the words: Old Ordinary.

Entering a narrow hall, there are large rooms on either side, the old dining-room, filled with fine old furniture, pewter, and so forth; a parlor, with the tap-room behind it, also appropriately furnished. Some old framed stage-coach bills give the schedule between Boston and Hingham, which line was owned by Mr. Wilder, one of this tavern's best known hosts. There is the typical large, low kitchen, and many specimens of the wooden ware for the manufacture of which Hingham was noted in early days.

Upstairs in the bedrooms are other interesting pieces of furniture, dolls, quilts, and so on. A narrow flight of stairs takes one to the attic, where the early roof, enclosed within a newer, larger one, may be seen. This inn did such a good business that it had to be enlarged.

None of Salem's old inns remain. From here one may turn off for Marblehead, quaintest of towns, first known as Marble Harbor, from the "marble stone" on both sides of the harbor. Here, in a cove, the ship *Desire* was built, the third in the Massachusetts colony.

In 1631, Isaac Allerton established a fishing station, and Marblehead fishermen soon had a reputation for hard drinking, while for a long time the Plymouth colonists complained that they were "too remiss" to have a church. On the grounds of the very old house almost opposite Oakum Cove, owned by the Misses Scott, Captain Kidd is said to have built himself a shanty, and in this cove other pirates, after first murdering all her shipmates, brought ashore and finally murdered a Spanish lady. For many years, Marblehead residents declared that on the anniversary of her death her screams might be heard.

The Old Tavern still stands close to the street following the shore, but has long been a private dwelling. The first stages between Marblehead and Boston were running in 1868, but the other early inns were probably mere drinking places, for at the time of Washington's visit in 1789 the town felt that it was too poor to entertain the President suitably.

Ipswich had many old inns, one of which survives, but so altered into a private residence as to be unrecognizable. Some have said that an old house standing near the railway station, part of which is now a museum, was an inn, but the writer has found no records to that effect. An inn and tea-room was, however, opened a few years ago in the very ancient house known here in Ipswich as the Burnham house.

This was built by Thomas Hart, yeoman, a tanner by trade, who came from England. In the town records for 1639 is: "Granted to Samuel Boreman one house lott one

[87]

aker a quarter of ground lying at the west end of the town having a house lott of Thomas Hartes on the west."

Hart probably built the house about 1640, and he and his family occupied it until 1755. In 1902 it was bought by Mr. Ralph W. Burnham, who made many changes in harmony with the old style, even purchasing another old Ipswich house and using its timbers to build the rooms that are now used as the tea-room and bedrooms of the inn. All the rafters used are old.

In 1920 it was purchased by the present owner, and opened as an inn.

From the tea-room, one enters the old kitchen, now a living-room, with a fireplace measuring nine feet across, and one of the earliest types of oven. An old clock in the corner, reaching to the ceiling, was built for this room in 1773 by Richard Manning of Ipswich.

At the other end of the room a door opens into a small entry, with the old front door, hand-made lock, huge key and hinges still in place. A short flight of steps leads down to the old parlor, paneled in pumpkin pine, with hand-hewn joists supporting the ceiling, one of these measuring sixteen and one half inches in width. Here, too, is a large old fireplace, the mantel carved in the dentil pattern, and on the cupboard door beside it are unusual "frog-leg" hinges. There is also a "night-cap" closet. This room was selected by the Metropolitan Museum in New York City as a perfect specimen of seventeenth-century architecture, and was reproduced for the Museum's American Wing.

Another short flight of stairs leads from the little entry to a large chamber above, where a bit of the inner wall has been removed to show the outer, arrow-proof wall. This wall is built of Ipswich bricks that were made of clay from the adjoining swamps, mixed with powdered clamshells and chopped salt-marsh hay. The walls of this room were plastered in about 1700. Here is another high, arched fireplace, and across the ceiling runs a huge beam which some early occupant found too low for his comfort. He therefore removed a section several inches thick from the lower side, which later was replaced again, but the joining can plainly be seen. In one of these upper rooms is a beam twenty-nine feet long.

An odd feature of the house is that, although apparently only one and a half stories high, there are five different

levels within, probably marking various additions to the original house.

In Gloucester the Ellery House, built for a parsonage in 1704, was opened as an inn thirty years later by James Stevens. Two years later he sold it to Captain Ellery, by whose name the inn was long known. The first Gloucester tavern whose location is known, it was for several years the meeting place of the selectmen, when they transacted the town's business. On "general training" days, it was patronized by the militia.

A Gloucester resident furnishes this item: "In 1749, the expenses of the town fathers at Captain Ellery's tavern ran up as high as £78, and the expense of a single meeting at the time of Mr. Stevens' occupancy was £3 18 sh. 2d for licker."

The house is now a private residence, occupied by a descendant of the Ellery family.

Groton had its old inn, first opened as an ordinary by Captain Jonathan Keep—the name ordinary is seldom used in New England—and when its first landlord proclaimed it a "temperance house," there was much grumbling. Later it was kept by three sisters, the Misses Hoar. Two rooms could be thrown into one by sliding up a partition, when space was needed for dances. Masons also held their meetings here. Later, the Central House was built on the site, and still later, the Groton Inn.

Last of Massachusetts inns to be mentioned is one in Newburyport, Wolfe's Tavern, which existed early in colonial days, for it was bought in 1743 by William Davenport and used as a private residence by him until 1762. Then he opened it as a tavern, hanging up a signboard with a picture of General Wolfe, under whom he had served when, as a captain, he had gone to the General's aid in Quebec.

Among this tavern's distinguished guests were the Marquis de Chastellux, Baron de Talleyrand, M. de Verdreuil, and M. Lynch de Montesquieu. De Chastellux wrote of the house as being "a mile from town." It was burned in 1807, while kept by Prince Stetson, who then removed to Salem. Benjamin Hale hung the old sign outside his tavern at the corner of State and Harris Streets, but after a few years, Stetson returned from Salem and took over the Washington House in Newburyport. The present Wolfe House is neither the original building, nor does it stand on the old site. None of Newburyport's many other old taverns remain.

## CHAPTER IV

*Another Route from New York to New Haven, and on to Rhode Island*

THE POST ROAD, after crossing King's Bridge, New York, branched from the Boston Post Road, and continued to Scarsdale. Here, a few feet below the present road level, stands a quaint, long, low building, the Wayside Inn, Scarsdale's oldest house, now the home of its Woman's Club. Although the exact date of its erection is not known, a house is first mentioned in the various transfers of the property in 1729. Probably this house, with alterations and additions, is the present club building. In 1765 it became the property of James Varian, who, after serving in the Revolution, returned home a cripple. His son, Jonathan, born in this house, distinguished himself in the War of 1812. The Varians are the first known innkeepers here. During the Revolution, Colonel Rufus Putnam of Washington's staff visited the Wayside Inn on a spying expedition, reporting that a party of Whigs in the tavern had declared that the British Army was not far away.

The story goes that when the British arrived, the owner of the Wayside Inn hid his two most cherished possessions, his Bible and his cow, in the cellar.

President MacCracken of Vassar says that one summer, when a child, he and his brother spent much time in picking old bullets out of the inn's shingle roof.

After Mr. Charles Butler bought the house in 1853, it was never again an inn, being used as a farmhouse. In 1919, his daughter gave it to the Woman's Club of Scarsdale.

[91]

# Early American Inns and Taverns

In stage-coach days, Varian's was the first stop on the road from New York to Albany, and was also a drovers' tavern. Three doors open from the quaint old porch which runs across almost the entire front. HL and strap-hinges abound; an old Dutch door admits to the hall, from which a narrow, steep staircase leads to the second floor, and there is also an old attic. Downstairs on the left is a large room which probably originally was three small ones. French windows and a broad terrace at the rear are modern improvements, affording a charming view over a pretty slope and plain, with the old name of Fox's Meadows. A second door from the porch opens into the dining-room, probably once a tap-room, with enormous fireplace and wall-cupboards; a third, into the present kitchen. The club has added further charm to the house by using old furniture and modern replicas of old rugs.

White Plains had some old inns, but nothing now remains of them. The Armory on Broadway occupies the site of the old Court House, near which was the Hatfield Inn, a first-class tavern, but local historians do not agree as to the exact location. Captain Hatfield, the owner, was in the King's Militia when the Revolution broke out, but his death shortly after left the question of his loyalty forever unsettled.

Somewhere opposite the old Court House was the Oakley Tavern, a drovers' or second-class house, whose proprietor, Miles Oakley, was paid to feed prisoners in the town jail. The site of this inn, too, is uncertain. It is believed to have burned down, and Isaac, son of Miles, opened another. His property, according to old records, was separated from that of his father by a mulberry bush, and needless to say, this marker has long since disappeared. It is possible that the present old hotel, the Carlyon Arms, with a ground floor apparently much older than the rest of the building, may occupy the site, or even comprise part of the second Oakley Tavern.

[92]

# Route from New York to New Haven

Not far from White Plains, on a crossroad, is Somers, originally a part of Cortlandt Manor. Somers did not receive this name until 1808, when it was so called in honor of a captain who distinguished himself in the Tripolitan War.

In stage-coach days, both the Red Bird and Eagle lines passed through Somers on their way to New York, connecting at Danbury with the Boston stages. In 1802 there were five inns here; one, Thorn's, later became a private residence, the others have apparently gone. However, the Elephant, built in 1823, is still standing. This is a three-storied brick house with a two-story addition, and on the second floor is a large ballroom. Its owner, Hachaliah Bailey, is said to have originated the menagerie business in this country. He imported the first elephant, Old Bet, and when she died, erected a granite monument, topped by a wooden image of Bet, in front of his hotel. Many distinguished men, including Aaron Burr, stopped here, and after Hachaliah sold the house it was later purchased by a cousin, Horace Bailey.

In North Castle there was an old inn kept by one Miller, who was killed in the Revolution, but his widow continued as landlady. At one time Washington used this house as headquarters.

From White Plains one may take either the route through Greenwich on to Stamford, or through North Castle, Salem, and Pound Ridge, to Ridgefield and other Connecticut towns whose taverns have been mentioned in Chapter II, thence to Farmington.

Here stands what is probably the oldest inn open continuously as such in the United States, the Elm Tree Inn, a tavern since 1660 or at latest, 1670.

The name of the original builder is not known, but old records show that William Lewis, who sailed in the *Red Lion* from England in 1632, after living in Hadley and

[93]

Northampton, Massachusetts, moved into this Farmington house in 1638, so it must then have been already built.

William Lewis died in the house in 1689, but his grandson, Philip, converted it into an inn before that year. The tavern-keeper's mother, Mary Hopkins Cheever, belonged to a prominent New Haven family. Her father taught the first school in that settlement, opening it in his own house, and New Haven's Ezekiel Cheever School to-day commemorates him. Again one sees that in early days, tavernkeepers were people of prominence.

Although from its exterior one would hardly suspect its great age, the Elm Tree Inn is especially interesting, because one can actually distinguish in the interior the original house. The hotel's entire front is comparatively new, but the front door is an old one, moved forward. At the rear of the entrance hall, beyond the office, a flight of stairs rises in the same spot where an earlier flight was built, and here still projects an iron hook from which used to hang a lantern, to light guests up the stairs. Here is the old chimney, with fireplaces on all four sides: in the hall, in the two rooms on either side, and in the modern dining-room at the rear, a small part of which probably stands on the site of an old lean-to kitchen. In the ceiling of the present hall can be seen part of the original overhang of the second story.

The smoking-room at the left of the hall is probably the former tap-room, with a large fireplace, Dutch oven, and wall-cupboard beside it. Stairs lead to the old cellar, paved with cobblestones. Opposite the smoking-room is the other original room, although greatly enlarged, but here one notices the uneven old floors.

Upstairs there were but three rooms; two over the tap-room and a large one over the sitting-room. This, like the one below, has been enlarged, but the original part is paneled in wood, some of the planks twenty-three inches broad, those in the floor twenty inches. The old walls on three sides are solid, although no longer strictly perpendicular, even as the ceiling has sagged, without endangering its safety.

HL hinges, the lock from the front door, with a key so massive that no one would care to carry it in his pocket, interesting pieces of furniture, china, warming-pans, et cetera, are carefully preserved by the present proprietor, who is enthusiastic over his charming old house.

Joshua Gay, in *Old Houses in Farmington,* remarks: "We will halt under the big Elm which overhangs the little house where Manin Curtis spent his life long enough to say that his father, Sylvanus Curtis, in company with Phineas Lewis, in 1762, the year after Sylvanus married, brought home from a swamp three Elm Trees. One was planted back of the Elm Tree Inn, one in front of the house of Mr. Curtis, and the third failed to live."

The big elm behind the inn, close to a piazza at the side of the tap-room, still lives, although reduced to a mere ten-foot stump, with a few leaves in summer. It is by record one hundred and sixty-four years old.

From Farmington one may easily reach Cheshire, a town of many old houses, one of which on Main Street, and now a residence, was the Beach Tavern. Cheshire was settled in 1723, and the turnpike from Farmington to New Haven passed through it. The tavern was built by Abijah Beach early in the 19th century, and kept by him until his death in 1821. It had other landlords after that, and part of it was used as a store. A ballroom, with a raised platform over the stairs for musicians, occupied the third floor, and was used for "balls, courts, exhibitions, singing schools and different kinds of public entertainments." In 1808 and for some years afterwards, the Free Masons met here.

At Cheshire's Military Academy, founded in 1796, the late General Joseph Wheeler and J. P. Morgan were pupils.

From New Haven another road, practically following an old one, runs through New London, burned by the British,—

[95]

apparently no old inn has survived,—and on to Norwich, a very old town. It had a number of taverns, two of which are now private residences.

The first Norwich tavern mentioned was kept by Sergeant Thomas Waterman, in 1679, and he was succeeded in 1690 by Deacon Simon Huntington.

In May, 1701, Sergeant Thomas Leffingwell was licensed to keep a tavern or public house, known as the Leffingwell Inn, on "Ye Common Street," and the eastern corner of the "Town Plot." It was a large, rambling house, with some of the rooms on a much lower level than others; and it contained a kitchen, a paneled "keeping room," and was provided with "blew and white china." Guests assembled here of an evening to drink rum, Geneva brandy, metheglin, or the popular flip.

Of bedrooms, there was one with "yaller bed curtains and hangings," another with a "sute of plaid curtains," one with "streaked linen," and another with "blew linti wooly." This inn was open for more than a hundred years.

In 1775, on the Plain of Norwich, there was the Lathrop Inn, with an assembly-room, and in the early years of the next century, two additional inns: Peck's, on the other side of the Town Green, shaded by a large elm tree beneath which the guests sat in summer, and Brown's, famous for its good dinners. On Bean Hill were Major Durkee's, Hyde's, and Witters inns; Hyde's in Franklin, originally part of Norwich, was popular with sleighing parties for refreshments and dancing.

An old account of a wedding dance given in New London relates that it stopped "at 45 minutes past midnight," but before that there had been "92 jigs, 52 contredances, 45 minuets and 17 hornpipes," danced by the guests. Dancing was popular in New England, in the period between strict Puritan days and the Revolution, which accounts for the many ballrooms in these old taverns.

THE WOMAN'S CLUB, SCARSDALE, NEW YORK

[*See page* 91.

INTERIOR, ELM TREE INN, FARMINGTON, CONNECTICUT

[*See page* 93.

THE BEN GROSVENOR INN, POMFRET, CONNECTICUT

[*See page* 97.

OLD SIGN OF THE NEW BEN GROSVENOR
INN

# Route from New York to New Haven

Innkeepers in the early days were looked upon as town officials, and to receive a license the applicant "must be of good report, and possessed of a comfortable estate."

In their prosperous days, stages to Boston ran through Norwich on Sundays, Wednesdays, and Fridays, often arriving on Sundays, with a loud blast of the horn, while people were in church. A resident by the name of Lathrop complained of this noise, but was informed by the State authorities that they would do nothing, as there were plenty of laws to cover the case if properly enforced. The Sunday stage ran by way of Providence and New London, following the Pequot Path, an early Indian trail, along which was laid out the first post road west from Boston, following the shore of Long Island Sound. On this road at Charlestown, Rhode Island, is the old General Staunton Inn.

From Norwich, on the Worcester turnpike, Pomfret is reached.

The present Ben Grosvenor Inn here is a mere infant, founded in 1872 by Benjamin Grosvenor, a direct descendant of Pomfret's first settler. The house was originally a farmhouse, built in 1765, at which time members of the Grosvenor family were conducting coaching inns in other houses.

Like the Elm Tree, this inn does not suggest its age, but here, too, the original farmhouse has been enclosed by the more modern two-storied large building, with a three-story front. Across the front extends a two-story piazza, more typical of the South than of New England. The house is built along old-fashioned lines, with many open fireplaces.

Through Pomfret, the road continues to Thompson, where is the last of our Connecticut inns still open as a hotel.

Built in 1814, it keeps the name of its popular host in those prosperous days, Captain Vernon Stiles.

Thompson is situated on two highroads, and it used to be said that more stage passengers dined daily at the Vernon Stiles Inn than at any other New England hotel. "Captain

Stiles was the beau ideal of a landlord, distinguished in person and manner, a genial host, a graceful speaker, an adroit politician. Catering to the youthful element as well, his spacious hall was ever at its disposal for parties, dancing and private theatricals. Thompson, bounded by two states which required several weeks' publication of marriage intentions, while Connecticut law demanded but one pulpit announcement, became popular as the Gretna Green of New England. Affianced pairs would drive to Thompson Sunday mornings, and be united in marriage at Stiles' tavern during the time intervening between church services." This finally became so arduous for the ministers that they resigned in favor of Captain Stiles, who as Justice of the Peace could perform the ceremony. "The wedding feasts, lubricated with stimulants from the tap-room, were merry occasions, which sometimes unfortunately led to Sabbath breaking, and undue conviviality." Thus a local historian.

After Captain Stiles' death, the hotel was for years a popular summer resort, and is now open only during that season.

A few miles away, on the road to East Thompson, there used to stand an old inn, Jacob's, at which Washington is said to have stopped, but this burned down some years ago.

Providence, Rhode Island, had many old taverns, and one famous hotel remains.

Roger Mowry came from Salem, and in 1655 was granted a license to "keep a house of entertainment in Providence." The original Mowry Tavern, later known as the Abbott House, consisted of but the "fire room," with an enormous stone chimney, filling almost one entire side of the apartment, leaving room for a steep flight of stairs to the loft above. Later it was much enlarged, and stood until 1900.

Roger Williams is said to have held prayer meetings in this tavern, and the Town Council met here, paying Mowry one shilling, sixpence for "house room," and "for burning the logs of this daies' firing." It also once served to guard an Indian arrested on a murder charge, since there was no jail in Providence.

The Turpin and John Whipple inns (1664) have gone. The Golden Ball Inn, later the famous Mansion House, is now an apartment house.

Built about 1763, the Sabin Tavern stood until 1891, and when it was torn down one entire room was removed to a private residence. This was the apartment in which, according to an inscription above the old fireplace: "June 9, 1772, was formed the plan for the destruction of the British Naval Schooner, *Gaspee*."

The *Gaspee* was sent by the British Government to enforce the revenue laws. On June 9th, the packet, *Hannah*, under Captain Benjamin Lindsay, passed the British ship, and neither struck her colors nor hove to when the *Gaspee* fired on her. Captain Lindsay, perfectly familiar with the waters, ran ashore, pursued by the *Gaspee*, which went aground off Namquit Point, and, Lindsay well knew, would be unable to get off before high tide the next day. Then Lindsay hurried to Providence with his news.

At ten o'clock that night, eight boats, their rowlocks muffled, set off from Sabin's Tavern, and rowed to within sixty yards of the *Gaspee*, without answering the sentinel's challenge. The *Gaspee's* captain next hailed, thereupon Joseph Bucklin fired, the captain fell, wounded, and without offering resistance he and his crew allowed themselves to be taken ashore.

The next morning, although at least one hundred men in a population of one thousand had participated, no one in Providence knew anything about the affair, nor in spite of vigorous investigation and offers of rewards by the British Government was anything learned.

Sabin Tavern, unfinished at the time, was run by James Sabin as "a house of boarding and entertainment for gentlemen." In 1785 it was sold to Welcome Arnold, one of the leaders in the *Gaspee* affair, and the room when removed was purchased by one of his granddaughters.

More than a century ago, the Mansion House already mentioned was a famous inn, and many entertainments were held within its walls. Washington visited it on May 29th, 1790, being greeted as he entered the harbor with discharge of cannon and ringing of bells. The Governor of the State met the packet at the wharf, and boarded her to greet the eminent visitor. A large delegation, including many students of Brown University, escorted him to the inn, then known

as the Golden Ball, and the next day a dinner was given in the State House close by.

In 1797, President Adams and family stayed at this inn, President Madison in 1817, Lafayette in 1824, all occupying Washington's room, "on the second story at the right of the balcony." The name of the house was often changed, but whether or not it was ever known as Amidon's could not be ascertained.

"The inn most esteemed in Providence is kept by one Amidon," the traveler Kimball states. Arriving one morning about nine o'clock, he asked for breakfast. " 'Breakfast is about through,' said Amidon, and added that he did not know 'how it would operate.' " Kimball had "already acquired so much acquaintance with this provincial phraseology

[100]

VERNON STILES' INN, THOMPSON, CONNECTICUT

[*See page* 97.

BALLOU'S TAVERN, PAWTUCKET, RHODE ISLAND

[*See page* 102.

of answering questions" that he persevered, and got his breakfast, but the next morning at six, being obliged to make an early start, "he went out to the kitchen, where he found Mrs. Amidon and several boiling kettles. Asking for a cup of tea, he was told 'Not at this time of day.' "

In early days, Providence decreed that "no howse of entertainment shall suffer any person to tipple after 9 of the clock at night, except they give a satisfactory reason to the Constable or magistrate." The fine for disobeying this order was "5 shillings for the Tavern-keeper, and 2 shillings six pence for the person who tippled." It is not stated what was considered "a satisfactory reason."

In Woonsocket stands the old Arnold Tavern. Richardson's history of this town, now out of print, states: "The next tavern at Woonsocket was kept by Thomas Arnold—he was licensed Sept. 15, 1739. In 1780, this house was enlarged by Peleg Arnold, son of Thomas, and again became a tavern."

The building, now a tenement, is still in good condition.

Warwick's David Arnold Tavern, a small, gambrel-roofed house, stands at what is now Champlin's Corners, but is no longer a tavern.

An old resident, Mr. H. Irving King, tells this story, which he had from Miss Mary Greene, who lived in the house until her death, at one hundred and five, in 1870. She had the story from Mrs. Arnold herself.

"When the British General Prescott was abducted from his headquarters in Newport, he was rowed up the bay, landed in Warwick Cove, and brought to the Arnold Tavern for breakfast. Mrs. Arnold bestirred herself to furnish the General with a substantial breakfast, but the captive ate sparingly. 'You don't seem to relish our victuals, General,' said the disturbed Mrs. Arnold.

" 'Madam,' cried the General savagely, 'do you expect me to under these circumstances?'

[101]

# Early American Inns and Taverns

"The General had been captured half dressed, and when his captors departed with him for Providence, good Mrs. Arnold took off her own neckerchief, her best one which she had put on in honor of her distinguished guest, and carefully wrapped the General's throat up with it, so he should not take cold in the morning air."

Portsmouth had "a small public house beyond the toll gate"; Smithfield had the Greenville Tavern, at which Washington stopped; Warren and Bristol Ferry also had their old inns, all of which, like the old Ballou Tavern in Pawtucket, where a business building now stands, seem to have entirely disappeared.

Of Newport, an early traveler wrote that it "has more than a common share of beautiful women; it has also some wealthy and very respectable inhabitants." In the early days of the 19th century, a resident of New York City wrote to a relative in Newport that the former city was growing so rapidly that he "believed it might some day be as large a city as Newport."

Here three buildings, once taverns, are standing: the White Horse and Pitt's Head, on Charles Street, both dwellings now, and Townsend's Coffee House, on Thames Street, altered into shops with rooms for transients above.

From Newport, if one motors down Cape Cod, at Barnstable, Massachusetts, is the Barnstable Inn, announced as the oldest inn on Cape Cod which has been open continuously.

Built in 1799 by Anne Eldridge, it was owned and operated by her and her descendants until 1922, when the present proprietor bought it. He has kept the interior as nearly as possible in harmony with the period of its building. Thus, while modern improvements at which the builders would have gasped, and pronounced them works of the devil have been installed, the sitting-rooms would not seem so changed. Copies of old papers cover the walls, one a reproduction of scenes from Scott's Lady of the Lake; in the big fireplaces, with their wall-cupboards at the side, old andirons still support great burning logs, and the furniture is chiefly antique. The modern dining-room and sun parlor have been added in such a way as to detract but little from the inn's look of age.

Directly opposite is the old Court House, and during court sessions judges visit the house as did their predecessors many years ago. The names of Abraham Lincoln, Daniel Webster, and Chief Justice Shaw are among those that may be found on the ancient register.

Kimball notes of Barnstable: "I breakfasted at a public house near the Court House. Only the female part of the family were in the house, the men of all the neighborhood being at work in the marshes, making salt hay."

He breakfasted at Eastham, and took shelter from a hard rain with a farmer at Truro, who was farmer, miller, and keeper of the lighthouse. Truro's is one of the oldest lighthouses in this section; the Hotel, especially the building now used as an annex, is old, and the same family still keeps hotel and lighthouse, and runs a large farm close by.

As Kimball traveled through Eastham, he "spied a glittering mansion of black and white," kept by one Captain Collings, and stopped for dinner.

Provincetown, now a summer art colony, quite overpowering the natives during the short season, has no really old inns, but the Red Inn, not far from the spot where the Pilgrim Fathers landed, as indicated by a bronze tablet, is a very old house, and has been an inn for perhaps twenty years. Except for necessary repairs, the present owner has kept as much as possible the atmosphere of bygone days.

Kimball mentions taverns at Edgartown, Marthas Vineyard, one of which was kept by a physician, the other by a Justice of the Peace; but says that throughout his travels he never found an inn kept by a lawyer.

## CHAPTER V

### *Old Inns of New Hampshire and Vermont*

FROM NEWBURYPORT, MASSACHUSETTS, a number of New Hampshire inns will be found within short distances, and there is a choice of two routes; or they may be combined without too much doubling on one's tracks. On the road to Dover, New Hampshire, but before reaching that town, by turning east at Greenland, Exeter will be reached. Here still stands the old Folsom Tavern, disfigured by the addition of a modern porch. Built about 1774, George Washington did not sleep here, but was entertained at a "formal collation," on November 4th, 1789, when he passed through the town on his way from Portsmouth to Boston.

Other old tavern buildings still stand here, but as private residences.

Returning to Greenfield, and continuing to Dover, one finds here the single survivor of several old inns, the others, of wood, having all been destroyed. This brick survivor, once the old Dover Hotel, stands in the center of the town, but for more than seventy-five years it has not been a hotel. About two hundred years old, two presidents of the United States and Lafayette were entertained here.

From Dover, the road to Manchester connects with another from Newburyport, and Suncook is but a short distance from Manchester. Here the old Kimball Tavern, still run as a hotel, is well worth visiting.

The main portion stands almost as it was originally, the

[104]

WYMAN TAVERN, KEENE, NEW HAMPSHIRE
[*See page* 107.

OLD INN SIGN, KEENE, NEW HAMPSHIRE

OLD BONNEY TAVERN, PENACOOK, NEW HAMPSHIRE
[*See page* 105.

KIMBALL TAVERN, PEMBROKE, NEW HAMPSHIRE

[*See page* 104.

THE ALDEN TAVERN, LYME, NEW HAMPSHIRE

[*See page* 113.

few changes, an addition at the rear, porches, and so forth, were made many years ago. Built for a tavern in 1780 by Deacon or Captain David Kimball, he ran it for many years, and a milestone set up by him in 1793, near the drive, was long used as a point for measuring distances. On it may be read:

1793
19 M. to
C. M. H.
35 M. to
H 6
M to C
Pembroke
D. K.

which means: 19 miles to Chester Meeting House; 35 miles to Haverhill; 6 miles to Concord, Pembroke, David Kimball. (Suncook is the rural delivery name; the town is Pembroke.)

The old part of the hotel consisted of eight large rooms, one of which still retains the original paneling of wide boards. The old chimneys are still in fine condition, built on brick arches beneath which one may walk upright, and with a flue for each room.

No old inn exists to-day in the actual town of Concord, originally part of Penacook Township, which name persists in a town a bit farther north.

Here stands the Penacook House, or, as it has been known since 1862, the Old Bonney Tavern. Except for repairs, the old inn has never been changed and is still open, having been so continuously for about one hundred and thirty-nine years.

In 1787, Captain John Chandler, a prominent business man, built it, and was the first landlord. He kept the house until 1818, was succeeded by his son-in-law, and it remained in the latter's family until 1850.

[105]

In 1862, Hannibal Bonney bought it. An old soldier, he had served in 1835 in the First Dragoons, U. S. A., and under General Sam Houston in the Texas War of Independence. Under Bonney, the old tavern's reputation spread into other states, for his wife was a noted cook, and traveling-men always tried to remain as long as possible in Penacook. Members of the Legislature used to drive up with their friends from Concord for one of Mrs. Bonney's dinners.

Mr. Bonney was succeeded by his son, and in 1915 the present landlord first leased, then bought it. This is one of the oldest hotels open continuously in New England.

The big old sign, with the old name: Penacook House, still hangs outside. The old bar still stands in what is now the office; the main rooms are beautifully paneled and finished in hard wood, and nine big fireplaces and four brick ovens may be inspected. Daniel Webster frequently supped here; Lafayette stopped on his visit to New Hampshire, and the house is still noted for its chicken dinners.

Penacook is a precinct of the present town of Boscawen, where in early days there were many taverns, for many immigrants passed through from Massachusetts, on their way to various points in New Hampshire and Vermont, while markets to the south were responsible for numbers of travelers in both directions.

Some of these inns long vanished were: Fowler's, at the lower end of King Street; Benjamin Coich's, in the section west of Beaver Dam Brook; another on Battle Street, kept by James Little; Jonathan Corser's, later made into a private residence; another still later made into Mr. Nathaniel Webster's residence; and Pearson's House, kept by Samuel A. Ambrose. The stable and yard of the last mentioned still exist.

The old Perkins Inn at Hopkinton burned eighteen years ago, and a modern inn of the same name stands beside the old site.

[106]

# Old Inns of New Hampshire and Vermont

In Hillsboro, the Pierce Inn is now owned by a society which intends to preserve it as nearly as possible in the original form. Already some changes previously made in the exterior have been rectified. Sometimes called "the birthplace of Franklin Pierce," it is not actually so, but the President was brought here when but six weeks old. No longer an inn, it is occupied by a caretaker and is an attractive, square, two-storied house, with a two-story piazza across the front, and down one side. The exact age could not be learned, but as Franklin Pierce was born in 1804, and the house was then standing, it is sufficiently aged.

From Hillsboro, Keene is not far. Here is the old Wyman Tavern, now a dwelling.

This house, according to a Keene resident and student of old houses, Mr. Clifford C. Wilber, was built about 1782. The Daughters of the American Revolution some years ago affixed a tablet with the date, 1750. Mr. Wilber believes that undoubtedly a house stood on this site at that time, but not the present one. This is believed to have been built by Captain Isaac Wyman, who took part in the Battle of Bunker Hill.

*Sanger's Journal*, a Revolutionary diary, contains many references to this old tavern. Under date of December 30, 1788, the former captain, now Colonel Wyman, advertised that "in future he would vend no more liquors, but would serve travelers with boarding and lodging and the best of horse keeping." Mr. Wilber explains that although this gained the Colonel the reputation as a pioneer in the cause of temperance, the real reason was the drunkenness and disorder prevalent in New England.

Colonel Wyman died in 1792, and the house may have been an inn after that, but has for many years been a private residence.

The old house was the meeting place of the patriots who went to Cambridge at the time of the Lexington alarm.

[107]

Other old taverns in Keene were: Richardson's, now razed, but standing as early as 1776, where was the first Post Office established by the State, and where tradition says that Queen Victoria's father, the Duke of Kent, once spent a night. The same story is, however, told of Richardson's Tavern in Groton, Massachusetts. The Ralston was torn down as early as 1827. Of this they tell that some women, trying to eavesdrop on a Masonic meeting in the room below, broke through the ceiling, but this story, too, is connected with another New Hampshire tavern.

Still another, the Shirtleff, became Harrington's Coffee House; remodeled in 1827, it was called the Eagle Hotel and is still in existence. In front of this hung an elaborate sign, painted by Charles Ingalls, a prominent local painter of the day. On one side was a picture of the hotel, on the other, a view of Keene's Main Street, the sign surmounted by a bronze eagle, made by another Keene resident. The sign was finally taken down and lost, but the eagle, mounted on a pillar near the sidewalk, remained longer. Then it, too, was removed, to surmount a temporary monument set up for the home-coming of soldiers of the World War, as it had previously witnessed the return of soldiers from the Mexican and Civil Wars.

In 1788, Lemuel Chandler opened a tavern on what is now Roxbury Street. It was described as "a two and one half story building, painted yellow, with a row of poplar trees on the north side of the lot." Later known as Ephraim Holland's Tavern, he afterwards opened "a new tavern nearly opposite the meeting house in Keene, at the sign of the Lyon and the Brazen Bell, and invites all Gentlemen, Ladies and Travellers to favour him with their company." This tavern burned down in 1822, and in December of the same year Keene's first brick hotel was opened on its site by George Sparhawk, landlord of the burned one. He named his new house the Phœnix, but it, too, was burned in

1836. This was considered the best hotel in Cheshire County. It had a hall running across the entire third story front, and was popular with dancing or sleighing parties from the neighboring towns. When it caught fire, an engine was carried up to the second story, but the flames could not be checked, although burning so slowly that almost all of the furniture was carried out.

The Cheshire Hotel was built, at a cost of twenty-five thousand dollars, on the old site, but the first landlord was unsuccessful. The second, Alvah Walker, kept the house full, and declared that the secret of hotel-keeping was to "feed 'em well." This house is still open.

The old Sawyer Tavern in West Keene, although no longer an inn, was standing a year ago. After the Battle of Bunker Hill, Colonel Abraham Wheeler of the Revolutionary Army removed to Ash Swamp, as West Keene was then called, and probably then built the Sawyer Tavern. His daughter married and kept the house for many years after her father's death, and the old sign is still in existence, showing a prancing tiger, with the date, 1811, above, and below: A. Wheeler.

In Fitzwilliam is another attractive old square house, two-storied, white with green blinds. The original tavern, built in 1796, known as Goldsmith's, was open until 1843, when it was removed and the present Fitzwilliam Tavern built on its site. Before the railroad came to this town in 1848, five lines of stages centered here, and many post-chaises, caravans and drovers passed along the Boston Road through the town. The hotel is still open throughout the year, and the dining-room has a noteworthy fireplace, although the present house is only seventy-eight years old.

Returning from Fitzwilliam to Keene, it is but a short run to Brattleboro, Vermont, and from here either of two routes will take one to several old inns.

By the first road, almost due north is the town of Newfane, Vermont. Here is another of the long, low, two-storied houses, with broad verandas, an attractive type of New England inn. For more than ninety years it has been run by the same family, who now keep it open only in the summer season. In 1835, when the grandfather of the present proprietor took it over, he moved the house to its present site, and it is difficult to be sure how many years the house had previously stood. The proprietor cherishes a book used as the hotel register in 1835-6.

Returning to Brattleboro and continuing west to Bennington, one follows almost the same route as the old road from Boston to Albany. Along this road, stops at places convenient for a half day's travel were frequent.

In 1829, Bennington is mentioned as having "a pretentious hotel," but the Walloomsac Inn, said to have been built in 1672, burned down fifty years ago. Stephen Fay kept it during the Revolution. North Bennington had the Bert Henry Inn.

North from Bennington, in Dorset, stood the old Cephas Kent Tavern, whose exact site is not now known. It stood on or near the site of a charming old house built in 1800, a private residence at least since 1900, and now the home of Mrs. Zephine Humphrey Fahnestock, the writer. The Colonial Dames placed a marker "on a convenient triangle of grass, in the middle of the road," Mrs. Fahnestock explained, adding: "I like to believe that even if the old tavern did stand across the way, it was moved when our house was built, and incorporated in it. Some one of Cephas Kent's sons built our house, and for many decades it remained in the Kent family."

Typical of New England, square, two-storied, with an old door and side and fan lights, is this house. The first Constitutional Congress of Vermont is said to have met in the Cephas Kent Tavern, and Vermont was admitted to the Union in 1791, so it is just possible that the present house or part of it was the old tavern of that time.

# Old Inns of New Hampshire and Vermont

North and west, almost to the New York State line, is East Poultney, which had the Eagle Inn. A private residence for at least forty years, its exact age is not known, for the town records were burned in 1840, but it stood in 1790. No old fireplaces or wall-cupboards remain, but it has a wonderful old cellar of brick and stone, and the ballroom occupying half of the second story may still be seen. Save for a small addition, the house is practically square, with a two-storied piazza.

In Revolutionary times, the Eagle was a noted meeting place for patriots, and here Captain William Watson offered his famous toast: "The enemies of our country! May they have cobweb breeches, porcupine saddle, a hard trotting horse, and an eternal journey!" This same Watson had a dog, Comus, and when he died the captain buried him in a wooden box behind the Eagle Tavern, marking the spot with a stone bearing this inscription:

> Comus is dead. Good dog, well bred,
> Here he lies—enough said.

Keeping on the main road to Orwell, a drive of but five miles brings one to Sudbury, where the Hyde Manor Hotel has for five generations been run by the Hyde family. Part of the present building is said to be at least one hundred and twenty-five years old.

From Orwell, a road leads to Chimney Point, where another old tavern has long been a private residence. The old tap-room and its fireplace have been kept as originally. At least part of the house was built in colonial days.

Following the general course of the Connecticut Valley, another road running north from Brattleboro, but east of the route just followed, brings one to Westminster and an inn still open, built one hundred and fifty years ago, of lumber said to have been brought by ox team from Boston. Originally a private dwelling, it became a tavern, and in 1775 the first county court was held in it, under the domina-

[111]

tion of New York Loyalists. This meeting was attacked by Tories, one man, William French, being killed, and three others wounded. The door through which the bullet passed is preserved in the Brattleboro Library.

On another road from Brattleboro, two more old inns may be visited. First, the famous Old Constitution House, at Windsor, which is now a museum.

Mr. Henry Steele Wardner, a native of Windsor, has written several articles on this former inn. He says of it that,

"In this house the Convention which formed the Constitution of Vermont in July, 1777, held its final sessions. It was then run by Elijah West, who had been the landlord for many years. The original site was on the east side of the main street of Windsor, the Connecticut River road, just south of what is now the street leading to the railroad station. It continued as a tavern until 1848, and was then turned into shops, and used for small manufacturing purposes. In 1870, it was moved several feet back from the street, and made into tenements. In 1914, the owners, the family of Collamer T. Fay presented it to the Old Constitution House Association, and they moved it to its present site, to land given by William M. Evarts. It is open to visitors during the summer season."

Mr. Wardner continues:

"Now and then, I have been asked how a man with a wife and four children could live in the old house, and also run a tavern. There may have been an ell, or a house used as an annex, for that property was owned by Elijah's wife, Hannah."

The Constitution Convention held in Windsor, in 1777, met in a second-story front room of the old tavern, and the Governor and his Council also met here while Elijah was landlord. Mr. Wardner does not believe that the Legislature met in the tavern, but in the meeting-house, and after 1784, in the court-house. The convention of 1777 was held

HOME OF ZEPHINE HUMPHREY, SITE OF CEPHAS KENT TAVERN, DORSET, VERMONT
[*See page* 110.

MAIN STREET, EAST POULTNEY, VERMONT
[*See page* 111.

NEWFANE INN, NEWFANE, VERMONT

[*See page* 110.

under difficulties. General Burgoyne threatened Vermont on the west, and because of the disturbing news from Ticonderoga, the Convention was on the verge of breaking up.

In Windsor was raised the first band of insurrectionists that made organized attacks upon the authority of the State of New York, and here the settlers voted to call their new state Vermont.

For many years after Elijah's death, the old tavern was known as Patrick's, after the next two landlords, and is said to have been given its present name during the 1840's, by the then landlord, Thomas Boynton.

Not far from Windsor, across the Connecticut River, is the town of Lyme, New Hampshire. More than one hundred years ago—no old resident can give the exact date—the Alden Tavern was built for a coach stop by Justus Grant. Until reopened as a hotel eight years ago, it had not been one for years. The old house, almost square, with a long ell at the rear, has three full stories and a high attic. Additions have been made so as to detract but little from its appearance of an old building. "Witch doors" with hand-made nails and floors of broad planks, may still be admired within. There is an old fireplace in almost every room, but a ballroom formerly extending the entire length of the house on the third floor has been made into bedrooms, and modern improvements installed.

The proprietor, Mr. E. B. Alden, is a lineal descendant of that John Alden who came to Plymouth, Massachusetts, with the Pilgrims, in 1620.

Although Portsmouth, New Hampshire, once had three old inns, nothing remains of them, nor of Montpelier's, nor of Seth Munson's Tavern which, according to *The Vermonter*, he kept from 1804 to 1830, together with a general store, within a dozen miles of Montpelier, on the toll-gate road from Burlington to Boston.

## Chapter VI

### A Few Old Maine Inns

**I**N PORTLAND, MAINE, it will be impossible to find the "very good inn" mentioned by Kimball.

Here he overheard the landlord pleading with "the barmaid" to come down and make a cup of tea for a fellow townsman, but the girl, Susy, was not at all willing, and finally only agreed to come down and look him over, before deciding about making the tea.

Kimball also speaks of a village on the site of Fort Halifax, a little below Taconnet Falls, where there was a well-built, well-furnished inn near the Ferry. Saco, Biddeford, Scarboro, Cape Elizabeth, and Portland are among the oldest settlements in Maine, but they were destroyed by Indians during the early wars, and no old inns apparently survive to-day.

In Freeport, a house was built in 1785 as a residence by Dr. John Hyde. Later it was sold, and became a tavern first known as the Jameson, then the Old Codman Tavern, under which name, although it has not for years been a tavern, it is still known. It is now occupied by three families.

It has twenty rooms, and has been kept in good repair. In the front northeast chamber, the Commissioners met in 1820 to arrange for the admission of Maine as a state, and here the papers were made out, but not signed. Although alterations have been made in the others, this room is practically unchanged.

Durham had an inn, but even the Post Office here has been discontinued.

[114]

# A Few Old Maine Inns

In Bath, Shepard's Inn, built in 1803 by some one of that name for a tavern, is in good condition, though not open as an inn. Until nine years ago it was owned in the Shepard family, and when the last member sold it, she removed much of the old furniture, mirrors, et cetera, to her home in another state.

The house is colonial in style; woodwork, mantels, even the nails, are hand-made. The irons from which the sign once hung still project from the outer wall, and in one room is the original wall-paper, brought from Italy by a relative of the builder. This paper is well preserved, and shows Italian scenery, with views of the Vatican. On the second floor, rooms could be thrown together by raising partitions and hooking them to the ceiling, and in the large apartment thus formed, the Bath Masons held a banquet at the time Bath Lodge was instituted, in 1804.

The last Maine inn located is that at Machias. The old Burnham Tavern on Main Street was built in 1770, seven years after the first settlers came to Maine, and is the only building in eastern Maine with a Revolutionary War record. It is now, fortunately, owned by the Hannah Weston Chapter, D. A. R.

A two-storied house with a low attic, and windows in the gable-ends, its old sign still projects from one end of the building, which has a chimney in the middle.

In the troublous days of 1775, this old tavern was the meeting place of Machias residents, come to hear the news of the day and discuss it; in this house the brave volunteers laid plans which resulted in the capture of the British frigate, *Margaretta*. "This engagement has been appropriately called the Lexington of the Sea," one of the Daughters said, "because it was the first naval battle of the Revolution." After this battle, wounded patriots were carried to the Machias Tavern, which then became a hospital. The capture of the

*Margaretta* seemed of sufficient importance for the United States Government to name a gunboat *Machias*.

In one of the tavern's upper rooms, Maine's second Masonic Lodge, Warren, No. 2, was organized, named after General Warren of Bunker Hill fame.

## CHAPTER VII

*Long Island, Staten Island, and New Jersey Inns*

IN very early days, there was a ferry from Manhattan to Flushing, the first boat a dugout canoe, or hollowed tree-trunk. Later, in stage-coach days, after crossing, the passengers took stages to Hollis, where Goetz's Tavern, built in 1710 and owned during the Revolution by Increase Carpenter, still stood a few years ago. There were three main roads on Long Island, the northern, southern, and middle, with many short crossroads, but at first the only stage route from New York ran from Brooklyn. Starting at the ferry, the stages proceeded along the King's Highway, part of the present Fulton Street, leaving at 9 A. M., stopping at Hempstead for dinner, and at Babylon for supper and the night. The second night, travelers "slept at Quagg or Quogue, breakfasted on the Shinnecock Hills, near Southampton, dined at Sag Harbor, and slept that night at Southampton." An old inn on the Jamaica Road, the Half Way House, was used as headquarters by General Howe, before the Battle of Brooklyn.

Not many old inns remain on Long Island, with its large estates, country homes, and suburban towns, but at Coram, where once were two, one survives as a private residence. Its exact age could not be learned, but the present owner's ancestor bought it in 1813 to 1816. Before that, it had been a tavern, kept by Goldsmith Davis, and at his death, by his son, who put up a sign: Temperance House. It was the town's voting place until 1883. The other old inn, "on the corner by the pump," was burned down before 1860.

[117]

At Middle Islam, two old tavern buildings are now residences, as is the Old Roe Tavern, at Setauket, which is mentioned by Washington in his diary.

The Canoe Place Inn at Hampton Bays stands on the site of a very old tavern, but every vestige of a former building, save the old signboard, was destroyed by fire in

1921. It is claimed that an inn stood here in 1657, fifty years before Queen Anne gave the house a charter, and that it existed twelve years before East Hampton was settled. It "was doing a brisk business when a company of New England folk, having landed at Cow Bay, purchased a tract of land from the Indians, and begun a settlement, were driven away by the Manhattan Dutch," and founded Southampton. Possibly this inn was the stage-coach stop mentioned. It is apparently the oldest inn *site* in this country.

The Mattituck House at Mattituck, still a hotel, was built in 1719 by Joseph Goldsmith, a blacksmith. From him it passed to Barnabas Terrell, and whether or not he kept it as a tavern, in 1762 it was open as one, kept by Terrell's son-in-law, John Hubbard.

Not quite one hundred years old is the interesting Clark House at Greenport, which was built in 1830 by Captain Clark and has been run by him and his family ever since. At first patronized largely by owners and officers of whaling ships, it later became popular with summer boarders from the city. It is filled with fine old furniture, china, et cetera, and one very interesting article is an eighteenth-century clock, made by Dominy of Montauk Point.

In 1774, a ferry ran from the King's Arms, Hoboken, to the Corporation Dock, at the Bear Market, New York! By 1807, another ferry was in operation between Cortlandt Street, New York, and Paulus Hook, or Jersey City. There was also an old ferry between New York and Fort Lee, near which, on the New Jersey side, used to stand Burdett's, a Revolutionary tavern. Other ferries crossed the Hackensack and Passaic Rivers, but one would search vainly for taverns near these ferry sites now.

Paterson had an old hotel, built in 1774, by Abraham Goodwin, at the foot of Bank Street, near River Street. Douw's Tavern, on the west side of the Hackensack River, stood a little north of the present Erie Railroad bridge.

In Hackensack an old tavern is still open, the Washington Mansion House. Built in 1751 by Peter Zabriskie for his residence, it later became a tavern, known in stage-coach days as the Albany Stage Coach. In 1825, the Weehauken Bank occupied the old tap-room for officers, and the Post Office was also housed in the old residence.

A piazza reached by a long flight of steps runs across the

[119]

front, which faces on Court House Square, formerly the Green, the side of the house extending along Main Street. On either side of the entrance hall are fine large rooms, one a dining-room, and a short flight of stairs descends to the basement. On the second floor are more large rooms. Almost all have the big old fireplaces, with wall-cupboards beside them, and the two large original chimneys rise through the middle of the house. Smaller rooms on the third floor make the total number twenty-three, so it was a fine old mansion, and with a ballroom.

Washington, who was a personal friend of Mr. Zabriskie, stayed here during the Revolution, presumably in the absence of the owner and his family, for meals were brought to the General from Archibald Campbell's Tavern across Main Street, where now a trust company building stands. The northeast room, No. 19, on the second floor, is pointed out as his, but, lest any visitor be tempted to carry away the key as a souvenir, the present proprietor has already replaced twelve such abducted keys, and who can say how many more were carried off before his day? Washington's room has the huge fireplace and cupboards of the other bedrooms, the fireplace tiles imported from Holland when the house was built, and in addition, in what seems a mere closet, is a secret staircase. Down this it is told that Washington escaped into the present dining-room and out through a window, while the Hessians were mounting the front stairs. Three or four thousand of these Hessians then occupied the town, presenting "a horrid frightful sight to the inhabitants, with their whiskers, brass caps and kettle or bass drums." A bronze tablet, placed on the house by the Bergen County Historical Society, commemorates Washington's stay here.

Mrs. Watson's Tavern is mentioned in 1766, and across the Green from Campbell's was one kept by Edward Van Beuren, the Hackensack House. This name was given to another at the corner of Main and Bridge Streets, which may have succeeded or included Abraham Ackerman's Tavern, existing before the Revolution. Painted and modernized, the building still stands as stores and offices. On the corner of Main and Salem Streets, the Hackensack Tavern was opened in 1833 by Isaac Vanderbeek, who bought for this purpose Jan Berden's residence, built in 1717. Popular for forty years, this tavern was torn down in 1921.

Taverns in neighboring towns existing as early as 1816, when they are mentioned as having been headquarters for a tax collector, are: John A. Hopper's, at Hopperstown, now Hohokus; Van Houten's in Saddle River, and Demarest's at Harrington.

A very old route from New York to points in New Jersey and Pennsylvania lay across Staten Island. After being ferried to Paulus Hook or other points, travelers took a stage for Bergen (Bergen Point was an old Dutch settlement), where were at least two taverns, the Half Way House and The Sign of the White Star, both of which survived until 1824. From here, another ferry took them to St. George, Port Richmond, and other places. Stages then carried them to the New Brunswick or Perth Amboy ferries.

The oldest tavern on Staten Island stood, according to local historians, on the site of the old Pavilion Hotel, built in 1815, burned not many years ago, and now replaced by a school building. The early tavern was built about 1640 by a Dutchman, Kieft, "an indiscrete and imprudent man," who treated the Indians so outrageously that he caused terrible trouble for other white settlers. His stone house, a story and a half high, known as the King's Inn, was during the Revolution occupied by a British commander.

The Steamboat Hotel at Port Richmond, built "long before the Revolution," was razed in 1855, but the old Port Richmond Hotel, built soon after the Revolution on the site of Fort Decker, known as the Decker House, and for a time the residence of the Winants, still stands and is now a chop suey restaurant. Aaron Burr died in this house.

The Swan at West Brighton has apparently entirely disappeared, and no one could be found to indicate even its site. At Sailors' Snug Harbor, close to the buildings which give the place its name, still stands a house built in 1770, and known as The Stone Jug, now quite modernized and a private residence, although not so many years ago a hotel. It is on the main highroad, a long, two and a half story stone house, with a wing.

Not far from the present ferry to Elizabeth, but a couple of miles inland, stands the old Bull's Head, at the place of that name. Opened in 1741, it was twice enlarged before the Revolution, and at one time was run by the Hatfield Gang, a notorious band of criminals. During their day, we are gravely assured, at least a dozen murders must have been committed in this tavern. Later, its reputation was whitewashed, for it became a popular stage stop and relay station between New York and Philadelphia. The old sign, the head of a bull, is plainly visible, painted on the side of the house, but the building is in a most dilapidated state, only one lower room occupied by a barber, and a lodging above.

Richmond Village, in the center of the Island, was once an important county seat, and here was the Cucklestone Inn, at which Major André once stayed, but it survived only until 1823. Purdy's Hotel at Princess Bay is still standing.

The old Fountain House, built in 1668, long stood in New Dorp, but is gone now, as is the Rose and Crown, built in 1695. This latter was headquarters for the British General Howe, and also for Hessian officers. Later, the first Richmond County courts were held in it.

The Black Horse, within the limits of New Dorp, on the highroad, still stands, but is so modernized that were it not for the old sign still in place few would suspect its identity. Built about 1754, in 1776 it was occupied by General Howe's staff, and in that year received its name. A lieutenant-colonel whom Howe styled, "my very dear friend Benton," owned a spirited black horse. One day while Benton was riding

him the animal bolted, and hurled himself and his rider against a stone wall, killing both. A British soldier there-upon painted a signboard with a picture of the horse, and the inn duly took the name by which it was ever afterward known. More than forty years ago, when it was entirely remodeled, although the old foundation walls were left, the owner threw the signboard away. A neighbor rescued it,

[123]

and when the present owner moved in gave it back. It was re-hung, and remained through the World War, then was taken down when the house ceased to be a hotel. The widow of the last proprietor cherishes it, and although every trace of paint has disappeared, the outline of the horse can be plainly seen.

Four miles from Tottenville, at Rossville, stands what is probably the oldest surviving inn on Staten Island, the Blazing Star, later known as Le Vaud's Hotel. This was a famous tavern, the starting point for stage lines, and a ferry used to run from behind it to New Jersey, at a point now known as Chrome. The house, although opened only two years ago, is in a most dilapidated condition, for the property on which it stands, together with an old farmhouse across the road, and a beautiful but equally dilapidated old mansion, is for sale, and the owner will not lease. Across the front of the picturesque old inn runs a porch; there is another in the rear, overlooking Staten Island Sound, and the decaying posts of the old pier are replaced by another some rods away. Doors from the front porch open into the old barroom, kitchen, and parlor, and into what was once a store. A ballroom on the second floor has been used until fairly recent times for dances, fairs, and other entertainments, and a Masonic Lodge still meets there. Otherwise the old house is deserted and forlorn, although the timbers and walls are solid. It is only a question of time when it will, like the other old inns on the Island, be torn down.

Near Tottenville, the Ferry Tavern, built in 1740, and after the Revolution kept by the Hessian Captain Delotz, was burned in 1866.

Other old-timers now gone are: Union Hotel (1764), Tottenville, at first a farmhouse, and the home of Commodore Vanderbilt's wife (the couple were married in its parlor); the Red Lion, a Revolutionary tavern; Cliff House (1794), near Fort Wadsworth; Nautilus Hall, pulled down to make room for a freight station, and Union Garden (1820), both at Tompkinsville; Bodine's (1815), at Castleton Corners, a stage house, later a residence; Bloomingview, a popular mail-coach stop, and later the residence of William H. Starin; and the Planters' Hotel (1820), popular with southerners, and pulled down only a few years ago. Bennett's, built in 1768, stood until 1870.

In the old village of Chapel Hill, across from Staten Island, settled in 1800, when shortly afterwards it had but thirteen houses, one was a tavern, Cornelius Mount's, the only inn in that part of New Jersey except at Middletown. Mount's later became a residence.

From Tottenville, as in old times, the ferry to Perth Amboy is well patronized. A short distance up the hill in the latter city, the modern Packer House stands on the old Crown Tavern site, which, as a tablet proclaims, has been occupied by a tavern or hotel since 1760.

On High Street, a few blocks away, is the beautiful residence of the last royal governor of New Jersey, now known as The Westminster.

In 1764 the Lord Proprietors ordered its erection, for "His Excellency, William Franklin, Captain General and Governor-in-Chief," illegitimate but always acknowledged son of Benjamin Franklin. William had accompanied his father to England, and at the time a degree was conferred upon the illustrious elder, the son was made a Master of Arts by Oxford University. When appointed governor, it was proposed that he make Perth Amboy his residence, but after visiting the town, he preferred Burlington, as being nearer his Philadelphia friends. Later, when the house was finished, he changed his mind, and in 1774 came to "sweet Perth Town," and moved into his beautiful new house. It stood then in a fine park, surrounded on three sides by water. Amboy Point was a popular resort, and thither the Governor and his friends, "dressed like a group of Watteau figures," used to repair at times, to watch the populace amuse themselves. Splendid entertainments were given in the Palace, as it was called; balls and theatrical performances in the large ballroom in the wing, for William had not inherited his father's simple tastes. In 1775, Benjamin Franklin came to implore his son to espouse the American cause, but failed to persuade him, and after being kept for some days practically a prisoner in his mansion, the Governor was finally arrested by the American forces. He had not even been neutral, but had continually urged loyalty to the king. After peace, he went to England, received a pension and a sum of money, and died there.

Shortly after the Revolution, the interior of the Palace was greatly damaged by fire. It was then sold to John Rattoone, who restored and enlarged it. For a time, Joseph Bonaparte contemplated purchasing it, but as he was unable to secure some other property which interfered with the view, gave up the idea. Early in the nineteenth century, it was the popular Brighton House, and then passed into the possession of Matthias Bruen, of whom it is told that he would not carry a penny in money, but always paid for his purchases, even to "a bunch of brass pickerel from the fish vendors of old Amboy" with checks.

One of his descendants declared that the house was haunted, and told the tale that,

"Promptly at midnight, the rumbling of a coach would be heard coming up the driveway; the sycamore trees would creak and moan, the dogs would bay, doors on each floor would creak, the heavy front door fly open to welcome its ghostly master."

In 1883, the house was used as a home for aged clergymen. Perhaps they exorcised the ghost, for the present proprietor of the house does not seem to be troubled by it.

Above a basement in which was the old dining-room, a long flight of steps leads to the beautiful old main entrance door; and from the broad hall, which probably originally extended through the house, although now there is a good-sized room at its rear, open spacious rooms with wide fireplaces and hand-carved mantels. The main building is of four stories and basement, its brick walls three feet thick, and there is a long wing containing the ballroom, now divided into smaller rooms. A secret passage used to extend to the Raritan River, but this has now been closed. The house was thoroughly repaired and restored when the present occupant moved in, and is a beautiful example of an eighteenth-century residence. Not strictly a hotel any longer, furnished suites may be rented.

The first ferry to New Brunswick was established in 1686, and by 1740, a stage was running regularly twice a week between New Brunswick and Trenton, the fare two shillings and sixpence.

New Brunswick's first tavern was Ann Balding's, opened in 1735 by the wife of a sea captain. The mayor and other town officers used to meet in it, and in February, 1735, passed the town's first paving ordinance there. In 1742, Paul Miller opened a second tavern on the north side of French, now Albany, Street, which was later kept by Brook Farmer, son of Thomas Farmer, Sheriff of Philadelphia, Collector of the Port of Perth Amboy, which again indicates the social rank of tavern-keepers in those days. Brook's house burned in the Revolution, and taking his sign, the Red Lion, with him, he removed to Princeton. Paul Miller also built the town's fourth tavern.

To obtain a tavern license in New Jersey in those days it was necessary for the applicant to "have the recommendations of 10 respectable freeholders, with a standing for good repute, for honesty, and for temperance." The tavern must have "at least 2 spare beds, and be provided with horse room," and the host might neither "game himself or herself, nor suffer any person to game for money." Prices were fixed by law. "For a good breakfast, 40 cents; good dinner, 50 cents; good supper, 40 cents; lodging, 12 cents; common breakfast, dinner or supper, 10 cents less." Innkeepers were forbidden to sell drink "on the Lord's day except for necessary refreshments." Considerable latitude seems left to the innkeeper as to what was "necessary."

By 1750, there were four or five taverns in New Brunswick; the oldest still standing is the Indian Queen, mentioned in 1778 in old records in connection with the ferry. It was probably built about 1741, then altered. Some years ago, when changes were being made, a wall two feet thick, eighteen inches of it of brick, the rest of stone, was uncovered. It has since been known as the Bell and as the Parkway, but is no longer an inn. Its first floor is occupied by stores, the rest as dwellings. President John Adams, his wife and suite lodged here when they visited the town, but they dined at the White Hall.

This house, originally called the White Hart, built about 1761, has also been altered into stores and apartments. At the time that the Adams party took their meals here, it was run by Nathaniel Vernon. Later, his widow married John Keyworth, and they kept the Steamboat Hotel, next door to the Bellona, one of the first steamboat hotels, run by a cousin of Commodore Vanderbilt. Neither survives.

Not far from New Brunswick, at Perryville, on the old Post Road to Easton, is the old Brick Tavern. The property on which it stands was purchased in 1788 by Cornelius Carhart 2nd, who built a substantial farmhouse and barn which are still standing. About 1802, he erected a tavern on his property, for the better accommodation of travelers. Its old sign, with a waving flag on one side, on the other a picture of General Jackson, is now owned by a resident of Flemington.

Perryville received its name soon after the tavern was finished, when news arrived of Perry's victory on Lake Erie.

[128]

BURNHAM TAVERN, MACHIAS, MAINE

[*See page* 115.

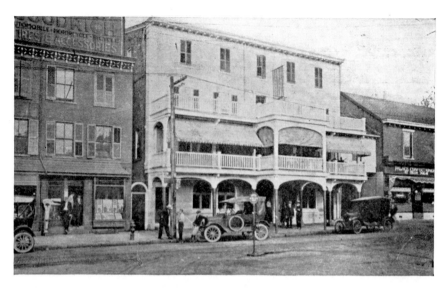

ARCADE HOTEL, MT. HOLLY, NEW JERSEY

[*See page* 133.

BOTTLE HILL TAVERN, MADISON, NEW JERSEY

[*See page* 137.

The old village of Bound Brook was on the pre-Revolutionary stage route, and an old military map names two taverns here: Tunison's, and the Bull's Head, near the present town of Somerville. Willam Kelley's At the Sign of the Buck, Bound Brook, was advertised in the New York *Gazette* and *Mercury* in November, 1772. He mentions that he has a stock of "the best English hay." Two years later he sold the house to Samuel Walker.

Posiah Stanbury had a tavern in Bound Brook, and here, too, was the Black Horse, kept by a man who told one guest that he was "not only innkeeper, but also weaver, shoemaker, farmer, farrier, gardener, barber, leach and doctor, and when I cannot help myself, a soldier."

The old Middlebrook Hotel, first known as the Harris Tavern, is said by some to have been built in 1700, by others in 1735. Raiders under Simcoe, known as the Queen's Rangers, native Americans loyal to the English, stopped in front of it one October night in 1779, and discussed the wisdom of burning it down, as they had burned many other inns in Somerset County, but they finally spared this one.

Later known as one of the finest inns on the stage route across New Jersey, it was the halfway house between New Brunswick and Somerville, and here horses were changed. This period lasted until the railroad was built, which in order to take a straight course, left the old hotel in a corner across the tracks, while a new turnpike added to its isolation. Ike Bennett, the old stage-driver at the time, refused to change his route, and for years crossed the railroad tracks with his stage and dined at the old inn. Although there were but few passengers, he continued to do this until one day his stage was hit by a train, and although he and his horses miraculously escaped injury, he drove no more.

The first Masonic Lodge in Somerset County was organized in this inn, and during the Revolution it was popular with officers and men of both armies. The building, with its low-ceiled rooms, still stands, almost as in those days, the old signboard remaining on its front; but it was sold last year, and although it has three times been threatened with razing and escaped, this time there seems little hope for it.

Somerville in olden days had Wood's Tavern, and an old building, once a hotel, still stands, much remodeled and now a residence, in Clinton. Its early landlord was Lieutenant Colonel Abraham Bonnell of the Revolutionary Army, and the house is still owned by his family.

Newton had a number of taverns, the first built probably about 1750 by Henry Hairlacker, on what is now called the Horton place. The present Cochran House, built by Dennis Cochran, existed under this name as early as 1800. An old tavern on the corner of Park and High Streets was kept in 1800 by Isaac Bassett, but was burned in 1856. Another of the same period, the Cross Keys, was later known as the Hoppaugh, then as the Ward House.

Blairstown's old tavern was some years ago altered into a handsome residence.

The present town of Johnson, first known as Log Gaol, was once the county seat of Sussex County, but a shifting of boundaries placed it in Warren County. Two stage lines crossed here; one from Albany to Philadelphia, the other to Stroudsburg, and there was a tavern.

A popular habitué, for he told good stories, used to stop here with his pigs, which he drove along the road to sell, never apparently having any trouble in coaxing the animals to follow him. He was always known as the Old Pig Drover, his real name being unknown. One day a traveler recognized him as a former merchant of Fayetteville, Tennessee, who had failed in business. Unable to pay his debts, he was so worried that he left his home, wife, and children, and later caused them to receive news of his death. He had finally come to his present occupation. With difficulty he was at last prevailed upon to return home, where he lived for many years.

Orange in 1798 had Mumm's Tavern, and for several years a tea-room was run in the historic Ball House at Maplewood. This had, however, never been a tavern, and now the tea-room has been given up.

Nothing remains of Newark's old inns. Gifford's stood in 1796 and later, with a signboard showing hunters and hounds, at the corner of what are now Broad and Market Street. Opposite were Johnson Tuttle's, and Major Samuel Sayre's. Before a tavern existed, a town meeting was held, and Henry Lyon appointed to keep one and "to prepare for it as soon as he can."

Nor can one find any old tavern now in Elizabeth, the old Elizabethtown, although this section of the country was "well inhabited by a sober, industrious people, who have necessary provisions for themselves and families, and for the comfortable entertainment of strangers and travelers." [1]

Before 1675, the only road laid out in New Jersey by Europeans led from Elizabethtown Point to the site of New Brunswick; it forded the river there and again above Trenton, then continued into Delaware, where it forked, one branch leading to Burlington. This was known as the Dutch Road.

In 1695 there were tavern-keepers at Piscataway, Woodbridge, and Elizabethtown, and before 1676, four Dutch families, one keeping a tavern, had settled at Burlington. Here until comparatively recently stood the Blue Anchor, now torn down.

The Indian Queen in "Elizabethtown" (Elizabeth), had been first a private residence. Here, in its tavern days, Kosciusko stopped. Two and a half miles from Elizabeth, there stood in 1764 the Roebuck, and that same year Michael

---

[1] *Barber and Howe's History*, 1845.

Cornelisse built a tavern, and a ferry was established from Elizabethport to Bergen Point. Four miles from Elizabeth, in Union, was the Meeker Inn, once famous, said to have been built in 1756, but since the Morris Turnpike on which it stands was not laid out until 1801, it was probably not built until later. This became one of the best known inns between Elizabeth and Morris and Sussex Counties, but it has recently been sold, and will probably shortly be razed.

From Perth Amboy another automobile road will bring one to Kingston, an important stage-coach stop on the New York-Philadelphia turnpike. This, before the railways came, was the most important thoroughfare between New York and the south. There were two popular inns in Kingston, the Withington and the Van Tilburgh, and both are said to have been favorite houses with Washington. The Withington was burned several years ago, and the present Union Line Hotel stands on its site. The Van Tilburgh met with a worse fate, for it became so dilapidated that it finally fell down, and a grocery store and dwelling now mark its site.

Princeton, half-way between New York and Philadelphia, was another important stop. The Nassau Inn, dating from the middle of the eighteenth century, still stands on the original site, although it is so changed by remodeling that there is not much of the original building left.

Farther down the same street is an old building, now occupied by several stores, which was a tavern in the eighteenth century. Although badly damaged by fire a few years ago, it has been repaired, and its exterior is much as it was originally.

Trenton, the old Trent's Town, had the Sign of the Green Tree, where John Adams stopped and commented on the four great walnut trees which gave the house its name. This was kept by the Williams family for many years. The Legioner, or Black Horse, kept by Robert Rutherford, was another old-timer. For both of these one must look in vain.

Bordentown had Kester's Inn; Mount Holly had the Arcade Hotel, a remodeled old hotel, open until recently, and the hotel on Mills Street in Mount Holly is also old. An inn said to be almost two hundred years old stood on the King's Highway in Moorestown, but has recently been sold and is to be torn down.

In 1820, at Cooper's Ferry (Camden), Cooper kept the horse ferry to Philadelphia, and also a tavern, a frame building with a long porch. From Camden, stages ran to Mount Holly, on to Middletown, Shrewsbury, and the Bay, and from a point near Sandy Hook a boat took passengers to New York.

Eight miles from Camden, part of the old Fish House stands, but with many additions. The Indian Chief at Medford in 1851 replaced an earlier tavern of the same name.

Haddonfield, however, has a fine specimen of an early inn, which fortunately has been taken over by the State as a museum. Patriotic societies have their club rooms here, and the old ballroom called the Washington room, is used for various community purposes.

This inn, the Indian Chief, stands on broad, tree-lined Main Street. One of the four large rooms on the ground floor is used by the Daughters of the American Revolution, and they have placed here many interesting souvenirs and pieces of furniture. Among the latter is a chair made of wood from the British frigate *Augusta,* which fired on and damaged the Steamboat House in Chester, Pennsylvania. The ship was raised from the river-bed after resting there for more than a century. Most of the rooms in the old tavern have large fireplaces, but the old hinges have disappeared from the doors, although a few of the old locks remain. A new sign hangs outside, but the old one, with merely a few feathers and stars distinguishable, is preserved within.

# Early American Inns and Taverns

In 1750, Haddonfield had the Creighton Tavern or American House, and in one of its rooms the State Legislature and the Council of Safety met. Dorothy Payne, later Dolly Madison, was a niece of Mr. Creighton, and liked to visit her uncle's family, for they were not, like her own family, Quakers. Mail-coaches stopped twice daily at the Creighton Tavern, and Dolly and her young cousins used often to ride in them for some distance after they left the house, and then walk back again.

Gloucester's first tavern was opened in 1696, and three more the following year. William Hugg's still stands, although now occupied by several families, and by the Gloucester County Fox Hunting Club.

Of a number of old inns in Gloucester County, some of them still used as hotels, the following are the most important: The Sign of the Seven Stars, at Repaupo, about two and a half miles from Woodstown, built in 1765, an inn during the Revolution, but now a private house. In the former barroom, the name of a man believed to have been an officer in the Revolutionary Army may still be seen, scratched with a diamond on a window pane. The Sign of the Buck, Westville, is now Toppin Inn; Old Seven Stars Hotel at Woodbury is now a residence, as is the Death of the Fox, three miles away, between Mt. Royal and Clarksboro, scene of some of the first mutterings against England before the Revolution. It was one of the Gloucester County Fox Hunting Club's meeting places, and here Philadelphia's First City Troop is said to have originated. Jesse Smith's in Woodbury is now Caul's Hotel.

Woodstown has still standing and in good condition, the oddly named Niggers' Glory, built in 1755 by Douglas and Mary Bassett. Rum was sold here for twelve and one-half cents a quart, and good meals for fifteen cents. Does this explain the name? The Woodsboro House, still open, was a hotel at least as early as 1797; the old Washington

[134]

House, on Main Street, with shops built into the front, is even older, and the Pole Tavern, recently torn down, was a "place of entertainment" in 1777. There is another very old inn at Sharpstown.

Salem was settled in 1675, and by 1729 had taverns, for these regulations were made for them: that they "should provide eatables for men, a hot dinner for 8 pence, supper and breakfast for 6 pence." But the taverns have gone, although a few brick buildings used in turn as residences, inns and again residences, still stand.

On the road from Perth Amboy to Lakewood, the town of Freehold offers some interesting inns. The old Union, which stood on the corner of South and Main Streets, was burned, and on its site erected what was later called the Belmont Hotel. Another, kept at the time of the Revolution by John Craig, has been turned into stores, but part of the old building is standing. Another, the Monmouth, opposite the Craig, has also been made into stores.

But the very old Our House Tavern at Ardena, six miles from Freehold on an old stage road to Farmingdale, is in existence. It is believed originally to have consisted of but two rooms. Fenton, leader of the Pine Robbers, who plundered and robbed farmers, is said to have been killed outside this house, in 1788. After he had committed many deeds of violence, two militiamen dressed as farmers hid in the bottom of a farm wagon, and drove to this tavern, where they had learned that Fenton was. They waited until he came out, then shot him, and later hanged him to a tree not far from Freehold. The honor of having been the scene of "Robber Fenton's" capture and death is claimed by another neighboring settlement, New Bedford, but Ellis' *History of Monmouth County* ascribes it to this Ardena tavern.

On the road from Freehold to Allentown, at Clarksburg, stands the Old Willow Tree Tavern. The year of its building is not known, but when some repairs were being made, the initials: L. W. M., and 1781 were found on a piece of sheathing. Benjamin Franklin and his daughter dined here, as did Joseph Bonaparte, who arrived with a retinue of servants. He is said to have so feared poison that he would eat no food that his own servants had not prepared.

Between Farmingdale and Lakewood, at Lower Suankum, is a very old tavern, now a private residence, which in 1800 was known as Paul Sears', although originally built for a private dwelling.

The Englishtown Village Inn was built in 1732, and the original house has been open as an inn ever since. Washington is said to have slept here before the Battle of Monmouth, and in the dining-room, he and Lord Sterling drew up the papers for See's court-martial. The interior has been kept as much as possible as in olden times, even to the antique furnishings.

Historic Morristown's inns have been destroyed, but the beautiful old Ford mansion, Washington's headquarters for more than six months in 1777, is preserved by the Daughters of the American Revolution as a show place, and is filled with interesting old furniture, china, muskets, documents and many souvenirs of the past. It is not too remotely connected, furthermore, with Morristown's first tavern.

This was built by Jacob Ford, one of the town justices, and according to local authority, may have stood on the Green, now the Park, or even where the Ford mansion now stands. The latter was begun in 1772, and occupied by the same Jacob Ford. The tavern existed certainly by 1740, and until 1755 court sessions were held in it.

The Norris Tavern was first built for a commissary storehouse, with a ballroom and Masonic lodge rooms in the upper story. Later, it became Dickenson's Tavern, kept by a captain in the Revolutionary Army, and here Benedict Arnold's court-martial was held. This building is gone.

On the north side of the Green, the famous Arnold

Tavern, also known as Freeman's, Hayden's, and Duncan's, was the chief hostelry of the town, built between 1735 and 1750, so since the Ford tavern was older, the Arnold must have been built before this earlier date. Washington spent some time at the Arnold Tavern, and in it met his aides, Baron Steuben and Lafayette. Colonel Hamilton's alertness probably saved Morristown from destruction. His office was in this tavern, and he became suspicious of a spy engaged by Washington, whom he, Hamilton, believed to be secretly working for the British. He therefore laid a trap. Busying himself while the spy was in the room on what appeared to be an extensive report of the American forces, ammunition, et cetera, but which really represented these as four times what they were, the Colonel had himself called from the office, and went out, leaving this report on his desk. When he returned, spy and report had both disappeared, confirming his suspicions. The British believed the Americans were too strong for them, and did not attack Morristown.

The tavern building was moved in 1886, and formed part of All Souls' Hospital, but in 1915 it was burned. It had entertained many distinguished guests, including Generals Sullivan, Lee, and Putnam of the American forces.

An old tavern, Larzelaer's, stood on the road to Basking Ridge.

In old times, this town was much larger than Morristown, and people from the latter place shopped in Basking Ridge. Settled in 1700 by Scotch Presbyterians, it had an old tavern, White's, later made into residences. The first courts of Warren County were held in this inn.

Madison's first tavern on Academy Hill was kept during the Revolution by David Brant, and had for a sign a bottle suspended from a corner post. The oldest part of the Bottle Hill Inn was built in 1804, and later enlarged, the last additions having been made about seventy-five years ago. From the name, there would seem to be some connection between the two. Perhaps the Bottle Hill Inn replaced the older. At all events, the former stood at the cross-streets where now is a modern bank building, and had it not been for the women of Madison, would have been torn down to make room for the bank. The women raised money, bought the old tavern, and moved it a couple of blocks down the street to its present site. The Historical Society reserves two rooms on the ground floor, the rest is leased for a hotel.

Entering a narrow hall, on the right is a small room, the original bar. When business increased so that more space was needed, a very large, low room, with a great fireplace, was added in the rear. This is now a dining-room, as is another old addition made for the purpose.

Except for modern windows, the old house is little changed. The Historical Society rooms have curious spatter-work floors, and contain some interesting souvenirs and old furniture.

Lafayette was entertained here in 1825, when thirteen young Madison girls, representing the original thirteen states, took part in a pageant in his honor.

Chester has an old hotel, the Chester, which was built about 1810 still open. But although Schooley's Mountain was a very popular resort more than a hundred years ago, owing to its mineral springs, and had at least four hotels, when the resort lost its popularity these all disappeared.

Hackettstown, near by, was not incorporated under that name until 1853, previously forming part of Independence. Silas Leonard had an inn here in 1791, and there has been an inn on the site of the present Warren House for more than one hundred and fifty years. The first, probably of logs, was replaced by a frame house, and in 1840 the latter was rebuilt. As early as 1823, the American House existed in Hackettstown.

In Washington, where almost all of the land was originally

[138]

owned by Major Carhart, whose son was mentioned as a tavern-builder, there was an early Windsor Tavern, on the site of which, in 1811, was built the Washington Hotel. This has been rebuilt, and the old name of Windsor restored to it.

From Trenton, turning north, it is not far to Flemington.

Here, in 1746, Samuel Fleming was licensed to keep a tavern in his log house, probably the first house in the settlement. Ten years later, he built Fleming's Castle, on the road from a mill to Howell's Ferry on the Delaware River. This road crossed the Trenton road, now Flemington's Main Street.

The old house has been but little altered by its various owners. A low roof comes down below the eaves, and inside, a winding staircase extends from the basement to the top floor. After Fleming died, the house was bought by Dr. George Creed, the first practicing physician in Raritan Township, and in 1840 by the family now occupying it as a residence.

Near Unionville, not far from Flemington, is an old house, now a private residence, which was once an inn. The oldest part was probably built about 1715, by one of the Prall family, large landholders in this section, and the *new* part added in 1780. This date, with initials, is carved in the old stair-rail, and when the house changed hands recently, a Franklin stove with the date 1780, and name: Hibernia Company, was found in one of the rooms. The outer walls are made of several thicknesses of oak, with clapboards outside, almost bullet-proof. A small window in the newer part is believed to have served for passing liquor to customers outside, and there is an old still in the neighborhood. Strap-hinges abound; there are two great chimneys and old raftered ceilings, and the building is being restored as nearly as possible to its earlier state. The old Trenton-Princeton highroad passed here.

[139]

In another direction from Flemington, at Larison's Corners, is a picturesque, long, low building, with a wide porch across the entire length. This is rapidly falling to pieces, although the stout old rafters are good for many a day. Only one end is now occupied as a residence, but when a tavern it was the scene of many festivities, and did a brisk business, for it is on the old York road.

Four of the lower rooms could be thrown together by opening wide folding doors, and an old resident declared that a fiddler was always kept on the premises to play for dancing. On the second floor is a unique feature; a small, square room, with no other means of ventilation, once the door is closed, but a window opening on a narrow hall. This room was used by gamblers, and through the window liquors were passed.

The General Training grounds were not far away, and after drill, soldiers used to be marched two abreast up the road, into the barroom, for a glass of whiskey at three cents, out another door, and back to the parade grounds.

North of Flemington, at Pittstown, is the Old Century, now known as the New Century Inn, after a fire which ten years ago badly damaged the interior. The stone walls are very old, and this is probably one of the two inns mentioned as existing here in 1845.

A mile north of Jutland is the old Brick Tavern; and at Everettstown another old inn, both of which are now private residences.

Emanuel Coryell, when he opened a ferry in Lambertville in 1732 near the present bridge, also built an inn, later replacing the first house with one of stone. It was for many years a dwelling.

Two miles from Frenchtown, but on the Pennsylvania side of the Delaware River, there stands at Irwinna an old house which has been by turns inn and residence, and is now the Riverside Inn. Many years ago, when a cellar for an

[140]

addition was being dug, the body of an Indian was found seated erect on his horse, as they had been buried.

In 1781, the Christian Church was built at Hope, New Jersey, and when, in 1844, an old tavern here burned, the church building was made into a hotel. Later it became the present bank building.

Chadd's Inn at Chew's, formerly Chew's Landing, and the Edward Middleton Inn at Mt. Ephraim, both old houses, were until quite recently still in use.

## Chapter VIII

*Pennsylvania Inns*

PENNSYLVANIA undoubtedly, during colonial days and later, had more inns than any other state, and of these many still used as hotels survive, as well as others altered into dwellings, apartment houses, or business buildings. Even without leaving the main traveled roads, the motorist will find numbers of them, and in Pennsylvania especially, certain typical features make even those that have been somewhat altered quite easy to recognize. Usually, like the old farmhouses in this State, built of stone, they are seldom more than two stories in height, with an attic with windows in the gable-ends; often the house is almost square, with perhaps an ell in the rear. Across the front one will find almost invariably a long porch, from which two doors open. The two doors are also typical of inns in other parts of the country, for one always led into the barroom, the other into a hall from which opened the inn parlor, or the family living-quarters. The New England inns were almost always of wood.

When one studies the history of Pennsylvania, the reason for so many inns is apparent. From early colonial days, the adventurous young men were always going in search of new lands, and while some from Massachusetts and Connecticut moved north or northwest into New Hampshire, Vermont or on into Maine, many of them, with others from New York and New Jersey, pushed westward into the unexplored tracts of Ohio, Indiana, Illinois, or still farther, even as from Virginia they were emigrating to Kentucky, Tennessee, Missouri, and Arkansas.

Except for some of the southern emigrants, going to the latter four states, all of these travelers passed through Pennsylvania, as did some of those from Virginia as well. In consequence, many inns were needed to accommodate the travelers, for not only were the inns small, but there must be houses for all kinds of travelers, from the aristocrat in post-chaise or coach, the wagoner or the humble teamster, down to the drover, and seldom did these different classes meet beneath the same roof. The inn which accommodated drovers would instantly lose class with stage-coach patrons, and it is told of one such inn that when it was practically forced one night to shelter a drover, he was admitted only on condition that he leave early the next morning, before the coach guests should see him.

There was in addition the common tap-room, where any one whatsoever would be accommodated, and of these taverns there were circulated many stories of robbery, and even of the disappearance of strangers.

The route of one party of New Englanders, traveling in 1788 from Providence, Rhode Island, to Ohio, as outlined in an early travel journal, will indicate the route of many others then and later.

After leaving Providence, they stopped at the Connecticut towns of Hartford, Farmington, and Litchfield; then proceeded to Ballsbridge and on to the North River, New York, where they took the Fishkill ferry to Newburgh; from Newburgh on to Warwee, Hope, Oxford, Easton Ferry, to Bethlehem, a rope ferry to Allentown, then Coatstown, Reading, Harrisburg, Carlisle, and then: "the roads were cut into deep gullies on one side by mountain rains, while the other side was filled with blocks of sandstone." After crossing the Blue, Middle, and Tuscarora Mountains, they "put up at an old tavern stand well known to the early packhorse men and borderers of that region"; then crossed the Allegheny Mountains into Pittsburgh, which at that time had a population of between four and five hundred souls, and had its tavern. Fifty years later, this little settlement was the third most important town in the Mississippi Valley.

The first stage from New York to Philadelphia ran in 1756, and took three days to make the trip.

In Easton, since it was on a main traveled road westward, one would expect to find old inns, and many inns there were, notwithstanding that they had to cope with unusual difficulties, for local historians assure their readers that visits from savage Indians were comparatively frequent, even as late as the middle of the eighteenth century.

Fourth Street was in early days Easton's chief business street, and one old hotel on it has thus far survived, the Barnet House, although its lease of life is now uncertain.

Christopher Engle built the hotel shortly after the Revolution, and sold it to Edward Barnet, from whom it took its name. He ran it until his death, after the Civil War. The Inn had a very large yard in the rear, which is still there, with accommodations for many wagons, carriages and horses. The whole place has not been changed in years, although of late the old hotel has been used chiefly as a rooming-house.

As to the old Easton ferry mentioned, David Martin of Trenton was granted a permit in 1741 to open a ferry at the forks of the Delaware River, which he did a few years later, and built a ferry-house as well. Local researchers have never been able to determine the exact site of this house; some insisting that it was on the south, others equally sure that it was on the north side of the river. If the latter, the so-called Vernon Ferry House is the original one built by Martin. In any case, he built and occupied this one, which was afterwards bought and run by Nathaniel Vernon,

BLACK HORSE TAVERN, NEAR SWARTHMORE, PENNSYLVANIA

[*See page* 180.

YE OLDE VALLEY INN, YORK, PENNSYLVANIA

[*See page* 162.

THE FIREPLACE, BLACK HORSE TAVERN, NEAR SWARTHMORE, PENNSYLVANIA

and it survived until 1924, when it was torn down. The logs of which it was built are owned by the Northampton County Historical Society, which hopes some day to use them in building a permanent home for the Society and its records.

The old Swan is still an Easton hotel, under the name of the Stirling, but this may not have been built before 1850.

White's Hotel, built of brick, once the finest hotel in this section, and where the meeting was held which resulted in the founding of Lafayette College, is now used as a market, offices and apartments. The Franklin House (1818) also survives. It was formerly known as the Green Tree Inn.

Jacob Opp's tavern, at the corner of Northampton and 2nd Streets, built about 1790, stands as stores and apartments, but will soon be torn down. The old Kaeshlein House, opened in 1754 on the outskirts of Easton, stands, but is no longer an inn. Outside of Easton, the picturesque old Uhler's Hotel is now a farmhouse, the present hotel of that name being a different building on another site.

Off the direct road, northward, is Stroudsburg, where is the old Indian Queen Inn.

Continuing from Easton along much the same road as the old one, a detour to the northwest brings one to the quaint old Moravian town of Nazareth, and although its old Rose Inn has not been in existence since 1858, the present inn stands on the site of another old one, built in 1771.

The Rose Inn was built in 1752 of stone, and was quite large for that day, for it had seven rooms. It took its name from the quaint and pretty agreement by which John, Thomas and William Penn transferred to their half-sister Letitia Aubrey, of London, five thousand acres of their lands in the Province of Pennsylvania, on consideration that she pay on the 24th of each June, on demand, *One Red Rose*, in full settlement for all "services, customs and rents." The fifth landlord of The Rose removed to Bethlehem and kept the Crown Inn in that town, which will later be mentioned. When The Rose was torn down in 1858, a shift in the road-bed had left the old house no longer on the high road. Its red paint had grown dingy, but some of its timbers were used to build a dwelling on the same site.

Long before this, traffic had warranted the erection of another inn on the site now occupied by Nazareth's modern hotel. Between 1811 and 1836, this second inn enjoyed a great reputation for its excellent food, and especially famous were the Shrewsbury cakes made by Betsy Schmick, sister-in-law of the proprietor. Up to 1836, all landlords of the two inns were Moravians, and The Rose was built under the auspices of that church.

The first approach to the flourishing city of Bethlehem is not apt to suggest old inns, but two famous ones were located here, one of which, though much remodeled, still exists under its old name.

The first Bethlehem "house of entertainment," as these taverns were often called in early days, the first in the Lehigh Valley, was the Crown Inn, built in 1745, but not at first known by any name. The present Philadelphia and Reading railway station marks its site.

Bethlehem's very first house of any kind was built in 1741, and a ferry across the river was opened two years later. In 1745, Adam Schaus had a public house near this ferry, but that same year a small clearing was made in the woods, and a white oak log house, of two stories, with high gables, was put up. The house measured twenty-eight by forty feet, and contained four rooms on each floor. Partition boards, flooring, even beading and fluting of the woodwork, were cut from solid timber, the nails were made by Bethlehem nailsmiths, latches and bolts of wood were, of course, also hand-made. This building stood for one hundred and thirteen years, and when torn down was sound to the core.

During this same year of 1745, on the King's Road from Philadelphia, a road was laid out from Bethlehem to Nazareth, but beyond were mere bridle-paths, and pushing on still farther, a few days' work would be required to cut through the woods to the Indian ford across the Lehigh River, to an island, now the property of the Bethlehem Iron Company. A bridle-path from Bethlehem to Martin's Ferry, at "the exact fork of the Delaware," was later made into a highroad.

The Bethlehem Inn was first called Ye Tavern Over the Water, the Bethlehem Tavern, and so on, but it was not regularly licensed until 1753.

Kept at first by members of the Moravian Church, when later they gave its management over to a salaried agent, it first became known as *Die Krone*, and a sign displaying a crown was hung out in 1760 before it. The new landlord

[147]

introduced the surprising innovation of furnishing his guests with table napkins.

Many persons fleeing from the Indians took refuge in this inn, and later, when the Indians were more peaceful, they themselves visited it as guests, though hardly welcome ones, since they usually clamored for strong drink. Gideon of the Delawares, who styled himself King, could, we are informed, drink three quarts of rum a day, and not get drunk.

On September 11, 1763, the first "stage wagon" started from the Crown, Bethlehem, for Philadelphia, returning on Friday of each week.

In 1777, many soldiers and civilians fled over the ferry near by, and past the Crown Inn, escaping from the British who were occupying Philadelphia. On July 25th, 1782, Washington is said to have stayed in this inn.

The last landlord and his wife died in 1825, and the house was never after that open as an inn, but was sold in 1857 for thirty dollars, to make room for the railway station. It is said that much of its timber was used in building new houses in Bethlehem.

The Sun Inn still stands, and is a comfortable modern hotel. Its original stone walls have been built into the present structure; the old north wall, with a walled-up window opening, may be seen in the present hall beside the stairs. The house was begun in 1757 and not finished for three years. It was of stone, two stories high, with a mansard roof, had a reception room twenty-four by sixteen feet, offices and kitchen, on the lower floor; a dining-room thirty-seven by eighteen feet, and three suites consisting each of a sitting-room and two bedchambers on the second floor, so it was an elegant establishment for its day. The large amount of travel had proved too much for the Crown to handle, hence this second inn on the other side of the river was necessary. It, too, was built by the Moravians.

# Pennsylvania Inns

Peter Worbas was the first landlord of this fine house, with its brass firedogs, shovels and tongs, Delft basins and china bowls, cups and saucers, and silver spoons. Many were the distinguished guests entertained here; Governor Hamilton twice dined at the Sun, and among other prominent men were Sir William Johnson, Richard Penn, John Hancock, John Adams and Lyman Hall, one of the Georgia signers of the Declaration of Independence, Generals Schuyler, Gage, and Greene, and M. Gerard, Minister Plenipotentiary from France.

In 1763, the first stage left the Sun for Philadelphia every Monday, returning from the King of Prussia on Race street every Thursday. Three years later, water was brought into the house by wooden pipes, and in 1778, a British officer declared that the accommodations at the Sun were equal to those of the first taverns in London. He had one of the second story suites mentioned, and found it well lighted, with a fireplace in every room, and keys to the doors!

Lady Washington and her escort of several officers spent the night of June 15th, 1779 at the Sun, and this inn also claims that Washington stayed here on July 25th, 1782, the selfsame date that his visit is claimed for the Crown. Since the Sun is still standing, and furthermore shows the fine old mahogany bed *in which he slept*, it would seem to have the best of the dispute.

The Marquis de Chastellux, that early and extensive traveler over our country, found this Sun Inn "very handsome and spacious," and notes that he was served with "venison, moor game, most delicious red and yellow bellied trout, the highest flavored wild strawberries, the most luxurious asparagus, and the best vegetables that I ever saw, with wine and brandy of the best quality, exquisite old Port and Madeira."

The first bridge over the river was built in 1794, and by April, 1799, a stage left Easton every Monday and

Thursday at 3:30 A.M., reaching the Sun Inn at six, and thence proceeding to Quakertown and on to Philadelphia, arriving at the Franklin Head on Second Street the same evening. The fare from Bethlehem to Philadelphia was $2.75.

One of the Sun landlords, John Lehnert, went in 1807 to Salem, North Carolina, where he kept the Salem Tavern until his death.

Early in the nineteenth century, the Sun was remodeled, a third story added, and the exterior plastered and painted. It then had the reputation of being the best inn outside of Philadelphia.

As a specimen of the huge repasts that were served in comparatively recent times, the following menu of a dinner at the Sun on Tuesday, November 8th, 1857, to one hundred members of the Historical Society of Philadelphia, is quoted in full.

*Soup*
Calf's Head

*Fish*
Boiled Rock, Sauce Monocasy

*Roast*

| Ribs of Beef | Chickens | Domestic Ducks |

Goose, Apple Sauce      Stuffed Turkey, Cranberry Sauce
Lamb with Jelly      Ham, Champagne Sauce

*Hot Relieves*
Boiled Turkey, Oyster Sauce                    Baked Calf's Head

*Cold Dishes*

| Boned Turkey | Chicken Salad | Beef Tongue |

Lobster Salad                    Boiled Ham

*Relishes*
Assorted Pickles      Worcestershire Sauce      Cold Slaw

[150]

# Pennsylvania Inns

## Relishes

Cranberry Sauce           Currant Jelly           French Mustard
          Apple Sauce      Celery      Catsup

## Vegetables

Turnips    Sweet Potatoes      Baked Potatoes      Mashed Potatoes

## Game

Saddle of Venison      Canvasback Ducks      Red Head Ducks
          Pheasants      Partridges on Toast

## Ornamental
Pyramid of Macaroni

## Pastry and Puddings

Mince Pie      Moravian Apple Cake      Bethlehem Streussel
    Apple Pie      Moravian Sugar Cake      Pound Cake
          Calf's Foot Jelly
    Forms of Vanilla and Strawberry Ice Cream
          Coffee and Tea

During Fries' rebellion, when a mob objected to the tax on window-glass, seventeen rebels were imprisoned in the basement of the Sun Inn, and were rescued by Fries. One historian believes that this may account for the tales of dungeons and subterranean passages said to exist in the Sun building, and which no one seems able to find.

Before this inn was built there was another on the same side of the river, opened in 1752 as a house of entertainment for Indians, and later used for white persons when it was too stormy to risk crossing to the Crown.

The Golden Eagle, a large hotel for its day, was opened in Bethlehem in 1823, on the west side of Main Street. Its site is now occupied by the modern Bethlehem Hotel.

The Moravian women early won a reputation with visitors for their beautiful embroidery and needlework. They were a musical people, too, and imported in 1754 from Europe

[151]

the first trombone quartet, for their noted Easter services in the cemetery, now attended by many strangers.

Fourteen miles from Bethlehem, at Quakertown, where the stages used to stop, is the Red Lion, built in 1770 and still open as a hotel. The present effect of the house is not at all old, with its woodwork painted in bright colors, but probably the kitchen, although the old fireplace is closed, and the adjoining room on the side, with two or three of the upstairs rooms, are part of the original building. At all events, the house has been open under the same name and on the same site since the early date given.

Kutztown, through which the modern road passes even as did the old one, has the old Kemp House, open until last summer (1925), although its fate is now in doubt. The present owner, the sixth generation of Kemps to own it, lives across the road, but takes little interest in the old tavern nor does he keep it repaired. A spring in its cellar forms almost a pond, and while in old times, when there was no ice, this may have been most convenient for keeping food in warm weather, it hardly adds to present comfort. A portion of this old two-storied stone house may date from 1740, and the date 1765 is displayed on one of the exterior walls. It contains fine large bedrooms as well as four small ones on the second floor, and the usual apartments, parlor, barroom, and so forth below. Almost every room has its fireplace, although most of these have been boarded up. Washington is said to have watered his horse here, on the way from Carlisle to Easton.

Kutztown had two other old inns, of which one, The Black Bear, modernized and no longer under this name, is still a hotel. The other, the Eagle, has also been altered, and is no longer an inn.

For many years, the Halfway House in Richmond Township, and Kemp's in Kutztown were the only taverns on the state road between Reading and Allentown.

# Pennsylvania Inns

In Schaefferstown, oldest settlement in Lebanon County, stands on the town square an old stone inn built in 1752 by the founder of the town. Before the Revolution, this was known as the Royal George, and was an aristocratic old inn. Later, its name was changed to the George Washington. It has an extremely well-built cellar, which sheltered many refugees during the French and Indian wars.

In Lebanon, on Market Square, stands the stone American House, built in 1771. On its façade are set two stones, with this inscription in German: "God bless this house, and all that go in and out of it. Caspar & Sawina Schneberly, 1771," and, "Maurer in Lebanon, Heinrich Rewalt," with "1771" carved ornamentally. A third story was added to the original building in 1855.

Another old stone building, altered merely to permit of a drug store on the ground floor, stands on the corner of Eighth and Cumberland Streets. This was originally known as the Buck Hotel, and William Henry Harrison stopped here during his visit to Lebanon on his presidential campaign.

In East Hanover Township, on the Swatara Creek, Adam Harper built a log tavern at so early a date that it was surrounded by Indian wigwams. Later it was replaced by a stone house which is still standing.

On the northwest corner of Fifth and Washington Streets, Reading, stands what was the Franklin House, the original two stories built in 1761. It is now stores and a rooming-house. In the barroom of this old inn, Martin Coleman, a local tailor, told a story of General Braddock's death which historians may dispute. It was to the effect that the British General was shot in the back by one of his own men, William Fawcett, because Fawcett's brother, also a soldier, had been struck by the officer with his saber.

Only recently was the Federal Inn, two years younger than the Franklin, torn down to make room for a bank.

[153]

# Early American Inns and Taverns

On the southeast corner of Fifth and Franklin Streets, stood Witman's, visited in 1788 by John Penn.

The present Mansion House was old before the Civil War, although it has since then been both enlarged and remodeled. The town pump once stood in the square in front of this house, and stages stopped here in the old days, even as the modern autobus and trolley do now.

In 1789, a two-horse coach, the first conveyance, ran weekly between Reading and Philadelphia, making the fifty-one miles in two days. Until 1826, the type of coach used between the two cities was that known as the "steamboat," open, uncovered, and holding twenty passengers.

From Reading to Lancaster a number of old inns will be passed on the highroad, and there are others in the immediate vicinity.

For instance, southeast of Reading on the road to Potts-town, is Baumstown and its Red Lion (1776), now turned into a tourist dining-room and ice cream parlor; Yellow House, which post office took its name from the old yellow painted tavern; Birdsboro, with its Mansion House (1751), now a private residence; Geiger's Mills, with the Plow (1781), the sign of which still exists; the White Bear, at Scarlet's Mills, greatly altered now into a private residence; and at Morgantown, the Morgantown Inn, still open. David Morgan built part of the present house in 1799, but an inn stood on the same site before that.

On the direct road to Lancaster, at Sinking Spring, is an old inn, named the Centennial in 1876, but known as Green's for many years before that. It has been modernized in appearance by a large wooden wing, and a third story added to the original stone house. It has modern doors and windows, and the present proprietor, who dislikes company—they say in the town that he dislikes guests equally—will grudgingly assure you that the house is not old. But a locality authority, Dr. P. C. Croll, a student of old times and

[154]

buildings in this section, states that the original part is well over a hundred years old.

Brinckley's at Wernersville is no longer an inn, but houses several families.

Womelsdorf has two old-timers: the Central House, now open only as a lunch room, and across the street, the Seltzer House, itself old, but the successor of a still older inn of that name, which stood on the same road, but several hundred feet nearer Reading.

The first inn, long and low, was built by Joseph Seltzer, probably in 1762, on what was then called the Tulpehocken Road. This, the first road laid out in this part of the country, as the result of a petition to the "Honorable Bench" in Philadelphia on the part of residents of the section, was opened in 1727. Many famous men stopped at the original Seltzer House, which was torn down more than fifty years ago, some of its well-seasoned timber being used in building modern houses in the town.

Washington, Daniel Rittenhouse, Robert Morris, William Smith, Provost of the University, Teuch Francis, who represented the Penns in 1793, when, on account of yellow fever, the Government had been removed from Philadelphia, were all guests of this old inn. They came "studying the country for a series of canals"; the first locks on the old canal between the Schuylkill and Susquehanna rivers had been built two years before. Washington was president of a canal company which proposed to furnish means of transportation for the produce of Pennsylvania farmers, to prevent these men from going farther west, out of the state, where rivers offered good means for floating their produce down to French ports in Louisiana. Some of these farmers even proposed to emigrate into French territory, and it was desired to prevent this if possible, for Washington and others felt that the country could not afford to lose such citizens.

Washington came to Womelsdorf again in 1794, during

[155]

# Early American Inns and Taverns

the whiskey insurrections, but on this visit he had dinner only, with the soldiers at the Central House. This inn was then kept by Conrad Strouch, who had stages and relays of horses, and it is certainly one hundred and fifty years old.

Perhaps forty years after the first Seltzer Inn was built, or in the early 1700's, John Seltzer, son of Jacob, built a larger one, two stories high, with probably three rooms on the first floor, which house, greatly enlarged, is the present hotel. Only one more generation of Seltzers kept it; the third, Michael, built himself a fine house next door, and retired from business. This house is still occupied by his descendants. Between house and hotel is a large yard, paved with cobblestones while Michael Seltzer was landlord. Before the railroad was built, teamsters with wagon-loads of iron ore from Cornwall used to stop over night at the Seltzer House, and on cold mornings often found their wagons so tightly frozen in the mud of the yard that they could not be moved for some hours. So the yard was paved, and the cobblestones remain to this day.

In Hamburg, between Reading and Harrodsburg, a road from the railway station crosses the river by a covered bridge, and entering the town, becomes State Street. Where this crosses Fourth Street, the principal business thoroughfare, is the American House. The oldest part on the corner is now a basement pool- and lunch-room, with an old kitchen adjoining, and in the story above is a modern grocery store. The other side of the house, the more modern, is now the hotel. Although the third story, the rear extension, and the kitchen here are fairly modern, the former barroom, dining-room, and bedrooms above are old, although only a few massive beams would now suggest it.

Farther south, on Fourth Street, is the Washington House, of about the same age, but looking older, for a portico still projects over the sidewalk along the entire front, and an old

[156]

signboard, with a supposed portrait of Washington, much re-painted, and with the name of the present proprietor added, still hangs in front of the house. The oldest part seems to be the rear, and a basement room was probably once the old kitchen, for it has a very large old fireplace. Otherwise, there is little to suggest its age: one hundred and fifty years.

Lancaster has many old inn buildings, as would be expected of the terminus of the very old Lancaster and Philadelphia turnpike.

The first stage of which there is mention ran here in 1754, as noted in the diary of Governor Pownall of New Jersey, who visited Lancaster in that year. The town was then called Hickory, from a tree of that species near a spring, and that was the name of its first tavern. The first on record in "Lancaster Town," was kept by a man named Gibson, in 1722, and stood on the old road from Philadelphia to Wright's Ferry, no longer a ferry.

The buildings of the old Cross Keys, frequented by court and county officials, and of the Sorrel Horse, on West King Street, are still standing. The former, one block west of Center Square, is much modernized, although the original walls remain, and it was open as late as in 1883 as a hotel. The Sorrel Horse, although it has decidedly come down in the world, retains many of the old inn features. Modern stores surround it in front and on the sides, but beneath an arch on the street, a driveway leads into the old yard, and once in here, the old building is unmistakable. There are the double galleries or piazzas running across the front, such as one sees in very old inn buildings here and in England. The house fronts only on this yard now, and is used for cheap lodgings.

The Plow, built in the 1750's, a one-story stone house, was recently torn down, as was the Swan, also known as The Golden Swan, or The White Swan. After this ceased to be an inn, it housed the offices of a newspaper, but a department store now occupies the site.

The Manor House, built in 1778, was burned, replaced by a new one, and that, too, is gone. Shober's, on the corner of Orange and Queen Streets, was torn down to make room for the Y. M. C. A. building, and on North Street, although a portion of the old Grape Tavern stands, it is now a store.

Another old house, the Fountain Inn (1758), where the courts met while the Court House was being built, occupied part of the site of the present modern Lincoln Hotel, and the Pennsylvania stands on the site of the old Globe.

At Lime and East King Streets, the Ship, another old inn, was torn down for a business block; the Balsamen, 121 East King Street, has been entirely remodeled into stores and apartments. A restaurant, however, at the corner of Orange and Spruce Streets, close to the railroad tracks, though painted and renovated a bit, is the old Sign of the Wagon, and any one examining the two and a half story stone building will not doubt its age.

The Pennsylvania State Arms, built in 1799, at which two years later Dr. Franklin stopped, was burned in 1811, rebuilt in 1813, and has now gone. Before 1810, there was a Lamb Inn, for there is a record of its sale to a new proprietor in that year. The number of old taverns formerly existing in Lancaster is large. In 1765 there were fifty-three licensed ones in the township.

The Lincoln Highway here follows the old Lancaster turnpike, along which, in 1777, a fourteen-year-old boy, Christopher Wolf, galloped with the post, which then often contained army dispatches. He cleverly eluded the many traps set for him by the British, and had a reward which must have been dear to his brave young heart. He was in Philadelphia when the news arrived of Cornwallis's surrender at Yorktown, and by hard riding, reached Lancaster at 1 A. M., and awoke the residents to rejoice.

# Pennsylvania Inns

On the outskirts of Lancaster, close to the bridge over the Canestoga River, stands the Canestoga Inn, still open to the public. The present house was built after the Revolution, but before that, in 1741, an old tavern stood on the same site. When the new one was planned, the old house was moved to an adjoining lot, and in 1839 was still open, known as The Grape, or Michael's, but it has now vanished. On the other side of the river there is another old inn building, and before the bridge was built there was a ferry and toll-house there.

Continuing east along the Lincoln Highway, the old Paradise Inn, once known as The Sign of the Ship, and still a hotel, will be noticed. There was another inn here, The Sign of the Stage, David Witmer's tavern, a three-storied, red brick building now used for stores and apartments. Originally of two stories, this was a famous inn, at which Washington is said to have dined, at a time when there were five taverns in the place. Although no longer a hotel, this is still owned by the Witmer family. The "upper block," which stood in front of this tavern, and which Lafayette mounted to be presented to the people assembled to greet him on his visit to the town, is owned by and stands in front of the country home of Judge Landis of Lancaster, whose wife was a granddaughter of David Witmer. They also own the old brass knocker from the tavern door.

There is a story told in connection with Washington's visit to this inn. Across the road was a hemp mill which the President was anxious to see in operation, as he was thinking of building one on his own estate. The mill hand was careless with the machinery; something went wrong, and he was injured, which so impressed the distinguished visitor that he gave up all idea of having such a mill.

After the inn was given up, the building was used for a

[159]

Post Office, a Young Ladies' Seminary, and an orphanage, before being converted to its present uses.

Farther along the road, on the south side, the old Sign of the Free Masons, now a private house, and the Sign of the Buck were both owned by the Witmers.

Not on the Lincoln Highway, but in this vicinity, is a private residence once known as The Practical Farmer, or Reynolds' Tavern, built in 1813. Its old sign is still in existence.

Returning to the main road, the Rising Sun Inn at Salisbury is still a hotel, but not under the old name. Where the trolley leaves the highway for a short distance, the old Slaymaker Inn, a famous one kept by Amos Slaymaker, who became a Member of Congress, stands across the road from the handsome summer home of the Slaymaker family, known as White Chimneys. Although greatly enlarged and modernized, this, too, is an old house, and some say that it, not the old house opposite, is the original inn.

The old Williamstown Hotel at Vintage, and one at Lemon Place are still open.

Continuing by the Lincoln Highway, instead of along the road which forks to the right, in Salisbury is the White Horse, where George and Martha Washington stayed when the British occupied Philadelphia, and Congress met in Lancaster; one mile below is the old Waterloo Tavern; near here is the Mount Vernon Inn; and at Compass, near the church, the Compass Inn, all of the Revolutionary period. Below Intercourse, At the Hat, now a weatherboarded farmhouse, is hard to distinguish as an old inn; none the less it is one. The sign, believed to have been painted by Benjamin West, is treasured in a private residence. The tavern took its name from the hatter who had squatted near by.

More than in any other part of the country, the old Pennsylvania inns recall those of England with their quaint names and signboards, and almost all of the old English

THE GENERAL GREENE INN, BUCKINGHAM, PENNSYLVANIA

[See page 164.

OLD ANCHOR HOTEL, WRIGHTSTOWN TOWNSHIP, PENNSYLVANIA

[See page 165.

JOLLY POST, FRANKFORD, PENNSYLVANIA

[See page 174.

names have been repeated here, or in the southern states. New England taverns in general were known by their landlords' names, or from the town in which they were located.

By following the trolley along the branch road near the Slaymaker Inn, for the highroad has shifted here, one comes to The Gap, a very old settlement originally on the highroad. Here were once several old inns whose buildings remain, but are no longer used for hotel purposes.

Beyond the third bridge over the railroad, a mile or more from the village of The Gap, stood one of these inns, built in 1726, and belonging to the Penn family. Indeed, they owned most of the land in this section. For many years this house has been a farm dwelling.

The Gap Hotel, a long, three-storied house directly on the old highroad, is said to have been built about 1750. When the highroad was shifted, another hotel, the Mansion House, stood across the road, a bit nearer the center of the town. The same woman owned both, and it was suggested to her to keep one still open as a hotel. She chose The Gap, which soon proved unprofitable; the other house, much more modern, built in 1838 for a private residence, once more became such, and is now occupied by a gentleman whose father and grandfather kept the White Horse, already mentioned. He, however, had no wish to continue in the hotel business

The Gap Hotel is now a private dwelling, the third floor used only for storage purposes, and all of its old inn fittings have been removed.

The Bear, in Elizabethtown, was originally a log cabin, built in 1730. Fifteen years later, a stone house replaced the cabin, and it is now a private residence, as is another Revolutionary inn, the General Washington, in Downington. The Duke of Connaught, which John Vernor was licensed to keep in 1735, is no longer an inn. The old Red Lion, about three miles away has disappeared.

[161]

We have followed the old Lancaster turnpike eastward, but before returning to York for another tour of inns, a few words about the old road may be of interest. It started from Market Street, Philadelphia, and ran a little east of the Darby Road, now Woodland Avenue. An old almanac cites twenty-one inns in the sixty miles between Philadelphia and Lancaster, but a later authority gives the number as sixty-six, and Mr. Searight lists all of them in his book, *The Old Pike.* Some have already been mentioned; others will be described in another chapter; but a few more are here listed for reference.

Two and a half miles from what was then Philadelphia's city limits, on the west side of the Schuylkill, was the Rising Sun, which now has an avenue named for it; the White Lamb, at the fourth milestone, near the present Wynnefield Avenue; the Sorrel Horse (Radnor); the Plough, remodeled into a handsome private residence; the famous old Blue Ball, at Daylesford, kept by Prissy Robinson, who quarreled with the railroad authorities over her heifer which had been killed on the tracks, and when she did not get the amount of damages she thought suitable, got even with the road by greasing the tracks until they were glad to settle; the Steamboat; Barley Sheaf; States Arms, still standing in Sadsbury; a General Wayne (not the one near Paoli), which later became a school; and a second Rising Sun.

Dr. Sachse quotes a droll old toast, apropos of these old inns:

"Here is to the Sorrel Horse that kicked the Unicorn, that made the Eagle fly; that scared the Lamb from under the Stage, for drinking the Spring House dry; that drove the Blue Ball under the Black Bear, and chased General Jackson all the way to Paoli."

Four miles east of York, although within the actual city limits, on the Lincoln Highway, stands Ye Olde Valley Inn, built in 1738 of stone. Now two stories and a half

high, the original part was a block house, the present northeast parlor, with rooms immediately over it. Built of limestone by a pioneer settler, John Greist, one of the first English Quakers to settle in this locality, in 1755 he sold it,
the new owner enlarged it, and opened the house as an inn.
While the railroad was building, the civil engineers stayed
in this house, but before that it was a famous tavern, with
a ballroom fifty by thirty feet on the second floor, now divided into bedrooms. As the landlord had the reputation
of serving good suppers, many parties were given here.
During the Civil War, in 1863, the Confederate General
Gordon and two of his officers stopped in the inn for refreshments, while the soldiers marched past. It was also
past this inn that in 1813 powder was carried in Canestoga
wagons to Perry at Lake Erie.

Through the house runs a broad hall, with rooms on either
side. The front room on the west was originally the bar,
with a parlor behind it, behind this the large old kitchen,
with an enormous old fireplace. Other parlors are across
the hall, and beyond them another hall and more rooms.
There are a number of bedrooms upstairs, besides the former
ballroom, and some of the old doors with their hinges and
locks remain.

The present proprietor, who runs the house as a hotel and
restaurant, is a dealer in antiques, so the old inn rooms are
appropriately furnished.

About a mile east of Valley Inn, a road turns off from the
highway to the right. If the weather is good—otherwise it
would mean hard traveling—by following this road until
it forks, then taking the road to the right and turning into
a lane, one will come to the old Schultz house, two stories,
of stone, and now a farmhouse. Built in 1737, it is the oldest house west of the Susquehanna in Pennsylvania. Members of the Continental Congress dined in this house on their
way to York on September 30th, 1777, then moved on to

[163]

hold their meeting in the old Court House, at that time standing in the center of the square.

In York itself, one block west of this square, there stands on West Market Street an old house with a history, duly set forth on a tablet affixed to the side wall. It was selected by General Wayne in 1781 for his headquarters, and was built about 1765. Two stores occupy the ground floor, to which an extension has been added in the rear. This addition and the second story are now a private residence, but the original house, two and a half stories high, with an attic above the half story, in the high, steep roof, is the only surviving old inn building in the city of York.

In Hanover, not far away, is a very old building which now serves the purpose for which it was built, a private residence. The pioneer Colonel Richard McAllister built his log cabin home here in 1745, and ten years later entertained Benjamin Franklin, during the French and Indian War. Later, a stone structure was built around the original log cabin, and for half a century it was a hotel, before again becoming a private dwelling.

The Five Mile House, or Wolf's Tavern, five miles west of York on the Lincoln Highway, was built about 1765. From 1780 to 1875 it was a noted inn, but is now a private residence, as is a large stone farmhouse, two miles farther on the same road but which was a hotel from 1760 to 1800. The Ten Mile house, still farther west, has not been an inn since 1800.

Another route from New Jersey into Pennsylvania runs through Lambertville, to New Hope, Pennsylvania. Here were two old inns, both more than a hundred years old, but they have been altered into apartment houses.

At Buckingham, on this old highroad, is the General Greene Inn, the oldest part of which was built in 1752. It received its name after the General made it his headquarters during the Revolution. The old signboard with his supposed likeness still hangs outside, and the kitchen, where he is said to have then eaten his meals, with an enormous old fireplace in one end, assuredly is a part of the oldest building. Lovers of antiquity will deplore the painting of the old room's paneling, extending from floor to ceiling, in bright pink and green, the work of a former tenant. On the outer door is still the old lock. The whole or at least part of the large dining-room may be of the original house; if the former, then it is probably several rooms now thrown into one. Probably much of the present front has been added, and the third story was built on sixty-seven years ago. The bannister of the stairs leading to the second story is hand-carved.

The old York Road, because of a large pond which prevented its continuing in a straight line, used to pass behind this house, where now an archway connects the kitchen with an outbuilding. When a quarry was opened near by, the pond almost entirely disappeared, so the road was straightened.

Not far from Buckingham, at Wrightstown, the Anchor Hotel, built about 1724, is still open. It, too, is changed in appearance by comparatively modern alterations and additions.

Doylestown had many inns and one survives, still in use as a hotel, standing near the site of the first tavern of all. The town is on two old turnpikes, one running from Philadelphia to the Water Gap, the other crossing at right angles in the town, connecting the Schuylkill and Delaware rivers.

The original Fountain Inn stood on the other side of the present Court Street from the later hotel, in what was a wood lot, and apparently its patrons had to cross this lot to reach it. The oldest part of the present hotel was probably built in 1752, but a number of additions have since been made to it, although as much as possible the old appearance has been kept, and there are many old door hinges and latches. The present proprietor is an enthusiastic collector of antiques, and has filled his hotel with old furniture, rugs, prints, clocks and ornaments of all kinds, so that much of the old-time atmosphere is preserved. Among his grandfather and banjo clocks, old books, etc., are several of the long horns with which stage-coach drivers used to announce their approach to an inn.

The exact age of the present house is hard to determine. An inn certainly stood where the present one stands at least as early as 1790, although the first recorded license was not given until in 1800, to Charles Stewart. But in early days, inns were often opened some years before a license was obtained or even asked for, so the old portions may actually have been built in 1752, or that date may apply to the building of a second house on the old site. In any case, the Fountain Inn is venerable, and Doylestown's only surviving old inn, although the buildings of several others are still standing.

The Ship has been torn down and replaced by stores; the Green Tree so altered into a handsome private residence that its identity would not be suspected; still another, two or three stories high originally, with a long double porch, is now a four-story apartment house. The Cross Keys, a tavern dating from about 1758, was, until twenty years ago, a farmers' inn. Standing at a crossroad on the way to Easton, it is now occupied by several families. Still another inn occupied the site of the present Post Office.

Thanks to the generosity of a resident, Dr. Mercer, Doylestown has a most interesting museum, whose tall, concrete building is plainly visible near the center of the town. Here may be seen a number of signboards from old inns, including that from the Robert Morris Inn at Morris- ville, with "My Word is My Bond," on one side, and many pictures of old taverns. There is a large collection, too, of farm and domestic implements of colonial days, one of the famous Canestoga wagons, a stage-coach, the body hung by leather straps; sleighs, shays, and many other articles which help one to form a picture of life in that period.

The Craigs, ancestors of Theodore Roosevelt, all took up land in Warrington, in Bucks County, but the family of eight brothers and sisters, with the latter's husbands, removed to Allen Township and founded what was long known as Craig's. One of the brothers-in-law bought land which later was the site of Craig's Tavern, now in Warringtonville.

In 1749, James Ratcliffe was licensed to keep a tavern on the York Road, probably where the Jamison Hotel now stands. He sold his tavern to John Barnhill, who married one of the Craig daughters, and Barnhill kept it until 1761, when he sold out and moved to Philadelphia. Here he bought two brick houses on Elm Street, between Second and Third, and in 1767 was still an innkeeper there. He and his wife were the great-great-grandparents of the late president.

Willow Grove has its old inn, the Sorrel Horse—names are repeated frequently in these localities—and at Bethayres is the Lady Washington, built in 1760, but called by this name after Martha Washington stayed there. The house still stands, but has been unoccupied now for some time, and previous to that was a private residence. On part of its grounds, a building occupied by a trust company was erected five years ago, and the old house will probably soon be torn down.

## Chapter IX

*Old Inns of Philadelphia and Vicinity*

PHILADELPHIA, long before it became for a brief time the capital of the United States, was always an important town. In addition to being the terminus for stage lines from New York—or the starting point for lines to that city, whichever is preferred—in addition to being the starting point of the very old Philadelphia and Lancaster turnpike, from here a line of boats plied to New Castle, Delaware, connecting in that town with stages for the south. Philadelphia had, in consequence, many inns from early days.

Patrons of these old inns were hearty eaters and drinkers. Their dinners consisted of roast beef, leg of mutton, ham, cabbage, a fat fowl, with ale, port, Madeira, or a glass of rum with hot water. The traveler's bed would be in a small room, with bare floor, white-washed walls, and plain curtains, for the city tavern, although it did accommodate travelers over night, was, according to an early historian, largely a drinking place, the rural inn catering more to those wishing to stop for a night or for a longer period.

In the most prosperous inn period, artists of some reputation did not scorn to paint inn signs. Woodside painted several; so did Matthew Pratt, who later studied under Benjamin West in London. Gilbert Stuart painted at least one sign, that for the King of Prussia. The great variety of Philadelphia inn signs was commented on by an English traveler in 1818, and a year before, another Englishman, Lieutenant Francis Hall, spoke of the landlords as "topping

[168]

# Old Inns of Philadelphia and Vicinity

men, field officers of militia, with farms attached to their inns." He thought them "apt to think that travelers rather receive than confer favor," but remarked that "they always give plentiful fare, particularly at breakfast, when veal cutlets, sweetmeats, cheese, eggs and ham were liberally set before us. Dinner is little more than a repetition of breakfast, with spirits instead of coffee. I never heard wine called for. The common drink is small cider. Rum, whisky and brandy are placed upon the table, their use left to the discretion of the company, who seem rarely to abuse them. Tea is a meal of the same solid construction as breakfast, answering also for supper. The daughters of the host officiate at tea and breakfast, and generally wait at dinner."

Another English writer (1822-23) complains of having to take room and board either by the day or week, but paid only $10 a week at Philadelphia's Mansion House.

Charles Dickens, in his much abused American Notes, remarked about twenty years later of Philadelphia, "It is a handsome city, but distractingly regular."

Probably Philadelphia's oldest inn was built in 1682 by George Guest, in a row of houses known as "Budd's Long Row." Of the Pennsylvania Farmers' Inn, once well-known, there still stands what is apparently but part of the old house, a three story and attic building, next door to the corner of Third and Callowhill Streets. The ground floor was evidently quite recently a saloon; above is a teamster's office. The Black Horse, on Second Street, south of Callowhill, may be identified in an old yellow brick building, now used for stores and offices, while the Red Lion, which "stood near the New Market," doubtless formed part of the present building, no longer a hotel, on the corner of Second and Noble Streets, and which will probably soon be razed.

One old inn, sadly fallen from its former estate, is still in actual operation and may be visited at the northwest corner of Girard Avenue and Second Street. This is the

[169]

Eagle Inn, now a four-story yellow brick building, with a store on the corner, and a basement cafe of which dubious tales are told, replacing the old dining-room. This building, or at least part of it, was a truly old inn, and an archway on the Avenue still admits to a typical old stage tavern yard, as formerly did another archway on Second Street, now closed. That portion of the house facing on the yard still has the old gallery across the second story, so characteristic of some of the old English stage-coach inns.

Until a very few years ago, the site of an old Philadelphia hotel was marked by a modern one. On the southeast corner of Market and Eleventh Streets, there stood first the United States, then the Mansion, and finally the New Bingham Hotel, the first of these, built in 1812, having been a famous house in its day.

The William Penn, a substantial brick building, no longer a hotel, still stands on the corner of Market and 38th Streets. This was an early stage stop for eastern coaches, and until 1897, the Newton Square stage started from the inn. The Bull's Head opposite, of similar style, replaced a former hotel of the same name. Two blocks below. on Market Street, there was another William Penn, now gone.

One more old building survives, although its lease of life will surely be short, for in the autumn of 1925 it was empty and dilapidated. This is the old Blue Bell Inn, on Woodland Avenue and 74th Street, built in 1766. Over Woodland Avenue, the Darby Road, Chester Pike, or King's Highway, as it has variously been called, Washington led his defeated army back from Brandywine, and he also passed along this road to victory at Yorktown. He drove over it many times, and at the Blue Bell was given his first welcome when he came from Mount Vernon to Philadelphia.

This apparently covers all old inn buildings still standing in Philadelphia save those in some of the outlying towns now within the city limits.

[170]

# Old Inns of Philadelphia and Vicinity

But if none others are standing, memories of many persist. In old narratives they are mentioned, and some may be heard of from the lips of old residents.

Very old was the Penny Pot House, a two-story brick building on the corner of Front and Vine Streets, which inn was later called the Jolly Tar, and disappeared long ago. In 1701, Penn decreed that the two landing-places near the inns should be left open for city and common use, and as early as 1683 he wrote that there were seven ordinaries where a good meal could be had for sixpence.

Benjamin Franklin, on his arrival in Philadelphia in 1723, went first to the Crooked Billet, on the wharf above Chestnut Street, and this house was called old then. The George Inn, at Second and Mulberry Streets, was a stop for New York and Baltimore coaches, and sported a sign showing St. George killing the dragon. This house was at one time kept by John Inskeep, Mayor of Philadelphia, and later a noted host was Michael Dennison, "the biggest landlord in the city."

The City Tavern, another noted resort where Washington used to sup, advertised in 1774 that it had "a long room divided into boxes, fitted with tables, and elegantly lighted."

Thomas Leiper, who connected his quarries at Crum Street by a railroad, in the very early days of that method of transportation, invited several gentlemen to meet him at a second Bull's Head, on Second Street, north of Poplar. In its yard, Mr. Leiper showed his guests his railway plan.

Near Centre Square stood the Indian Queen, usually known as the Centre House, for another inn, on the east side of Fourth, below Market Street, for which Woodside painted a sign in 1800, claimed the name of Indian Queen, although younger than the other.

On the east side of Second Street, in what was known as Greenwich, stood the Yellow Cottage, originally built for a country home, surrounded by lilac bushes and standing on

[171]

the side of a hill sloping up to Front Street. When the house became an inn, guests used to indulge here in various sports, such as quoit-throwing, attempting to walk blindfolded up the hill, only to discover that they had walked in a circle; rifle-shooting at a target, throwing an ax, large stones, or a fifty-six pound weight.

The Purple and Blue Tavern, another old one, was a favorite resort with the military, until a new proprietor changed its name to The Quiet Woman, with the picture of a headless woman for a sign. This, for some reason, so displeased his patrons that he had to leave the inn, presumably taking the offending sign with him.

One would now look in vain for the Spread Eagle, on Market and Ninth Streets, which was a stage house in 1814, for when it was built, the stages which had been leaving for Harrisburg, Sunbury, and Pittsburgh a block below on Market Street, moved up to this hotel. Later, and until after 1850 it was known as the Philadelphia House.

Of Germantown's many inns, only two buildings now stand in recognizable form, the former Green Tree and the Washington, both on Main Street, now Germantown Avenue.

The first of these, now a parish house, substantial, of stone, little changed externally save for new windows and fresh paint, was built in 1748. This was the home of David and Sarah Pastorius, and they kept the tavern until 1754. David was one of Germantown's earliest settlers, and at his dugout, in October 1683, the thirteen original settlers met to draw lots for their home sites.

Known in turn as Widow Mackinnett's, the Hornet's Nest, and the Green Tree, it was in this tavern that in 1750 a meeting was held to organize a Germantown public school, and the Germantown Academy.

At 6239 Germantown Avenue stands the old Washington Tavern, said to have been built in 1740, but it has fallen on evil days. The corner room was occupied fairly recently as a saloon, but when seen last autumn, the whole building was deserted and forlorn. What looks like the old stable is now an automobile repair shop, and the old stable yard remains. The property was for sale, and probably the buildings will soon be torn down.

There is such difference of opinion about the age of Philadelphia's popular Valley Green Inn that it is impossible to determine it. Somewhere between seventy-five and one hundred and twenty-five years lies the truth. It has, at all events, long been popular with Philadelphians both in winter, for sleighing parties, and in summer for those frequenting the beautiful shady grounds. The present innkeeper, who runs it under the supervision of a committee of women, says that it is one hundred years old, and at all events, the locale is both beautiful and of historic interest.

Of old inns outside of Philadelphia there are so many that the present volume does not pretend to include them all, but merely the most important, and those on main traveled roads. On by-roads will be found many others, some so altered into private residences that their former history would not be suspected.

Frankford, now of course within city limits, was settled by the Swedes long before the central part of Pennsylvania. The first Englishman to take up land here, Thomas Farmer, purchased it in 1679, but as he did not receive his patent until 1688, he was antedated in this respect four years by Thomas Waddy.

While eastern Pennsylvania, western New Jersey, and Delaware were occupied chiefly by the early Swedish settlers, travel was largely by boat. Even much later, a popular route from New York south was by coach to Philadelphia, thence by boat to New Castle, Delaware, and again by stage to Havre-de-Grace, Baltimore, etc.

With the coming of English settlers, wagon travel was

[173]

still difficult, because of the *many stumps in the roads*. By
1733, a stage line ran to New York via Burlington and
Perth Amboy, and three years later another left Butler's
Death of the Fox, in Strawberry Alley, Philadelphia, for
New York, taking three days to make the trip. All stages
to New York ceased running in 1836, when the Philadelphia
and Trenton Railroad was opened.

The Philadelphia-Bristol turnpike is Frankford's Main
Street, now Frankford Avenue, and this was the direct
route between Philadelphia and New York. Recently this
road has been straightened in places, and will now be the
shortest automobile route between the two cities. That
part of the road running through Frankford out into the
country was also the chief thoroughfare for farmers bringing their produce into the city. During British occupation
of Philadelphia, Frankford was disputed ground and several skirmishes occurred in and near the village, for the
British tried to keep the road open, that the farmers might
bring in food supplies, and the Americans tried to close it.

Previous to 1800, Frankford was a charming country
village, with broad, shady streets, houses set in gardens, no
pavements, or later a macadamized strip in the middle of
the forty-five-foot road, with dirt on either side which in
bad weather became deep mud. (The Bristol Turnpike was
one of the first roads on which Macadam tried his new
method of road making.) Silas Dean, a Connecticut dele-
gate to the Continental Congress held in 1774, in Philadelphia, wrote of Frankford's "beautiful road, bordered on
each side by meadows which reminded me of the Connecticut Valley at home.'

By 1800 the town had six taverns; one very old, if not
the oldest, the Jolly Post Boy, or as it was later called, the
Jolly Post, stood until very recently. Just how old it was
no one seems to know, but in 1768 it was referred to as "the
noted inn called the Sign of the Jolly Post," when it was

[174]

advertised for sale. It then stood "in about 20 acres of land," and had "a young orchard of 200 apple trees." A row of stores has replaced the old tavern, near the Orchard Street station of the Frankford elevated railway, but in the side wall of the present building may be seen the old south gable, and in 1912 a bronze tablet was placed to commemorate the tavern, for Washington, Lafayette, and many other noted men were its guests. On the night of the grand ball given in Philadephia by General Howe, it was from the Jolly Post that Captain Allan McLane and his dragoons started out to set fire to the British palisades, the glare from these flames breaking up the ball.

During the Harrison presidential campaign after the Mexican War, a log-cabin facsimile of the general's reputed birthplace was set up outside the Jolly Post, with a barrel of hard cider on tap. Parties of Philadelphians used to drive out in summer to eat strawberries or peaches and cream in the old inn's garden, or in winter sleighing parties used to make it their objective.

In the spring of 1881, a battalion of the United States Army under General Hancock, marched in the path of the Continental Army from Trenton to Philadelphia, on their way to Virginia, to commemorate the victory of Yorktown. They stopped at the Jolly Post.

Another old inn, which stands—or stood recently—at 4219 Frankford Avenue, is more than two hundred years old, since the property belonged to one family, the Pauls, for that length of time. It became an inn in 1760, and continued as such, under different names, through the Revolution. In 1840 it was known as the Golden Fleece, and was kept by Captain George Snyder, a veteran of the War of 1812. Later it became the Park Hotel, and although stores have been built into its front, it is still a hotel. A two and a half story, pebble-dashed, double house, the first building and loan association, the Oxford and Provident, met here in 1831.

A few hundred feet north stood an old inn, known through the nineteenth century as the Cross Keys, or Mrs. Rice's, after one very popular landlady, famed for her cooking. This inn is mentioned as early as 1745 in local newspapers. During the Revolution it was kept by Colonel Benjamin McVeagh or M'Vaugh, commander of the local militia. He died there suddenly in 1786. A line of omnibuses ran from here to the city, and important local bodies used to meet in this inn, a wide, double house, pebble-dashed, and painted in colonial colors.

Near the Cross Keys was the General Pike, kept in the latter part of the eighteenth and early nineteenth centuries by Robert Thornton.

The old Robin Hood, which may or may not be responsible for the saying: "All around Robin Hood's barn," as is claimed for it, was torn down not so many years ago to make room for the trolley-car barns.

Last of the old inns to have wholly disappeared is the extremely popular Seven Stars, known also under other names. It stood on Allen's Lane, between Main Street and the Oxford Pike, and was for a time the village voting place. Rebuilt in 1858, it was then advertised as at the junction of the two streets. Known also as the Lewis House, a picture of it in 1912, advertising it under its old name of the Seven Stars, shows it as a three-story building, with piazzas on two sides of the lower stories. It was torn down about a year ago, and a bank building now occupies the site.

The famous Wheat Sheaf, not far from Frankford, which existed as early as 1767 and was kept by John Hall, a warden of Trinity Church, Oxford, has long since gone, but The Sun Tavern or Ale House, a much older building, stood until a few years ago, surrounded by the North Cedar Hill cemetery.

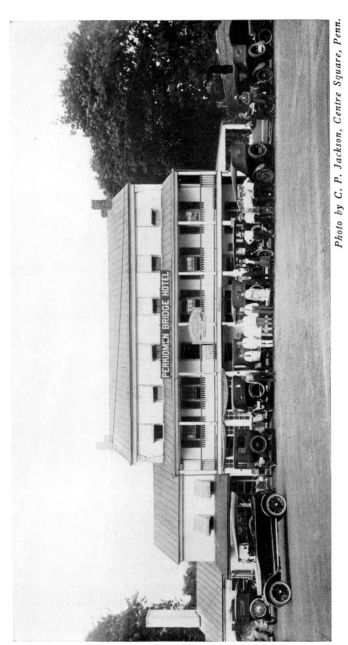

PERKIOMEN BRIDGE HOTEL, PERKIOMEN, PENNSYLVANIA

Photo by C. P. Jackson, Centre Square, Penn.

[See Page 178.

KING OF PRUSSIA INN, KING OF PRUSSIA P. O., PENNSYLVANIA

[*See page* 179.

THE OLD FIREPLACE, KING OF PRUSSIA INN

# Old Inns of Philadelphia and Vicinity

A remarkable old lady of ninety, long a resident of Frankford, and with an excellent memory, recalls an inn which when she first knew of it was considered very old, a drinking place with a bad reputation. The inn has gone, but the memory of its sign has survived, a bee hive, with bees flying around it, and beneath the following lines:

> "Here in this hive we're all alive,
> Good liquor makes us funny.
> If you are dry, step in and try
> The flavor of our honey."

The Sorrel Horse, on Second Street Pike, where the old Byberry road crosses it, was a favorite resort with drivers, and is said to date from 1754. The building of the old inn at Dunk's Ferry on the Dunk's Ferry road, is also standing.

In Collegeville, the General Wayne; the Green Tree in Holmesburg, and the Washington, between the two, are all standing, but although there were many inns along this road, but few now survive.

The old Red Lion at Torresdale is still open. It originally was directly on the highroad but the straightening of this makes the new road but a few rods away. Beautifully situated on a charming stream, the old inn had until last year been kept by three generations of the same family.

Although a concrete floor has replaced the original of wood in the old barroom, it, with another room across the hall and bedrooms above, probably constituted the original inn. Many years ago a two-story addition was built. Almost every room has its old fireplace, and many of the old doors and hinges remain.

It was in 1730 that Philip Ames, an Englishman, petitioned for a license to keep a public house "near Poquessing Creek, on the highway from Philadelphia to Bristol."

[177]

This was the Red Lion, and it is said to have been open continuously from that year. In 1781, part of Washington's army camped around the inn, on their way to Yorktown.

The famous Robert Morris Inn, at Morrisville, is now for sale, the old stables having recently burned down. The signboard is, as mentioned, in the Doylestown Museum.

Returning once more to the vicinity of Philadelphia, a number of old inns will be found near Norristown. Two miles away is the Jeffersonville Inn, bearing the date 1804. If any existing part of this house is really so old, it is the rear.

The Trooper, farther along the same road, on the right-hand side, a long, low, two and a half storied house, painted white, has not been an inn for many years. Another old house, The Lamb, at Trappe, is now only an oyster bar. It dates from 1742, and, save for a more recent ell, is little changed. Upstairs are eight bedrooms, each with a fireplace, and every one different. Washington is said to have slept in the upper right-hand front room. When repairs were recently made to a ceiling it was found that the laths under the plaster were, like the floors, of solid oak.

An old sign with the picture of a lamb used to hang outside, and later the same animal in electric lights was displayed. Opposite the inn is the second oldest Lutheran Church in the country, in which services are held on the second Sunday in August of every year. A new building close by is used on other occasions.

Other old inns on this road are Shepard's, now remodeled into apartments, and The Fountain, no longer open.

The Perkiomen Bridge Hotel bears the sign: "The oldest hotel in the country." It may be the third oldest, for the original portion is said to have been built in 1701. This, the eastern end, contains the kitchen, with an enormous old fireplace into which a large modern range easily fits, and a dining-room, probably originally two rooms. A huge old

[178]

rafter supports the ceiling. Above are two or three old rooms. The large three-story addition, now the main part of the hotel, is at least fairly old in part, for Washington dined in the back parlor at the left of the hall, now a lunchroom. In the barroom, a mark some three feet above the floor on a door molding, shows the height to which the river rose in 1869, flooding the house. The old stone bridge over this river is the oldest in the county, and was built in the early 1700's.

A most charming old inn, open to serve meals, is the King of Prussia, four miles from Norristown.

Outside still hangs the venerable signboard, supposed to have been painted by Gilbert Stuart, showing the King of Prussia, somewhat marred by wind and weather, astride a horse, decidedly wooden as to legs. Built in 1709, the old house is as staunch as ever. The original two rooms on the right as one enters, have old fireplaces across adjoining corners, as have the rooms above, now private dining-rooms. On the left downstairs the rear room is the old kitchen, with an enormous fireplace in which two persons may sit comfortably in chairs. The old crane is still in place, as is the old oven, and up in the wall of the chimney is a small niche for keeping food warm. In front of the kitchen is the old bar. From the kitchen, a steep, narrow flight of stairs testifies to its age, and one may admire massive old beams, and some of the old doors and hinges. The original stables and spring-house are still standing.

The inn was given its name by the builder, a native of Prussia, only a few years after the Elector of Brandenburg had made the duchy of Prussia into a kingdom, and established himself as King Frederick I of Prussia.

The Skippack House, along Skippack Road, and formerly known as the Farmers' and Mechanics', is at least one hundred and twenty years old, for records show that it was licensed then. It may be older.

# Early American Inns and Taverns

Not far from Swarthmore, The Lamb, directly on the highroad, and beautifully set in shady lawns, and the Rose Tree Inn, adjoining the property of the Rose Tree Hunt Club, with its unusual dumb-bell track, are old inns that have only recently closed, and probably not permanently.

Charmingly fitted out, with alterations made so as to preserve as much as possible its old character, is the Black Horse Inn, on the corner of the Baltimore Turnpike and the old Middletown, or as it is now generally called, the Great Edgemont Road. Built in 1739, this is a large stone house, with a modern terrace, dining-room and sleeping-porches recently added at one end. The original part, from the position of the old rafters now bared on the ceiling of the large living-room, was probably two or possibly four rooms, with a hall between, kitchen beyond, and bedrooms above. Years ago, another hall was added at one end, with two rooms on the ground floor and rooms above.

When the present owners bought it, they removed the plastered ceilings, and now the old rafters and boards are visible. A fine fireplace in the living-room is the old one. The kitchen is to be remodeled, as it is dark and hard to ventilate, but when we saw it, a range fitted easily into the old fireplace. Workmen will find it no easy task to pierce these thick old walls. The cellar is as it was when the house was built, and if the gracious hostess will take one upstairs to the aged attic, one may see the ancient wooden pins holding the roof timbers in place. Many old doors with strap- and other old hinges are in place in this charming house, and old fireplaces and cupboards abound.

In the old addition downstairs, the beautiful front door, with side and fan lights, is set in a rounded alcove, which is, according to architects, an unusual feature. A new sign similar to the old one now hangs outside, but the original is carefully kept within.

[180]

# Old Inns of Philadelphia and Vicinity

This tavern was licensed in 1737, the name Black Horse having been given it fifty years later.

The original petition to open a tavern, which was signed by fifty residents of the section (near Media), set forth that the petitioner was frequently obliged to keep travelers on the road from Chester to Great Valley, indeed was "much burden'd with Travellers passing and Repassing on said Road . . . which your petitioner finds to be somewhat chargeable, and prays to be allowed to keep a Publick House of Entertainment." He met with some opposition, for there were those who feared that "a Publick House would be bad for the neighborhood," but eventually his petition was granted. He declared that his house was only three-quarters of a mile from the Presbyterian Church, and would be most convenient for those attending services in cold weather to stop in, warm, and refresh themselves. The old part of the present Presbyterian Church not far away is still standing, and is the church to which he referred.

The Seven Stars, with its quaint double porches, still stands at Village Green, but last winter it, too, was closed.

The actual building of the old Red Lion stands at Ardmore, but is used for an automobile business; The Buck (1735) has been remodeled into apartments. Hatboro's Crooked Billet, now a private residence, was built soon after the inn of the same name in Philadelphia.

The original grant of land on which stands the General Wayne at Merion was given by William Penn in 1704 to a man who sold it to an Englishman for twenty-five perch of stone, and the latter again sold it for twenty-five shillings. The main part of the inn was built in the same year, 1704, but additions have been made at both ends and in the rear.

The old barroom, now a dining-room, was once the village Post Office, and also its voting place.

Washington's room, the southwest second-floor front

chamber, has a large old fireplace, as has the adjoining room, and both have "maple sugar closets," at one side of the chimney, narrow cupboards in which maple sugar was stored.

The original floors remain in the old part of the house, and several old doors. In the past one hundred and ten years the house has been owned by but three families: Lieutenant Streeper, of the Continental Army; Mr. William Young, who kept it for fifty years; and Mr. Odell, who now runs it with his mother. He was a lieutenant in the A. E. F.

Recent digging opposite the house, to lay a drain, brought to light what proved to be old stone railroad ties of the first railroad from Columbia to Philadelphia. To these ties, wooden rails were fastened by iron spikes, and a few of the spikes were still embedded in the stone.

A small building opposite the inn was a smithy during Revolutionary days, and its smith shod both British and American soldiers' horses. Until a few months ago it was still occupied by a blacksmith, but he found business too light and gave it up.

The Washington Inn, Valley Forge, was not an inn at the time of the memorable encampment of the Continental Army, although an old mansion had stood on this site before 1768, and was then the home of Colonel Dewees. He built large ovens in his cellar to bake bread for Washington's troops, and the soldiers called the house the "Bake House." Enlarged, this is the present inn. Although officers were not quartered in it, several courts martial were held here. A row of chestnut trees is said at that time to have extended from Radnor to Valley Forge, and these trees were used by our soldiers as points from which to signal. One sole survivor was long pointed out.

Seldom does one see such a picture of dilapidation as is presented by the once famous Bird in the Hand, on the old Gulph Road. Not far from the overhanging rock beneath which Washington stood to address his troops on the way to Valley Forge, after crossing the stone bridge at the spot where Witmer, a Quaker, had a ferry before building the first bridge, one comes to a decrepit old stone building which probably was part of the inn stables, and later, as an old sign proclaims, a general store, long abandoned. A little farther along is the inn, said to have been built in 1754, while others say that this is the fourth inn of the same name to stand on the same site. At all events, Witmer died before 1764, and an inn undoubtedly stood there earlier than that date.

The house is so ruined that it does not seem possible that merely pilfering hands could be responsible. Not a window-sash remains, hardly a door, yet the thick stone walls, the once fine woodwork, the mantels and window frames once white, all testify that it was originally a substantial house. Of the two large rooms on the first floor, each with a door-way opening on the rickety old porch, only one may be entered, for a huge gap in the floor of the other, down into the cellar, and another in the ceiling above, make this room dangerous to move in. In the other room the floor indeed remains, but there are great holes in the ceiling, and few would care to trust themselves on the narrow stairs at one side of the old chimney. The present owner, before the building had fallen into such a state, although it was no longer an inn, refused either to sell or lease the property. It is hard to believe that anything short of fire or an explosion could thus have wrecked the building, which resembles a house in the devastated area of France immediately after the war. I was assured that nothing of the sort had occurred.

The Media Hospital was once the Anvil Inn, built about 1806. The old Pineapple Inn (1737), near Concordsville, has been made into a residence.

On the turnpike from Philadelphia to Ambler, a three mile run brings us to Blue Bell Inn, built in 1776. The walls are the original ones, but the entire interior was rebuilt and remodeled in 1917. The room in which Washington slept is shown, and the house is open as a restaurant.

Two miles from the Blue Bell, at a crossroad, stands the old Broad Axe, still open, with old fireplaces and deep window recesses showing the great thickness of its old walls.

Diagonally opposite is a still older house, now a residence, but formerly the Split Crow Inn. In bygone days, a man committed suicide in one of its two attics, and his blood stains are said to have remained for years indelible. The present owner says she has vainly hunted for them, nor has she ever seen his ghost, said to wander over the old house. Both of these two inns are well over one hundred years old.

From Broad Axe, it is three miles to the Three Tuns, also open. An old sign hangs outside, braced a bit to preserve it, and the old bar is intact. The front part of the house dates from 1740, and the man who built it, an Englishman, is said to have bought three tuns of liquor with which to start his inn business; hence the name. The present proprietor believed this to be the only inn of the name in this country, but there is another in Baltimore.

At Montgomery Square is another inn of the same general style, about one hundred and fifty years old, and which has not been open as an inn for nearly fifty years, although from time to time liquor has been sold on the sly by its different owners. Asking an old resident who had volunteered this information, and also that the house was again for sale, if these violations of the law explained why the house had been closed, he said:

"No, they never got pinched."

"What did happen, then?"

A pause. Finally:

"Oh, well, they died or got sick," was all that he would say.

Four miles farther on the same road is the Spring House,

built in 1719, but rebuilt in 1822. The front of the house and the old barroom are certainly old, as is the staircase leading directly from the barroom; the other flight and entrance hall are much more modern, but the outer walls are very thick. This house, too, is still open; the old stable is a garage.

Two miles beyond, at Gwynedd, is the William Penn, two hundred and nine years old. Here again the barroom is old, as are the narrow front hall, another room across the hall, and the rooms above. Broad piazzas, a large dining-room and other rooms have been added quite recently, so that at first glance the house is almost modern looking. Still open for guests, this has been continuously an inn for more than one hundred years. Daniel Acuff bought the property in 1818, and the following year petitioned for a license, which was not granted until 1827, but an old account tells that "about the year 1700, William Penn and his daughter, Letitia, rode out from Philadelphia to visit the Welsh Quakers who had settled at Gwynedd." They stopped at the house of Thomas Evans, which was later known as the William Penn Inn.

At Centre Square, an inn built before 1758 and rebuilt about sixty-five years ago, used to be known as the Wagon Inn, and is still open. Although much remodeled, one may see twenty-five-foot joists in the ceilings of the ground floor.

The present Fortside Inn, only some thirty years old, stands on the site of the old Blue Tavern, built one hundred and fifty years ago, in a historically interesting locality. The southern end of Flourtown's Inn is said to date from the days of Washington, but the main portion is modern. Farther down the road, the old Black Horse is now a residence, although the interior is practically unchanged as yet.

At Barren Hill, not far away, the Lafayette, part of which is said to be one hundred and fifty years old, was kept by the former proprietor for forty-four years.

# Early American Inns and Taverns

Open only during the motor season, and chiefly as a restaurant, the old General Warren Inn, now called the Warren, was built in 1745, and is now slightly off the high-road, although plainly visible. Major André stopped here with the forces which attacked Paoli. In 1777, Peter Mather bought and ran it. His daughter, Sally, lived to a great age, and used to tell how, when she was seven years old and her brother ten, she was awakened by her mother's screams. She remembered seeing her father led out between two British soldiers, one of whom had grasped him by the throat. He and other men of the neighborhood were kept out all night "under the poplar tree," to watch the Hessians pass. They were then allowed to return home without further molestation, but the soldiers carried off everything of value in the tavern except the sum of fourteen dollars. This house was rebuilt in 1831.

Fourteen miles west of Philadelphia, in Radnor Township on the Lancaster Pike, was the Spread Eagle Inn, believed to have been built in 1788. A small stone house, kept by Adam Ramsower as a House of Entertainment, stood here as early as 1769. In 1772, the property was sold to Jacob Hinkel, and the inn given the name of the Spread Eagle. During the Revolution it was a favorite meeting place for the patriots of the neighborhood. In 1796, the landlord was John Siter, and when the Lancaster Turnpike was finished in that year, this inn was a stop for mail, post accommodations, and relays, and a village grew up around it which was called Sittersville. In 1836, the landlord was Stephen Horne, and some time later, George W. Childs bought the property and turned it into a home for Indian girls. In 1886, when Mr. Sachse wrote his history, it stood, though unoccupied, yet between that day and this, all traces of the old building have apparently disappeared, for the large house now standing on the property, a private residence, was built between 1836 and 1846, and is now owned by a Philadelphian, Mr. A. L. Diament. There is a Spread Eagle Inn close by, also on part of the original property, and some believe that it is located in what were either the old stables or some part of them, but no one seems able to verify this. The present attractive inn may at least be said to stand near the old site.

The Eagle, on the West Chester turnpike, was burned down some years ago and replaced by a new one on the opposite side of the road. The old Drove, in Edgmont Township, is now a tea-room.

Others in this section—and there were many—have either been altered into apartments or private residences, or replaced by business buildings.

But two old inns survive of many that once existed in West Chester. The Green Tree, so remodeled, with its entire lower floor made into stores, that nothing suggests its age (1786), and The Turk's Head, for which two dates of its building are given, 1747 and 1761. Perhaps the second date is that of rebuilding. Opposite the Court House, kept by a former proprietor of the Green Tree, it is a popular lunching and dining place, and although the ground floor facing the Court House has been made into stores and the former bar a drug store, part of the house on the side street is said to be the original building.

## CHAPTER X

### *Other Pennsylvania Inns*

ON THE ROAD from Philadelphia to Wilmington, at Ridley Park, a dilapidated old building close to the highway was the White Horse Tavern, built in 1729. For years it has not been an inn.

Chester offers much of interest to those fond of old buildings. The town was settled by the Swedes in 1644; William Penn visited it in 1682, and named it in 1701. Since Chester was a boat stop as well as on the stage route, it had many inns. King's Road, now Third Street, was for years the town's western boundary. Nothing now remains of the tavern on the west side of Edgmont Avenue, above Third Street, built in 1733, and kept, in 1787, by James Pennell, who had a tame bear which did tricks to amuse the guests. Pennell removed with his bear to the Black Horse at Middletown (presumably the Black Horse mentioned in the last chapter), and here the animal one day became angry and killed his owner.

The Washington Hotel, on Market Street (1747), still open as a hotel, was first called the Pennsylvania Arms, the name being changed later in honor of the President. Upstairs, in the second story right-hand room, he wrote at midnight the only report of the Battle of Brandywine that he ever sent to Congress. This was in 1777, and twelve years later, Washington was received and welcomed at this same hotel by the people of Chester, as their president.

Although the front of the house has been changed, and

[188]

the old archway formerly leading into a yard built into a theater, some of the old features remain, such as the piazza across the second story front, converted into a sun-parlor, without greatly altering the appearance.

The Steamboat Hotel, at Front and Market Streets, was built for a private residence in 1765 by Francis Richardson, after inheriting money from his aunt, the widow of Chief Justice Lloyd. Mr. Richardson believed that Chester was destined to be an important port, and invested so heavily in wharves and warehouses that, at his death, his property was sold by the sheriff to pay his debts. During the Revolution, the British frigate *Augusta* fired on the town from the river, one shot piercing the nearest gable of the Richardson house. Afterwards, the owner cut a window around this hole, and the window still remains. In 1826 the house was licensed as a hotel. Now only about one-third of the original mansion remains; to this a one-story addition has been built on the front, and the first floor now serves as a railway office, the rest being let as a lodging.

A negro, Laban, was killed in the house, and his blood was said to have left an indelible stain—apparently all murders of the time were characterized by this—while his spirit used to wander over the building. Those wanderings are to-day sadly cramped.

Francis Richardson, son of the builder, went to England when very young, and became a captain in the Coldstream Guards, an honor never before given to one not of royal birth.

The Stacey House, another old tavern at which Lafayette is said to have stayed in 1777, adjoining the Blue Anchor, later called Hope's Anchor, and still later, when kept by John West, The White Swan, have both long since disappeared, as has the Plow and Harrow, on the left side of Fifth Street, which was kept by Mary Withey. She had the reputation of keeping the best tavern in the colonies, and she dressed Lafayette's wound, after the Battle of Brandy-wine.

The old Boar's Head, built early in the eighteenth century, on an elevation where Second, Third and Penn Streets are now, has vanished; the Blue Bell (1765), at the corner of Second and Market Streets, is now a residence.

Before continuing our imaginary journey from Chester to Wilmington, there are other inns in the central, southern, and western part of Pennsylvania which merit a visit.

On the direct road from Washington, D. C., through Hagerstown, Maryland, and Greencastle, Pennsylvania, lies the town of Mercersburg. Along all that part of the present Lincoln Highway, before reaching and after leaving Mercersburg, many old inns are still standing, although often so transformed into private residences or modern-looking hotels, that it is difficult to distinguish them. Between Fort Loudon and Chambersburg, Pennsylvania, a few of these old inns are: The White House, kept in early days by Patrick McDowell, born in 1770, and who died in 1846, so the inn is truly old; the Gillan Hotel; a hotel owned by Bart Zeiger; the Bratton Hotel, east of St. Thomas; and a house where Campbell's Run crosses the highroad, near the present Parnell Inn.

President Buchanan is connected with Mercersburg in the following manner. James Buchanan, Senior, was clerk in a store at Stony Batter, at the foot of North Mountain, not far from Mercersburg. When he set up in business for himself in that village, people from the "West" as they then called it, brought their produce to exchange at his store for salt, cloth, and other needed articles. In 1788 he married Elizabeth Speer, and on April 23, 1791, the future president was born in Stony Batter, where he lived until, in 1796, the Buchanan family removed to Mercersburg. Here the merchant built a fine store and home. Later, this property was

[190]

turned into a hotel, the Mercer House. A modern hotel here now has little to suggest the old one.

The Mansion House was originally a quaint, two and a half story building, with an old swinging sign, and a pump in front. It was a stage-coach stop, but now it, too, is a modern hotel of three stories.

In the book entitled *Old Mercersburg*, a picture of the Mansion House as it was in stage-coach days is shown.

One of the earliest inns here was the Washington Inn, believed to have been the birthplace of Governor William Findley and his brothers.

Another old house, which burned down some years ago, stood on the top of Loudon Mountain, and at one time was kept by David Fegley. His daughter, Susan, waited on President Buchanan when he stopped at this inn on his way to visit his birthplace. Susan's brother, a Congressman, was a friend of the President.

Continuing from Mercersburg, McConnellsburg is reached. Its Fulton House has a unique distinction. Although the old portion was built about 1793 and the new part added in 1820, the Father of His Country never stayed here, nor did Lafayette, as the present proprietor notes, conscious of this as an unusual fact. In all these years, the attractive old hotel, its limestone walls twenty-four inches thick, two stories high, with broad double piazzas, has remained open.

While admitting that Washington "never enjoyed even a sandwich here," the proprietor is at pains to point out that four presidents have visited the house. John and Abigail Adams for one night occupied the front room at the right of the stairs, on the second floor; Zachary Taylor, William Henry Harrison, and James Buchanan were also guests, the latter always stopping here when on his way to spend the summer in Bedford. And the Siamese twins spent several days here before Barnum discovered them!

This house has entertained guests since the days when there was no wagon-road west, only a pack-trail. Later, it was headquarters for the fast stages of the Pittsburgh-Philadelphia route, and is now on a popular automobile road.

The old road from Philadelphia and Lancaster County, over the Blue Ridge Mountains to Shippensburgh and Bedford, and across the Allegheny Mountains to the headwaters of the Ohio, was in early times a much-traveled road, although at first barely passable. Traces of the old Pennsylvania Road and Turkey Foot Branch, since known as the Chambersburgh-Pittsburgh Pike, may still be found a few miles west of Bedford.

In 1758, the Forbes Road ran from Lancaster, through Carlisle, Bedford, and on to Pittsburgh, and was one of the most important thoroughfares to the west.

All along the old turnpikes were taverns, where relays of horses were kept, meals and lodging furnished, and in Penn-

*Photo by C. P. Jackson, Centre Square, Penn.*

THE WILLIAM PENN INN, GWYNEDD, PENNSYLVANIA

[*See page* 185.

FULTON HOUSE, MC CONNELLSBURG, PENNSYLVANIA

[See page 192

sylvania and the south, the taverns were neighborhood re-
sorts. Along the old Cumberland Road, as described by
Mr. Searight in *The Old Turnpike*, three cents a glass was
the usual charge for whisky toddies, and rather more for
wine. But "it was considered a lasting disgrace for one of
the stage taverns to entertain a wagoner." The tavern would
instantly in such a case lose caste. Wagoners must look to
other taverns for accommodations. Most of these ancient
houses along the road from Lancaster to Pittsburgh have
disappeared.

On the present road between Washington, Pennsylvania
and Pittsburgh, is an old town which once had many inns.
After crossing the bridge over the Monongahela River at
Brownsville, one enters the town of West Brownsville, built
on the site of an old fortification. The birthplace of James
G. Blaine, the town stands on land once owned by Indian
Peter, and when surveyed, in 1769, it was called Indian Hill.
Peter died in possession of the land, and it passed to his
white wife and their eldest son. Widow and son sold the
tract in 1784 to Neil Gillespie, great-grandfather of Blaine,
for forty shillings, payable in instalments of money, iron,
and one negro. The bridge over the river then stood a short
distance from the present north end in West Brownsville,
where the road makes a sharp turn. On the south side of
this angle stood a tavern, kept by Samuel Adams, and later
by John Huston. This house was always crowded. Later
it was torn down and a brick one built in its place, and this
continued prosperous. The new house was open before
1840, and at that time it was not unusual to see fifty wagons
standing near. Until 1882 it was open; then the Pennsylvania Railroad bought the building, moved and enlarged
it into a depot for the town.

At the foot of River Hill there was another old inn, the
Vincent Owens House, and a ferry across the river. This
inn was closed in 1845. Two miles west, in the hamlet of

Malden, a stone tavern was built in the days when residents believed that theirs was destined to be an important town. A stone in the front wall of this building, with Kreppsville cut in it, was placed there in 1830, and another with "Liberty," and figures of a plow and a sheaf of wheat. In 1925, this section was laid out in house lots, so, although standing last November, the old house has probably disappeared.

One chronicler of olden times gravely tells that in early Pennsylvania days, the people, although by no means drunkards, were in the habit of drinking much whisky. Women entertained their women visitors with "whisky made palatable with sugar, milk and spices." Morning bitters were commonly taken, as was "a dram before meals."

The very first tavern in this locality—hardly that indeed, but rather a house whose owner entertained travelers— opened in 1774, by William Huston, was a cabin on the old trail followed by pioneers journeying between the Ohio River and the mountains. It was known as Catfish Camp, and Huston is said to have been the only white man then living in that part of the state.

In 1781 James Wilson was licensed by the first court held in the county to keep a public house of entertainment, at Catfish Camp, in what is now Washington. This was a building of logs, and here judges of the Supreme Court stopped. Wilson kept the tavern until he died, in 1792, and it continued open, although enlarged, the logs covered with weather-boarding. In 1815, it was given the name: At the Sign of General Wayne, by a new proprietor, and was a tavern until 1840.

Where the William Henry Hotel now stands, Charles Valentine built a log house, and in 1791 was licensed to open his tavern At the Sign of the White Goose. The next proprietor, John Rettig, changed the name to The Swan. He was succeeded by Julian Valentine, who in 1819 advertised that "Columbus, A Male Elephant, the first and only male

[194]

in this country," might be seen "at Mr. Valentine's Tavern in Washington for three days, between the hours of 9 A. M. and 5 P. M., for 25 cents, children under 12 half price."

Various proprietors succeeded at the old stand, until the most popular of them all, Joseph Hallam, took it over in 1840. Travel and the freighting business along the old National Road were then at their height, and Hallam, who had been a wagoner himself, understood drivers' tastes, and catered to them. Not until eight years later was the old house razed, and replaced by a new brick building, called the Valentine House, after its early proprietor. Its old brick stables were still standing a year ago, built for stage-coaches when the brick hotel was erected. The old Good Intent stage line made its headquarters here, and even after travel on the old road decreased, many people still went by stage from Washington into Pittsburgh, Waynesburg, and other towns in this section.

A third story was added to the inn in 1880, and the name changed to the Allison House. It was partly destroyed by fire in 1899; used for several years as a rooming-house, then a new hotel was built on its site, first known as the Hotel Siegel, then the William Henry, as at present. Thus for one hundred and thirty-five years there has been a hotel on this site.

James Workman, after keeping a tavern, the site of which is not known, was landlord of the Sign of General Jackson, just below the Sign of the Globe, on the corner of South Main and West Strawberry Streets. David Morris had bought the latter house in 1798, but enlarged and improved it, not opening it until ten years later. Morris remained landlord for thirty-eight years, entertaining five presidents: Monroe, Jackson, Harrison, Taylor and Polk, and also Daniel Webster, Lafayette, Henry Clay, and the Indian Chief, Black Hawk. Morris's wife, a sister of Robert Fulton, was famous for the good meals which she cooked.

[195]

# Early American Inns and Taverns

Mr. Earl Forrest tells that Morris opposed the building of the National Pike, fearing that a good road would enable travelers to make so much better time that they would not need so many hotels. "But," he adds, "he lived to see the time when he could not accommodate the many guests the National Pike brought to his doors."

General Lafayette's visit was a notable event in the town's history. He was given the greatest welcome ever known in that day, for more than twenty thousand persons gathered to welcome him. After Morris died, in 1834, his widow ran the hotel for a year, then it was used as the Post Office, but never again as a hotel, and it was torn down in 1889.

A George Washington House has existed under this name in Washington since 1863.

Michael Kuntz in 1791 opened a tavern, and part of this building was included in the George Washington Hotel built in 1863. On the same site, a hotel of this name, remodeled, still stands. Kuntz called his stone tavern, The Sign of the Buck. Joseph Huston, cousin of William, the first settler and innkeeper, was its landlord, when it was known as Huston's Home Inn. He died in 1812, and his widow sold it to James Sergeant, who ran it for three years. Then Mrs. Huston returned, and James Fleming, whom she had married, kept the old tavern.

Early in the nineteenth century there were two hotels named for Washington; one in the town, and one at Pancake, on the outskirts, standing, oddly enough, on the Mount Vernon Farm in that village. The first one, in Washington, was kept by the same man who had the Pancake house, and Mr. Forrest tells how, when hunting through old newspaper files, he found this advertisement:

"James Dunlap begs to inform the public and his friends that he has just opened a PUBLIC HOUSE at the sign of GENERAL GEORGE WASHINGTON (lately that well-known stand THE BLACK HORSE, occupied by Capt.

Charles Fox), in the town of Washington, where he intends to lay in a choice assortment of wines and spirituous liquors." This was dated February 3, 1804, and as the tavern was already in existence, it would be truly old now, but a business building occupies its site on the east side of South Main Street.

Dunlap was a prominent citizen, Brigade Inspector of the Washington County militia, and was known as Major Dunlap. He owned the Mount Vernon Farm east of Pancake, where in 1815, he opened a roadhouse: At the Sign of General George Washington, but two years later, he advertised farm and tavern for sale. He sold part of the farm to Jonathan Martin, and the latter, in 1825, built a brick tavern, which still stands, although no longer an inn. That same year, Dunlap took over the Washington hotel At the Sign of General Jackson, already mentioned, which had then become known as Auld's. The new proprietor promptly changed the name to the Jackson Hotel, which was appropriate, since the General had been entertained there, and meanwhile sold his Mount Vernon property, which was a popular wagon tavern during the days of the Canestoga wagons, but then known as Rettig's, after the new proprietor. It was burned after the newer Rettig's was built. The Jackson Hotel became The Travelers' Inn and Stage Coach, then the National, again General Andrew Jackson, the Railroad House, then Auld's again.

Another Washington hotel-keeper, McCammant, in 1801 opened At the Sign of the Cross Keys, in an old building on the southeast corner of Main and East Wheeling Streets, where now is a business building. He kept this tavern for twelve years, and is said to have died from the bite of a mad wolf. His widow continued the business for two years, then advertised her removal to "a well-known stand, the Sign of Gen. Washington." She soon moved back again, and in 1831 advertised that she would "furnish dinner and

[197]

horse feed for 25 cents, and boarding and lodging for jurors and others attending court for $2 per week." Later known as the Philadelphia and Kentucky Inn, this was never a hotel after 1844.

In Washington, as in other localities, it was necessary to obtain a license to keep a tavern, and prices which the host might charge were fixed by the courts. In 1781, when Washington County was organized, these were some of the prices set:

Whisky by the half pint, $4; breakfast or supper, $15; dinner, $20; lodging with clean sheets, $3; one horse over night, $3; one gallon of corn, $5; strong beer per quart, $6. (At that time Continental money was worth little more than German marks a few years ago.)

Mr. Forrest also describes a very early Washington sign-board which depicted a white boy, trying to scrub white a colored boy, standing in a tub of water, and the name: Labor in Vain.

The Rising Sun, opened in 1816, has now entirely vanished. Its landlord, Briceland, came from Briceland Cross-roads, now Florence, where he had kept a tavern for several years. General Jackson and his family stayed here a year after John N. Dagg succeeded as landlord. The house became very popular, sometimes as many as one hundred teams standing around it at night. The barroom was popular with wagoners on the National Pike, and in April, 1823, a carpenter, James Guy, got into a dispute with one of the wagoners, Patrick Gallegher, both being drunk. Mr. Dagg several times ordered them out, but finally they became quiet, so he allowed them to stay. As the barkeeper started to take Gallegher to his bed, however, the latter made a leap at Guy, who pushed Gallegher against the door, his head striking the latch forcibly. Mr. Dagg put Guy out, then Gallegher, but the latter fell, striking his head on the pavement, and died the next morning. Dagg was tried for murder, but acquitted. About 1838, he became landlord of the Mansion House, on the site of a little red frame building, known as The Spread Eagle, then the Eagle, finally the Sign of the Eagle. The Mansion House became Washington's chief hotel, but was burned in 1868.

Other old Washington inns long since gone are: General Wayne, Buck, Commodore O. H. Perry, Fountain Inn, Indian Queen, Green House, Schmidt's Hotel, White Goose, Swan, Mermaid, General Brown, Franklin, and John Wilson's Tavern.

Washingtonian chronicles do not name the inn referred to in Colonel Hay's diary in 1788. He says, ". . . in the morning, at half past eight, arrived at Maj. McCormick's, in Washington, where we breakfasted. This is an excellent house, where New England men put up."

In 1820, the National Road Stage Company ran coaches leaving Washington every Monday, Wednesday, and Friday at 4 A. M. for Cadiz, Ohio, there connecting with stages for the Lakes, thus forming a continuous line to Lake Erie.

Lucius W. G. Stockton, a prominent stage line owner, lived in Unionville, and kept fast horses. He often stopped in Washington to dine and rest his horses, when driving from Unionville to Wheeling. He could cover this distance in twelve hours, and once raced a locomotive on the Baltimore and Ohio Railway, in a buggy drawn by one horse, and won the race.

## Chapter XI

### Delaware and Maryland Inns

FROM THE DAYS of the early Swedish settlers, Delaware had inns, although the earliest ones did not keep travelers over night, as a rule, but were rather drinking places, where "flipp, egg-nogs" and punch made of rum were consumed. In this part of the country, "ordinary" was the name given to eating houses, and later, the title of coffee house distinguished those more aristocratic. Owing to the lack of good roads in Delaware, there was not so much travel here as in other sections, but the first steam passenger railroad in this country, the New Castle and Frenchtown Rail Road, in 1832, here succeeded the stage-coaches.

On the direct route from Chester, Pennsylvania, to Wilmington, Delaware, a few miles before the latter city is reached, one will pass at Naaman's Creek a most attractive old house, where now luncheons and dinners are served. This is the Robinson House, bought in 1738 by Thomas Robinson from Dublin, who married a wealthy widow in the colony. Just how long it had then been standing has not been definitely determined, but on the grounds is an old blockhouse, believed to have been built in 1654, by John Risinghe, Governor of the Swedes.

In this blockhouse, Swedish colonists used to take refuge when warned by the friendly Indian chief, Naaman, that the Indians were on the war path. Although not now open to the public, if the owner can be persuaded to show it, visitors will find it quite as interesting as the large old Robinson House itself. The huge fireplace in the square lower room of the former blockhouse occupies the entire story, and steep old stairs lead to an upper room, where two of the original four musket holes, one on each side, remain now, the other two having been cut into windows. An old spring and smoke-house, possibly equally as old as the blockhouse, has been joined to the latter building, and forms an attractive little residence.

The large house has been carefully restored, not modernized, by the present appreciative owners, who, oddly enough, since they are not related, have the same name as the original owner. After a period of more than sixty years, during which the old mansion had been put to various uses—some say that it had even been a questionable roadhouse—it had come to need repairs sadly. Originally a summer home for the Robinson family for more than a hundred years, from time to time they had made various additions to the original building. Several of these Robinsons are said to have been sea-faring people, and some ship timber was used in building additions. By opening a door from the main hallway or living-room which extends from front to rear of the house, may be seen an old staircase, with a sliding panel, through which Light Horse Harry Lee, an intimate friend of the Robinson family, and hence thoroughly acquainted with the house, escaped, while British soldiers guarded the other two staircases. Later, Lee captured the officers of a British frigate near by.

"Mad Anthony" Wayne, brother-in-law of the owner, was a frequent visitor, as was Washington. When the British were advancing in this section, during the Revolution, Washington directed Light Horse Harry Lee to remove and hide the millstones from the mill on the creek close by, so that the British would be unable to grind their corn. This was done, and many years later, one of these millstones was found buried in the old orchard. It had been split in half by a young cherry tree, and one piece now forms the hearthstone in the big hall running through the house.

Grubb's Landing, on the Delaware, had a very old inn, The Practical Farmer, through which, during the Revolution, a shot from a British frigate passed.

Wilmington was founded as Fort Christiana, by the Swedes, in 1738, although a small settlement may have existed still earlier. What is said to have been Wilmington's first house stood on Front Street, and was later the site of the Buck Tavern, torn down in 1900.

In colonial days, a direct route from Lancaster and southern Pennsylvania passed through the town, as did another highroad to Newport, Christiana, etc. Wilmington stages left David Brinton's Indian Queen—now vanished—at the corner of Fourth and Market Streets, at eight o'clock every morning, arriving in Philadelphia four hours later. Southern mail-coaches stopped at the Indian Queen at 7 A. M. every day, for breakfast.

Another stage line left the Swan, later called the Gibson House, and the Lynch House. On the south side of Fourth Street, between Market and Shipley, stands a four-story building, with an Italian restaurant on the second floor, and a fairly old doorway. The rest of the house has been modernized, but it, or a part of it, was the Swan.

Northern and southern mail-coaches in 1812 and 1813 passed through Wilmington; the former from Robbinstown, Maine, to Washington, the latter continuing from the latter city to St. Mary's, Georgia.

To-day the Wilmington-Philadelphia turnpike practically follows what used to be known as the King's Road; the first road in this section, a mile or more nearer the shore, was originally an Indian trail along the Delaware, from Naaman's Creek to Tinicum, and later a bridle-path.

Eli Lamborn, who controlled the post coaches between

# Delaware and Maryland Inns

Wilmington and Philadelphia, as an old historian states, "at one time or another was landlord in most of the early Wilmington taverns."

The first Wilmington tavern, believed to have been The Foul Anchor, was built in 1740, on Water Street. A lawn in the rear sloped down to the Christiana River. This was a tavern only until 1830.

In 1800, Billy McDougal had a tavern on the edge of the marsh at Tatnall Street and Delaware Avenue, which he called The House That Jack Built, but which was better known as Bull Frog Tavern, because of the numbers of frogs in the marsh near by. When French refugees arrived from France and San Domingo, they taught the people of Wilmington to cook and eat these noisy neighbors.

Although at first glance one would hardly suspect it, the three-story building, with high, steep roof, on the southeast corner of Market and Third Streets, was once the Sign of the Ship, whose first landlord, in 1789, was John Marshall. He was followed by Patrick O'Flynn, who changed the name to the Happy Retreat. O'Flynn was an ardent patriot, and never tired of telling how Washington, Jefferson, Aaron Burr, Commodore Perry and others had been guests in his house. It was Lafayette's headquarters, and Louis Philippe also dined here. When O'Flynn died, it was kept by General Wolfe, but in 1835 the old tavern was sold, and altered into a store and apartments.

This and the Swan are the only old inns whose buildings may be seen in Wilmington. Gone are the Indian Queen (1789), the White Hart (1785), later called the Washington House, the Cross Keys, which stood on the old King's Road, on the part now called Adams Street, near Delaware Avenue.

Through Newark, Delaware, the British army passed in 1777, just before the Battle of Brandywine. A famous old inn, St. Patrick's, was owned and run here in 1750, by John

[203]

Pritchard, and remained in his family for almost one hundred years. Although it is gone, the present Deer Park Hotel was built in 1851 on its site. The Newark Hotel, licensed in 1757, and where Washington is said to have stopped, was torn down.

From Newark, the highroad continues to Baltimore, but if, instead, one turns south and east from Wilmington, a drive of about six miles brings one to New Castle. On the way, at the Post Office of Red Lion, stands the old tavern, now a private residence, which gave the place its name.

The original inn stood half a mile north of the present one, near Pigeon Run and the Presbyterian Church there. This was burned, and the present building of brick and wood was built in the village by a French Huguenot refugee, a lady of some means, who opened it as a tavern. The French lady met and married an Englishman, during her early days as a landlady, and he helped her to run the tavern, and also farmed his own land in the vicinity. It is said that this was one of the few early inns at which Washington did not stop, but Lafayette spent a night in it. The house was rebuilt in 1820, but closed as an inn about 1837, when the railroad made it no longer profitable. It was then used as a residence, and remained in a family related by marriage to the original owners, until very recently. The old sign is still owned by them.

New Castle is one of the oldest towns in the country. Settled by the Swedes in 1638, it was first a fort, and has been known by eight different names from the original Indian Quinnimacook to the present one given it in 1654 by Sir Robert Carr, when the British succeeded the Dutch owners. It has the oldest Court House in the United States still in use—part of the present building—from which, as one Enoch Anderson records in his diary, in 1776: "We took out of Court House all of the Insignia of Monarchy, all the Baubles of Royalty, and made a pile of them before the

Court House, and burnt them to ashes. A merry day we made of it."

New Castle was the landing for boats from Philadelphia, and here stages were taken to Frenchtown, from thence boats across the Chesapeake, then stages on for southern points.

The Old Packet Tavern, on the Strand by the river, was a famous New Castle Inn. It was destroyed by fire in 1824. A very old diary, recently found, kept by "a lady book agent" in 1830, tells how she sat on the porch of this house and watched the passengers come up Packet Lane from the boats; Indians, Quakers, "Frenchmen with their boxes," and so on.

There are no records as to the exact year in which an old inn opposite the Court House was built, but it was in use about 1741. Later known as the Gilpin House, Washington lodged here in 1774. It still stands, but has fallen into disrepute, and while open, is not really an inn. As one old resident describes it: "it has been renovated and re-renovated," but something of the old building's walls remains. Old double porches across the front have been removed, modern store-fronts replace the original, but the sides of the two-story-and-attic building are but little changed.

Two doors below is a very old brick house with a new front, where Penn stayed on his first visit to New Castle, and there are a number of other very old houses, built for private residences surviving in this quaint old town, with its early Green, dating from the time of Peter Stuyvesant.

In Smyrna, the State Legislature first met, and in 1787, Joshua Fisher built a hotel, known in 1827 as the Indian Queen. Fifteen years later it was turned into a store. The present Post Office now stands on its site.

Eight miles from Smyrna, on Duck Creek, is a large old brick building which in stage-coach days was a tavern.

Dover, laid out by order of William Penn, in 1683, has the second oldest State House in the United States still in use, built in 1722 for the Kent County Court House. It stands on the east side of the Green, and on the south side is the present Court House, built on the site of the old one. The old one was erected in 1699; thirty years later it was turned into a tavern, famous under the name of the King George Tavern. When the Revolution broke out, the name was changed to the George, then it was demolished for the present building.

On the north side of the Green stood the Biddle Tavern, later replaced by the Capitol Hotel. Here in 1782, the Assembly gave a banquet to celebrate the birth of the Dauphin of France, later to be known as the unfortunate Louis XVII. On the northwest side stood the Harris Tavern, later called the Steamboat Hotel. Both are gone.

In 1724, John Rees had a tavern in Dover, which he sold to John Bell, in whose family it remained for one hundred years or more. Its sign was a portrait of George III, and after the Revolution, this was changed for one of Washington. For several years this house was the headquarters of the Democratic Party, but it was burned in 1863.

Not far from Dover is the old town of Camden, called Piccadilly by its first settler, Daniel Mifflin, then Mifflin's Cross Roads, and since 1788 by its present name.

The Daniel Mifflin House, built in 1783 at the crossroads, as a residence, later became a tavern, and is still used as a hotel, save that about five years ago, the corner room on the first floor was made into a store. The house has been somewhat remodeled. None the less, it has much of the old-time appearance, as has the old town, with its broad, shaded streets.

The present hotel at Milford on the Maspillon, the Central, is neither old nor suggestive of age, but one end of it is part of the former residence of Martin de Waehle, a French aristocrat, born in Paris in 1763, who built this American house twenty-five years later.

[206]

# Delaware and Maryland Inns

A few other old inns on out-of-the-way roads may still be found, but because of the comparatively light travel by stage in this part of the country, old inns outside of Wilmington were not numerous.

From Wilmington the road to Baltimore runs through the old settlement of Havre-de-Grace. In stage-coach days, an inn stood on both sides of the river, but the present Lafayette House on the farther side, although an old building, has but recently become a hotel. It was built about 1737 of brick imported from England by a gentleman of means, who owned a large tract of farming land near what was then called the Lower Susquehanna Ferry. A rope ferry this, travelers from Philadelphia to Washington were obliged to remain over night here. The owners of the old mansion often entertained distinguished guests under their roof, among them Washington and Lafayette, those determined tourists.

Of the many inns that once existed in Baltimore, but one old building survives, and no longer is an inn. This, the Three Tuns, will be described later. Modern hotels now occupy the sites of two others.

In 1752, Baltimore Town consisted of two hundred inhabitants, and twenty-five buildings, four of these of brick. Of the brick buildings, one was a church, and two were taverns. These were "low-browed, hip-roofed houses, out of line, like an undressed regiment, painted blue, or yellow or white." The present city originally consisted of three towns; Baltimore Town, Old Town, and Fell's Point. Sixty acres of the land on which old Baltimore stood were purchased by the city commissioners from the "Messieurs Carroll" for not quite six hundred dollars.

Up to 1772, there were only passable roads for wheels out of Baltimore, these leading to Fredericktown, now shortened to Frederick, and Annapolis, although there were a number of bridle-paths, and "rolling roads," for transporting tobacco, which was packed in well-hooped hogsheads, and rolled by at least two men to the place of shipment.

Between 1805 and 1810 three turnpikes were begun, and by 1825 there were seven good roads from Baltimore, running to all four points of the compass.

In 1752, Payne's Tavern, of brick, on the corner of Calvert and Bank, now Mercer Street, and its rival, Rogers', on the northeast corner of Calvert and Baltimore Streets, are noted in early annals. Valentine Larsh, a Pennsylvania German, built a tavern at the southwest corner of Baltimore and Gay Streets in 1753, and five years later, another German from the same State, Jacob Myers, built one on the southwest corner opposite. Two others are mentioned as standing in 1861.

Taverns near the wharves, although much needed, were smaller than the more elegant stage inns. By 1772, there were so many packets and stages coming to Baltimore that more coffee houses and hotels sprang up to supply the demand.

This same year of 1772, which saw the building of so many taverns, marked an attempt to introduce a startling innovation: the use of umbrellas as a protection against sun and rain. But this was called "ridiculous effeminacy," and only when physicians urged their use to keep off "vertigoes, epilepsies, sore eyes and fevers," were they finally adopted. Early umbrellas were made of oiled linen, with rattan sticks, imported from India by way of England.

In 1778, William Stenson moved from his old tavern to a "modern and extensive coffee house," on the corner of South and Baltimore Streets, and four years later, Daniel Grant announced his removal from the Indian Queen to what was soon to be the famous Fountain Inn, on Light Lane (now Street), between Market Street and Ellicott's Wharf. The Carrollton Hotel was later built on this site,

THE ROBINSON HOUSE, NAAMAN'S CREEK, DELAWARE

[*See page* 200.

THE RED LION INN, RED LION, DELAWARE

[*See page* 204

THE OLD SIGN BOARD OF THE
RED LION INN

MIFFLIN HOUSE, CAMDEN, DELAWARE

[*See page* 206.

WASHINGTON HOTEL, PRINCESS ANNE, MARYLAND

[*See page* 211.

THE HALL OF ROSE HILL MANOR, FREDERICK, MARYLAND

[*See page* 211.

THE OLD STONE TAVERN, FREDERICK, MARYLAND

[*See page* 211.

and when it was burned in 1904 the Southern Hotel was erected on practically the same site.

The Fountain Inn cost ten thousand dollars, had a ball-room, hair-dresser's rooms, and stables for eighty horses. Many notables were entertained here. In 1792 Grant was still its host when President and Lady Washington, with their suite, visited Baltimore, and the President was given "an elegant supper, during which many toasts were drunk, amid the discharge of artillery by Captain Stodder's company." As late as 1870, part of Kaminsaky's famous old inn, a two-story brick and timber building, stood near the site of the old Fountain Inn.

Other early taverns long since vanished are: The Golden Horn, White Swan, Golden Lamb, Black Horse; the Hand Tavern and Yard for market people, on Paca Avenue, near Lexington; the Black Bear, General Wayne and the May-pole.

At Paca and Baltimore Avenues, Cugle and Frost kept "a stylish hostelrie," for western travelers, horse dealers, and cattle drovers, the Three Tuns. This remains, a mournful relic. One must look behind low, encircling shops for this old building, with its steep roof and dormer windows. Originally built around three sides of a square, with a great stable-yard, a tall granite column, surmounted by three iron tuns, stood in front of the house. Column and tuns have long since gone, nor has the place been an inn for many years.

The General Wayne, with the old sign showing the General standing beside his horse, stood until 1881.

In Baltimore Old Town, the Bull's Head stood on Front Street, the Rising Sun on High Street. Old Town was "the pet of the eastern shoremen, long after it ceased to be the pet of presidents." The Indian Queen here was popular under Gadsby. At most of these inns, stages called regularly, or started from them.

[209]

# Early American Inns and Taverns

Not until 1792 were there sidewalks or paved streets in Baltimore. The need for the latter had been forcibly demonstrated a year earlier, when a drummer boy got into so deep a mud-hole on Baltimore Street that he and his horse were extricated with difficulty. About this time, a line of stages was established between Baltimore and Philadelphia, and a year later, this was extended to Alexandria. Stages also ran to Frederick, and Annapolis, the road to "Fredericktown . . . from time immemorial passing Red House and Cook's taverns."

Annapolis began existence as the Town Land at Proctor's. In 1694, it was Anne Arundel Town, and the following year received its present name. An early French writer says: ". . . in that very inconsiderable town at the mouth of the Severn, of the few buildings it contains, three quarters may be styled elegant," and the term surely still may be applied.

Many are the stately, beautiful old houses here, and one of the finest, the mansion built for himself by the gentleman who afterwards became Governor Paca, is now a famous hotel, Carvel Hall. Much of the old-time atmosphere has been retained, for the front portion is the old house, built in 1703; the additions have been made at the sides and rear. The hotel annex is another very old house, the Brice. Here are the spacious rooms of the period, the broad halls; and one should notice in Carvel Hall the curious balustrade of the stairs leading from the second to the third floor, in curious zigzag work.

The earliest taverns mentioned in Annapolis annals are the Blue Bells, which existed at least as early as 1747, and the Annapolis Coffee House, which early became a private residence.

The Peggy Stewart Inn, although it has been an inn for only a few years, is housed in an old building, but not in the actual Stewart residence, a charming old mansion a few doors away. From this mansion, Peggy Stewart watched the sinking by her husband of his ship, and the burning of the twenty-three hundred pounds of tea which it had carried, for his indignant fellow citizens refused to allow him to land this cargo at a time when the colonists were protesting against British taxes, and especially were refusing to drink the taxed tea.

In 1840, the City Hotel, on Church and Conduit Streets, was proud of its ball, supper, and card rooms.

Annapolis is also proud of having possessed the first theater in the United States. As early as 1752, this was presenting Shakespearean dramas, and in 1771, a new theater of brick was built.

Picturesque old Frederick has an old stone tavern building, but many years ago it was given over to housing several families. It stands, practically unchanged outwardly, on West Patrick Street, where the main highroad from Baltimore forks, the branch going to Cumberland and Harper's Ferry.

On the road out of Frederick to Gettysburg, the old Johnson mansion is now Rose Hill Manor, open for guests in the motoring season. This was built in 1770 by the first governor of Maryland, Thomas Johnson, and is most attractive, set in fine grounds. The interior is practically unchanged, save that an archway has been cut in the old hall.

In Hagerstown, where the Cumberland Road joins Potomac Street, the walls of an old tavern remain, and the old stable-yard may be traced in the rear.

Down in Somerset County, at Princess Anne, is the Washington Hotel, built a hundred and fifty years ago, rebuilt in part early in this century, and still open as a hotel. Its parlor and library, each twenty-two feet long, have their original floors, and a few old doors with hand-made hinges and latches remain. Two stairways ascend side by side, in the front hall; in the men's lounge, the sides of the mantel have been worn by the feet of those who propped them against it for more than a century, for in spite of modern heating, the old fireplaces are still in use. It is a picturesque, interesting old house, and many are the distinguished citizens who have slept within its walls, including Maryland's first Attorney General, Luther Martin; Judge Salmon P. Chase, Governor Carroll, statesmen, politicians, officers of the Army and Navy, and so on.

From Baltimore to Washington, one turnpike runs through the little town of College Park, where stands the old Rossburg Tavern, and Bladensburg. The latter had two old taverns, although neither is in use as such. The Indian Queen is probably a building on the left-hand side of the road, modernized, and occupied by several families, but the old stable-yard is still in evidence. It dates from the early 1700's. The Washington House, almost opposite, was built in 1732 of bricks imported from England, but save one room in which the old paneling and large fireplace remain, the interior has been torn out and remodeled. Here, too, the stable-yard remains, but the house has not for years been an inn.

## CHAPTER XII

### *Old Southern Ordinaries*

TRAVELING by stage-coach in Virginia in the early days
must have been perilous, for as late as 1842, when
Charles Dickens made such a trip, at which time at
least the latest improved type of stage was in use,
his experiences, as graphically set down, do not move one
to envy him. On this trip, after proceeding by steamboat
from Washington to "Potomac Creek," he then took stage
for the journey to Fredericksburg, and thence by railroad
to Richmond. He says:

"Soon after nine o'clock we came to Potomac Creek, where
we are to land, and then comes the oddest part of the journey. Seven stage-coaches are preparing to carry us on. . . .
There are four horses to each coach . . . the coaches are
something like the French coaches, but not nearly so good.
In lieu of springs, they are hung on bands of the strongest
leather. There is very little choice or difference between
them; and they may be likened to the car portion of the
swings at an English fair, put upon axle trees and wheels,
and curtained with painted canvas. They are covered with
mud from the roof to the wheel-tyre, and have never been
cleaned since they were first built. . . .

"The first half mile of the road is over bridges made of
loose planks laid across two parallel poles, which tilt up as
the wheels roll over them and IN the river. The river has
a clayey bottom and is full of holes, so that half a horse

[213]

is constantly disappearing unexpectedly, and can't be found again for some time." [1]

Making due allowances for some exaggeration, the journey must have been appalling, even though they were able to "do the ten miles or thereabouts in two hours and a half; breaking no bones, though bruising a great many." [2]

Later, when traveling in Ohio, he gives another account of stage travel which must have been typical of the whole country at an earlier period. On this occasion, he and his party hired "an extra" stage-coach, to carry them from Columbus to Tiffin, Ohio, where they were to take the railroad.

"We started off again, in high spirits, at half-past six o'clock next morning, very much delighted to be by ourselves, and disposed to enjoy even the roughest journey.

"It was well for us that we were in this humour, for the road we went over that day was certainly enough to have shaken tempers that were not resolutely at Set Fair, down to some inches below Stormy. At one time we were all flung together in a heap at the bottom of the coach, and at another we were crushing our heads against the roof. Now, one side was down deep in the mire, and we were holding on the other. Now the coach was lying on the tails of the two wheelers; and now it was rearing up in the air in a frantic state, with all four horses standing on the top of an insurmountable eminence, looking coolly back at it, as though they would say: 'Unharness us! It can't be done!' The drivers on these roads, who certainly get over the ground in a manner which is quite miraculous, so twist and turn the team about in forcing a passage, corkscrew fashion, through the bogs and swamps, that it was quite a common circumstance on looking out of the window, to see the coachman with the ends of a pair of reins in his hands, apparently

[1] *American Notes*, Charles Dickens.
[2] *Ibid.*

driving nothing, or playing at horses. . . . Never, never once that day, was the coach in any position, attitude, or kind of motion to which we are accustomed in coaches." [3]

Not the least of benefits from the automobile is the improvement in our roads. The motorist out of Washington, D. C. to-day will encounter no such perils, and surely will not anticipate arriving at his journey's end battered and bruised.

A delightful trip out of the city, along a fine road, will bring one to the sleepy and once important Virginia town of Alexandria.

Although Alexandria's two old inns have practically disappeared, a visit to that quaint old town is worth while. Certainly no one should fail to visit the historic Carlyle house, around which years ago was built a hotel, the Braddock House, now completely altered.

This Carlyle mansion, built in 1752, is now preserved as a show place, and is filled with old furniture, ornaments, et cetera. Each room is named, and the Blue Room was the scene of the conference between General Braddock and the governors of the Five Colonies, at which Washington, then a lieutenant, was present. It will be recalled that Braddock refused to listen to the young American's advice concerning the plans for the Indian campaign, and lost his life in consequence. This conference was further responsible for the system of taxation adopted by Great Britain which resulted in our Revolution.

The house was built as a handsome private residence, on the site of an old Indian fort. From the terrace at the rear there is no longer the extensive view of the Potomac, which then came much nearer. A tunnel led to this river, and in the cellar of the house are dungeons, in which Indians were imprisoned. At present, to reach the house, which is open to the public by paying a small admission fee, one must cross

[3] *Ibid.*

[215]

the vestibule of an apartment house. This building and others adjacent stand where was the Braddock House.

The builder of this hotel was a clever man. He went north, bought a quantity of mahogany timber, brought it back to Alexandria, and sold it for enough money to build his house. He was also wise enough to preserve the old Carlyle house as an additional attraction for his guests.

At the corner near by is the Bank of Alexandria, first financial institution authorized by Virginia's General Assembly, of which Washington was a patron and depositor.

On the southwest corner of Royal and Cameron Streets, is all that remains of the famous old Gadsby Tavern, now a mere shell. Across its old brick front still runs the sign: City Hotel, but according to an old resident, it has not really been a hotel for probably seventy-five years. The lower floor is occupied by a junk shop, but the fine window-moldings, and one old fireplace, with paneling reaching to the ceiling, though begrimed and blackened, are still beautiful. The second floor contained the ballroom, removed in its entirety, and set up in the American Wing of the Metropolitan Museum of Art, New York City. One old Alexandrian remarked that "the Museum people" replaced the old wainscotted walls, doors, etc., with "wood that was a lot better than what they took." The upper floors of the building are now divided into cheap lodgings.

In 1820, mail-coaches left Alexandria before dawn, that is practically the route of the modern highroad between Alexandria and Fredericksburg. This was first known as the Potomac Path, an Indian trail, later it was a telegraph road. Over it Rochambeau and Washington passed, on their way to Yorktown.

"Although the inns in Virginia are sometimes bad, yet they might reach Fredericksburg before night, traveling the fifty miles in sixteen hours.

The oldest white man's road in Virginia ran over what

*Courtesy of the Fredericksburg Chamber of Commerce.*

THE RISING SUN, FREDERICKSBURG, VIRGINIA

[See page 217.

THE OLD ASHBY TAVERN, PARIS, VIRGINIA

[*See page* 219.

THE SIGN OF THE GREEN TEAPOT, YANCEY'S MILLS, VIRGINIA

[*See page* 219.

upon the whole they are better than those in other states. Those in the back country here are preferable to the inns in many of the most inhabited parts of New England," wrote the Duc de la Rochefoucauld, in the eighteenth century.

In Virginia, ordinary was the usual name for the inn or tavern of other localities. They were usually furnished with billiard tables and bowling alleys, and were great gambling rendezvous. At the various "court houses," as county towns were called, the ordinaries were centers of social and political life.

Mrs. Wakefield, an early English traveler, wrote: "We can scarcely pass ten or twenty miles without seeing an ordinary. They all resemble each other, having a porch in front, the length of the house, almost covered with hand-bills. They have no sign. These Virginia taverns take their name from the person who keeps the house, who is often a man of consequence." Early travelers seem quite generally impressed with the class of men keeping taverns in America: retired army men, justices of the peace, parsons' sons, and so on.

In the interesting old town of Fredericksburg, a Revolutionary tavern is now cared for by the Association for the Preservation of Virginia Antiquities. This, the Rising Sun, built in the 1760's by Charles Washington, the President's brother, was Fredericksburg's first Post Office, and, of course, a meeting place for the patriots. Both Washington and Lafayette stopped here. A small story-and-a-half house, it is now filled with fine old furniture.

At the Maury Hotel, once the Exchange, Charles Dickens was entertained in 1842; and the Indian Queen, now vanished, was a noted inn.

Although ordinaries were plentiful in olden times here in Virginia, comparatively few are still standing. The armies fought back and forth over her soil during the Civil War, and, too, many of these houses were not built for permanence. As in other parts of the south, travelers, even though strangers, were quite generally entertained in private homes, leaving the ordinaries to accommodate the humbler class of traveler who could be comfortable in them.

On the corner of Broad and Ninth Streets, Richmond, part of The Swan, a noted tavern, survives in the present building. The Swan was kept in its early days by Major Morse, probably a Revolutionary officer. Judges and lawyers frequented it, and it had a high reputation for good food, comfortable beds, and excellent company. Edgar Allan Poe stopped at this inn on his last visit to Richmond.

From Richmond, a road runs southeast to Gloucester, where Ye Olde English Tavern was standing recently; then on to Yorktown, where Ye Olde English Tavern, established in 1775, is still open to travelers.

The plot of ground on which this hotel stands was sold in 1691 for one hundred and eighty pounds of tobacco, on condition that a house be built there within a year's time. As this was not done, the land was forfeited, and sold again on the same terms to a widow, who seems to have kept the agreement. Eight years later a man was murdered in an upstairs room of this house by one of his slaves.

The original house was opened as a tavern in 1725, and although remodeled, has been a hotel ever since. Both Washington and Lafayette are said to have stayed here, but the present proprietor refuses to state this as a fact.

Those who are willing to leave the main roads will find in the northern part of the state, in Fauquier and Warren Counties, other old inns.

From Richmond, a highroad runs north to Ashland, and a short distance east, in Hanover, is a tavern built nearly two hundred years ago. Its exact age is not known, but since taverns in county seats derived their patronage largely from frequenters of the courts, it can not have been built much later than the Court House here, or 1725. It is still in good condition and still used as a hotel. Kept in its early days by John Shelton, father-in-law of Patrick Henry, the younger man often took the elder's place. In the old Court House he made his maiden speech, in 1763, and early in his career also spoke in the Gloucester Court House. The Marquis de Chastellux, author of *Travels in America in 1780-1782*, also stayed at and described this Hanover tavern.

In Fauquier County, two miles east of the village of Aldie, is an old stone building, long supposed to be what remained of Nevill's Ordinary, where George Washington spent his first night while on his way to begin a survey for Lord Fairfax. But a resident of this section recently made extensive investigations, and convinced himself that the tavern kept in 1748 by George Nevill was not this, but another building, unoccupied for years, in what is now the village of Auburn, twenty miles south of the Aldie tavern, which is the William West or Watts' Ordinary.

On the Lee Jackson highway, at Middleburg, is another old ordinary, the Beverage House.

Just before reaching Ashby's Gap, in the Blue Mountains, there stands in the village of Paris a tavern which was operated for many years by Thomson Ashby, until his death in 1850. A lieutenant in the War of 1812, he was an uncle of the noted Confederate cavalry officer, General Turner Ashby. When Thomson Ashby died, his family continued to keep the old tavern until after the Civil War; then it was sold to Abner Slack. He kept it open until about forty years ago, since when it has been the private residence of members of the family.

Beyond the Gap, on the Shenandoah River, is the site of another ordinary, kept in the middle of the eighteenth century by Captain John Ashby, one of the leading settlers of the Shenandoah Valley. He distinguished himself as a scout in the French and Indian War, and Washington, in his *Journal*, mentions spending a night in March, 1748, in this

[219]

ordinary. From about 1760, it was run by Joseph Berry. Both landlords also operated a ferry across the river near the ordinary, known as Ashby's, then as Berry's Ferry. Part of a very old building which is still standing is pointed out as either the original tavern, or a portion of it.

There are a number of sites of old inns south of this highroad, which may be investigated if one has the time and does not mind poor roads.

On the old stage road between Richmond and Charlottesville, there were many ordinaries, some of which have been torn down; a few survive. At Boyd's Tavern Post Office, stood a tavern which was purchased from its owner, Boyd, before the Civil War. The inn was burned in 1868, and the second owner's son rebuilt it on the old site, using the same chimneys and foundations. As Shepherd's Inn, this was open as long as stage-coaches ran between Richmond and Charlottesville, but is now a residence. A separate building containing the original bar is still standing a short distance from the house, and here Lafayette and his soldiers stopped to refresh themselves. Originally a log building, it has been weatherboarded, but is in a very dilapidated condition.

Lafayette camped about three miles from this tavern, and some cypress trees, marked with French soldiers' initials, still stand near the residence now occupying the old camp site.

In Charlottesville, the old Colonial Hotel, still open, is at least one hundred years old, for it was built when Thomas Jefferson visited the town at the time when he was planning the building of the University of Virginia. He had a room in this hotel, often making long sojourns. As the University opened its doors in 1825, no one can deny the hotel's claim to age. Patrick Henry and James Monroe were other distinguished guests. The greater part of the old building was recently torn down, and replaced by a large addition to the hotel. The small portion of the old building that still remains is probably doomed to the same fate shortly.

Many other ordinaries once stood here in Charlottesville, but have now gone. The Eagle Tavern on Court Square, built shortly after the Revolution, is one of these, although its site has been used for a hotel ever since, and it is said that in building the present Monticello Hotel, and the large new adjoining building, some of the old timbers were used. The old Eagle Register is kept here, and among famous names in it are: Jefferson, Madison, Monroe, William Wirt, Patrick Henry, Edgar Allan Poe, Generals Lee and Jackson, and two modern presidents, Woodrow Wilson and Theodore Roosevelt. The old Swan Tavern, kept by Jack Jowett, is gone.

West of Charlottesville, at Staunton, is a residence called Sunnyside, which was for a long time a tavern, under the name of Clarksville, established before the University was built. In Oxford style, students in disgrace with the faculty were, for a time, sent to this inn to rusticate, but it was found that the inn bar furnished these students too much enjoyment, so private families were induced to board them. This house is now so modernized that it does not suggest an old ordinary, save that it is very close to the road.

One mile west of Ivy is another modernized residence, which in 1805 was the Hardindale Inn, and recently a tea-room.

Farther West, in Yancey's Mills, is The Sign of the Green Teapot, now, and for the past twelve years, open as a tea-room and small hotel. The present owners state that it is more than two hundred years old, and was long a tavern, the present tea-room having been the barroom. A white frame house, with green blinds, it is very attractive, many of the old features having been preserved. There are, for instance, the original old floors, doors and windows—although

[221]

with modern panes of glass—the big old fireplaces are still in use, the old mantels are here, and the house is lighted by candles and lamps.

Between Greenwood and Afton is a rather small old brick house, a private residence now, and not suggestive of an inn. None the less it was one, and is more than a century old.

North of Charlottesville, on the road from Stony Point across the mountains, was an old inn with surely the oddest name: Pinch-'em-Slyly! The site is still to be seen on the private grounds of Mr. John B. Minor, but the inn, which had not been in use since 1790, was torn down in 1827.

The Rising Sun, another ordinary, eight miles from Charlottesville, served those traveling over the Three Notch Road, and was frequented by drovers. It is told that two of these expressed a wish to meet a certain well-known character, Fountain Wells. On their return from selling their stock, with pockets filled, they spent the night at this Rising Sun. After supper, the two drivers played a game of poker with a stranger, who, after winning all their money, bade them good night, adding: "Gentlemen, you have met Fountain Wells!"

An old inn that remains practically unchanged, off the beaten track, is the Michie Old Tavern, between Free Union and Earlysville. Here is a fine old chimney, the flag walk is old, and on the second floor is a ballroom, but the large frame building is now occupied as cheap apartments, and is rapidly tumbling to pieces.

Williamsburg's very famous inn, the Raleigh, with its Apollo Room, scene of many festivities, for the house was a social center, was burned in 1857. Cuckoo Tavern, in Louisa County, connected with the famous ride of Jack Jowett, and Tarleton's raid, is now much altered, and a private home.

The old Cumberland road, opened in 1818, the only highway of its kind, since it was wholly constructed by the Government, and formed part of the National Road, largely followed Nemacolin's Path, the old trail which ran from the Potomac to the Ohio River. From earliest times, this was used by traders. The road cut by General Braddock for his unfortunate expedition, as far as the orchard where he died, and one later known as Washington's largely coincided with the later Cumberland road, which joined another running from Baltimore to Boonesboro. All along this road, as early as 1830, were taverns, some of which are still standing, and "every cabin in all the western wilderness was a tavern, where if there was lack of Bear and Cyder, there was dried meat." The first tavern in the west was on Braddock's Road.

The old Northwest Turnpike from Winchester, Virginia to the Ohio at Parkersburg, was laid out by a company incorporated in 1827. Although as early as 1770 there was a settlement where Wheeling now stands, this was for many years frontier country.

White Sulphur Springs has, however, been a popular resort for more than a century, and its large hotels are successors of the original log cabins. Not far away, near Big Sewall Mountain, the old Star Tavern still stands; at Kanawha Falls the Stockton Tavern building remains; and in Lewisburg is Colonel Crow's. At Clarksburg, in 1798, Felix Renick describes in his *Journey Made by an American Pioneer*, the landlord of one tavern as "an apparently good, honest, illiterate landlord, who had recently been appointed one of a commission to lay out the road between Cumberland and Marietta, Ohio. This worthy said that "*by the straight line*, the road was seventy miles long, but coming back, they found a shorter one."

Running south into North Carolina, on Albemarle Sound is the old town of Edenton, one of eleven which existed in the State between 1729 and 1787. Named after Charles Eden, an early governor of the colony, it was one of the several capitals which North Carolina tried out before determining on Raleigh. A good road early ran from this town to Bath, and from thence to New Bern and Brunswick, but the first post did not come through until 1769, and then only once a month. Before the Revolution and for many years afterward a famous old tavern stood here, known as Hornblow's. It was burned long ago, and a modern hotel, the Bay View, stands on its site.

Hertford, north of Edenton, had a picturesque old inn, the Eagle, a long, rambling, two-story wooden house, with a double portico running its entire length, but this was burned to the ground twelve years ago.

No old inns remain in New Bern, another of the oldest towns in the State. South of Wilmington, at Southport, is a charming old hotel, established in 1842, and still popular. The lower portion of the house, built of brick, is shown by town records to be one hundred and thirty-four years old. The upper frame portion was added in 1852. This is the Stuart House, on the south side of Bay Street, its wide piazzas almost washed by the Cape Fear River.

The first landlady, Mrs. Mary E. Stuart, came to Southport from Tennessee, after her husband had been killed in the Battle of New Orleans. She bought the house and opened it as a hotel. Living to be eighty-nine years old, her daughter succeeded her, and has run it ever since.

One of the traditions of the house, which has for years been a stopping place for judges and lawyers, is that every lawyer must sleep in its garret before he can be raised to the bench. "There have been just enough exceptions to prove the rule," Miss Stuart says.

Ships coming into or leaving the harbor, passing her garden, often salute Miss Stuart, and dip their colors. This custom originated one day when the daughter of a ship captain was swimming in the river, and the current

STUART HOUSE, SOUTHPORT, NORTH CAROLINA

*[See page 224.*

SALEM TAVERN, WINSTON-SALEM, NORTH CAROLINA

[See page 2

threatened to sweep her away. Although nearly sixty years old, Miss Stuart plunged in and saved the child.

In Raleigh there still stands the house of Joel Lane, which in 1771 was an ordinary. Peter Casso's Inn is still in use. Here Jacob Johnson, father of the president, was employed as a hostler, and his wife, Betty, was a weaver. The future president was born in the old inn, and was named Andrew by "pretty Peggy" Casso, daughter of the inn's owner, on her wedding night.

The inn at Barclaysville, not far from Raleigh, where Lafayette dined in 1825, on his tour of the State, is no longer standing.

Westward, at Hillsboro, is the modern Colonial Hotel. Part of the building, originally a log house, is believed to be one hundred years old, but the whole house has been remodeled and changed as much as its name, for since 1865 it has been known as the Occoneechee Hotel, the Corbinton Inn, and only for about four years as the Colonial.

In Danbury, about a century old, still open, is the Mc-Cauless Hotel, a name which it has borne for fifty years. It was built by Nathaniel Moody, a prominent merchant, then passed to Dr. McCauless, who lived to a great age, but always refused to tell what that age was. His son, quite an old gentleman, is the present landlord.

The house is put together with wooden pegs, and oddly enough, although the inner part of its walls is of soft brick, none show in the apparent frame structure. In two of its sides live swarms of wild bees, which came down from the mountains. Two North Carolina governors, Robert Glenn and Thomas Bickett, boarded here when beginning their law practice, and years ago the house was a summer resort.

One of the earliest in the State is the Salem Tavern, at Winston-Salem, and still open as a hotel.

A frame house was built here in 1772, and run as a tavern

[225]

by the Moravian Church. When this burned, in 1784, a new brick house was built on the same site, and opened that year.

The first landlord, Jacob Meyer, was given lengthy instructions in German by the church for running the tavern. He was warned that "the guests who come here are of very different dispositions and customs, yea, even occasionally enemies and spies," so it was hoped that these guests "may be served by our Brother and Sister in every respect in such a way that their [the guests'] consciences may tell them that we are an honest and a Christian people, such as they have never before found in a tavern."

These landlords were not allowed to engage in any other business, but received board and lodging for themselves and their families, one hundred and fifty dollars a year, and if the season was profitable, at the end of the year one-third of the profits. Guests must be served, the landlord was cautioned, with "wholesome and plentiful food," also the beer, liquors and wines must be "good and unadulterated." Rooms, windows, beds, and crockery must be kept clean, and the landlord was further enjoined to treat his guests with "kindness and cordiality, but not encourage them to be intemperate or run themselves in debt."

The old tavern soon was the scene of many hot disputes between Patriots and Tories, "there was much drinking and fighting amongst the soldiers, and broken heads and quarrels were frequent." Finally, soldiers of both armies were from time to time quartered in the town, and visited the tavern. Many distinguished men were guests at the tavern as well, and some of these left without paying their bills. The inventory of April 30th, 1781, contains the following:

## LOSSES

For entertaining the Officers Armstrong, Sheppard and Cummins—
2 pounds, 1 shilling, 6 pence.

# Old Southern Ordinaries

For entertaining Maj. Winston twice—8 shillings.

For expensive entertainment of Col. Cleveland and six other officers and feed for horses—2 pounds, 18 shillings.

For ten cords of wood burnt by the soldiers, and feeding fifteen horses for four weeks for which there is no ticket—4 pounds.

Col. Gunn also remained in debt for his entertainment—1 pound, 7 shillings, 6 pence.

For 6 cows, 1 ox and 2 year old heifer—lost 30 pounds.

Total—40 pounds, 16 shillings.

"On November 8th, 1781, Gov. Martin, ex-Gov. Richard Caswell and sixty-three members of the legislature arrived in Salem for the purpose of holding a meeting . . . On the night of the 24th, the alarming news was brought that a large body of Tories were near town and intended to make an attack for the purpose of seizing the body of the Governor. It was a cold, rainy night, and all night long two companies of soldiers patrolled the streets and guarded the building, but no attack was made . . . In the inventory of April 30th, 1782, there is mentioned among the assets of the Tavern 'One Ticket [voucher] from Governor Martin, 15 pounds, 17 shillings, 8 pence.' " [4]

In spite of war times, water was brought into the tavern from near-by springs in 1778. After the fire, the new house, two stories, with a steep, tiled roof and a stone-paved kitchen, with two great fireplaces, was the largest building in town.

In 1850, after heavy losses, the Church authorities sold the tavern for five thousand dollars to Adam Butner, and for years it was known by his name. Twice, a new dining-room was added to the old building, a ballroom, and other apartments, but later these additions were removed and made into houses, so that at present the tavern is about as it was when first built.

Many stage lines passed through the town from early days and until finally superseded by the railroad, so the

[4] *The Old Salem Tavern,* William S. Pfohl in Winston-Salem *Union-Republican.*

tavern did not lack for guests, and even since that time its ballroom has often been used for balls and other entertainments.

In South Carolina few old inns may be found. A stage route ran in 1776 from Philadelphia to Charleston, and an old agreement in 1835 leased the Rantowles House establishment in St. Paul's Parish, Colleton, on condition that the lessee "doth covenant, promise and agree to keep a respectable, well found, and well ordered house of entertainment for the accommodation of travelers."

In 1824, a Camden paper carried the advertisement of: At the Sign of the Eagle and Harp, with a picture of a two-story, square house; an announcement of the Camden races, in the same paper, gives notice that a meeting will be held at Ballard's Tavern. It would be hard now to find these two taverns.

Four miles from Charleston, on Broad Path, a building more than a hundred years old still stands. For many years it was a famous tavern, but in 1812 bore a most unsavory reputation, for it was kept by a couple who, before they were finally arrested, convicted, and hanged, are believed to have robbed and murdered many travelers who lodged there. Broad Path is the country road from Charleston, and where it forks, there stood another old tavern, the Quarter House, built before 1721, which has long since disappeared.

Mrs. Leiding tells that in 1740, the indigo planters of Prince George, Winyah Parish, in what is now Georgetown, formed a social club which met in the Oak Tavern, on Bay Street. This club flourished, but a building long known as the Winyah Inn, now a Masonic Temple, was the old Georgetown bank. A picture of this house shows a large yard, with sheds in the rear, so perhaps it was at one time an inn.

The Joseph McCullough House is about one hundred years old, and still stands on the old stage-road between

Greenville, South Carolina and Augusta, Georgia. Built of brick, covered with plaster in soft coloring, it originally had a piazza on the second floor, each end of which was later enclosed to make a room. The owner used it as his residence as well as an inn, for he was merchant, landowner, and innkeeper. It is still owned by his descendants, but not occupied by them.

Only one old inn has been found mentioned in Georgia, Tondee's Tavern, which stood on the northwest corner of the present Whitaker and Broughton Streets, Savannah. At the beginning of the Revolution, the Sons of Liberty used to meet here, but it was torn down many years ago.

If there were old inns in Florida, it has proved impossible to locate any. During the Spanish occupation, travelers doubtless, as in New Mexico and California, were entertained in convents or Government houses. In Alabama, two or three are still standing, and records of others exist. Through the courtesy of Mr. Peter A. Brannon, of Montgomery, a list of some inns existing between 1810 and 1830 along the Federal Road, through the Creek Nation, to Mobile, has been furnished.

At Leighton, a house now a residence, was an inn, or perhaps one should call it a "house for paying guests." At all events, the father of the Confederate General Gregg entertained travelers here at a charge. Said to be more than a hundred years old, it was in the early days for many years an inn.

Eighteen miles east of Montgomery, now a negro house, is a former tavern at which Lafayette stayed in 1825, and it was used as a stage stop until well after 1840.

This Federal Road entered Alabama at Fort Mitchell, and left the State at Mobile. The Creek Indian Treaty stipulated that "stopping places for travelers through the Nation be provided." These were between thirteen and sixteen miles apart, and the Government regulated the charge for meals as follows: Breakfast, fifty cents; dinner and supper seventy-five cents. Stage horses were changed at each stop.

The coaches were usually run either by a company or by individuals who derived most of their profits from a Government contract for carrying the mails, and they troubled themselves little about the passengers' comfort.

A post route was established in 1818 from Fort Mitchell, via Fort Bainbridge, Fort Jackson, then by Mims Ferry to St. Stephens.

After leaving Fort Mitchell, the first inn, consisting of several log cabins, was at Uchee Bridge, three miles west of the fort, and in 1820 this was kept by a young man from Philadelphia, whose partner was a half-breed. It seems not to have lasted long, for in 1830 the stage stop was on the Government Reservation at the Fort, was known as Crowell's Tavern, and kept by a brother of the agent. Commissioned officers stationed at the Fort boarded here.

Royston's Inn, fourteen miles west of the Fort, was described in 1830 as "a tolerable country inn," and must have been welcome after the earlier days, when there was no stop between Fort Mitchell and Fort Bainbridge, so that travelers were obliged to make the journey to the latter place in one day.

The inn at Fort Bainbridge was kept in 1820 by Captain Kendall Lewis, a former United States Army officer, who married an Indian, and also had for silent partner an Indian, Big Warrior, as seems to have been quite the custom. By 1830, it was kept by a Mrs. Harris, her husband acting as head waiter, and was the best inn in all the Creek country. By special request, travelers might have *private towels*, and even a basin of water in their own rooms, instead of using the basin and roller towel in the hall. They might even have rooms with single beds. Guests without privileges, however, were expected to *shave in the hall*. In 1836, this house was known as Cook's, and from 1818, when the road was cut through from Pensacola to Fort Mitchell, was an important stop.

In 1830, Captain Walker, who was apparently another son-in-law of Big Warrior, was keeping a tavern between Fort Bainbridge and the Line Creek Tavern at what is known as Pole Cat Springs, half a day's journey from Walker's Race Track, and near Fort Hull. This was the last white man's dwelling in the Creek country, and good meals were served, with white bread; guineas, pea fowls and poultry were raised by this landlord.

Walter B. Lucas kept the Line Creek Tavern mentioned as early as 1820, in the present village of Waugh. Ten years later, Mrs. Lucas was managing it admirably, serving for dinner chicken pie, ham, vegetables, puddings, pies, preserved fruits, or strawberries, plums, and other fruits. Wine and brandy were served freely, and she charged seventy-five cents for such a meal.

The first tavern in Montgomery was a log cabin on the north side of Decatur, then Market Street. The sufficiently high rate of three dollars a day was charged here. Two years later, the Globe Tavern, a two-story, frame house, also on the north side of Market Street, was built. Later, this was called the Indian Queen, but in 1830 it was burned down. In the same year as this tavern, the Montgomery Hotel came into existence, later called the Lafayette Tavern, after that general had been entertained there. This quite large house for the times, ninety feet long, sixty wide, two stories high, with a double veranda running its entire length, still stands. In 1821, the Mansion House was built where later the Exchange Hotel succeeded it.

In 1820, a one-roomed cabin was built about ten miles south of Montgomery, and in this a family lived, and also accommodated for the night the stage driver and such guests as might be obliged to stop here. Known as the Bonum

House, it served poor meals, and the landlady had the reputation of being ill-tempered—the crowding might well explain this. Meals were put on the table at the hour the stage was due, and if it were late, the guests had to put up with cold food.

The next stage stop was at Wood's Tavern, presided over without pay by Colonel Wood of the militia. Dinners were poor here too, but beer brewed from molasses was relished by the guests.

A log cabin came next, none too good a protection from the weather; then came Fort Dale, with a fairly good tavern, whose landlord was a member of the legislature, and had quite a library.

Major Taylor kept the tavern at what is now Greenville, where, although small bedrooms were to be had, he furnished no bedding but scantily filled feather beds.

Ten miles below this was another tavern, later called Price's, then the stage proceeded to Murder Creek, and when possible, left the tavern by moonlight, via Burnt Corn.

Beyond where the Mobile and Blakely roads fork, the first tavern was kept by a Georgian, and there was a school near by where Latin and French were taught, the head master receiving what must have been a large salary for those days, seven hundred dollars, and he had two assistants.

For almost forty miles beyond, there were for years no houses of any kind; the next inn was kept by a man who owned two thousand head of cattle, but furnished his guests neither milk nor butter.

On another route were Price's Inn, whose landlord was the stage driver; Cooker's; Longmyre's, kept by a woman who acted as physician for the neighborhood within ten miles; and next Duncan MacMillan's, where there were separate bedrooms, good coffee, and family prayers every evening, but the man who drove the stage between this and

[232]

THE MC CULLOUGH HOUSE, NEAR GREENVILLE, SOUTH CAROLINA

[*See page* 228.

OLD ALABAMA INN NEAR MONTGOMERY

INN NEAR ST. FRANCISVILLE, LOUISIANA

[*See page* 236.

Mrs. Longmyre's is said to have been "a most profane man."

Peeble's was kept by an educated, well-to-do planter, then came Mrs. Mills', well thought of in the neighborhood. She raised all her products on her farm, and supplied her guests with venison and wild turkeys. Then came Macdavid's, two rooms with a hall between, with only a roller towel for general use.

Of the next settlement of Blakely, nothing now remains but its once famous Washington Avenue, still bordered with live oaks, hung with gray Spanish moss.

In 1822, John Fowler of this village was authorized to "set up, keep, maintain and run a Steam Ferryboat between the city of Mobile and the town of Blakely," for five years, said boat to be large enough to transport six horses at a time. The usual traveler did not stop at Blakely's, where the boat met the stage, but went directly on to Mobile. Five miles from Blakely, on another road, there was a tavern where Judge Burns served a good breakfast, the coffee being especially commended.

The first stage route east from Montgomery was established by Lewis Calfrey and Major James W. Johnston, at one time proprietor of the inn at Fort Mitchell, and by 1823, two trips each way were made weekly. The first mail was brought by these stages to Montgomery in 1821; before that it had come west once a week only, on horseback.

For many years after there were settlements in Alabama, it was in part almost a wilderness, where bears and panthers came close to isolated plantation houses, and deer abounded.

Mississippi was even less settled. A traveler in 1860 mentions that Fort Gibson had a tavern, and speaks of a few log cabin taverns, but for the most part he stopped at houses along the way for food or lodging, either being entertained free, if the house belonged to people of means,

[233]

or paying the usual charge of one dollar for supper, lodging, breakfast and horse food. Alexandria had three taverns, and this "and Natchitoches were the only towns of any size in this section."

In 1872, another traveler mentions a "huge, barn-like tavern" at Meridian, Mississippi.

While still a French possession, Louisiana had her inns.

An early traveler down the Mississippi describes visiting New Orleans in 1804, and taking lodgings at Mme. Fournier's, for forty-five dollars a month. He speaks of Bayou, two miles back from the town, as having "a place of public entertainment, the Tivoli, a new affair, at which is a ball once a week. None of the streets [of New Orleans] have pavements, and after rains" they walked on "a long line of single logs, set in the line of the roadway. Shrimps are eaten here," he continues, "also a dish called gumbo."

Another traveler's diary tells that in 1806 he "took board with a French innkeeper" in New Orleans, where he several times helped make peace in barroom brawls, whereupon the landlord came to him, and suggested: "You make peace in my house—you tend bar—I give you boarding and $50 a month—you make peace." The traveler accepted.[5]

In New Orleans, there is still standing on St. Peter's and Charles Street a building which was once a famous tavern called *Le Veau qui Tete* (The Sucking Calf). This is more than a hundred years old, the architecture Spanish. Its proprietor would have none but well-bred guests, and his cooking was renowned. He served both *table d'hôte* and *à la carte* meals.

A few of the old taverns along the levee, patronized by river men, are also standing.

In 1723 to 1730, New Orleans consisted of a small, cleared space near the river, surrounded by ditches filled

[5] George Sampe in *The American Pioneer.*

[234]

with refuse. The aristocrats lived chiefly on plantations outside the town.

The St. Louis Hotel, which stood until quite recently, was originally built to include a hotel, bank, ballroom, and stores. It was nearly destroyed by fire in 1840, but was repaired and reopened. A picture of it at that time shows it as a four-storied building, with double galleries across the front.

In 1841, the St. Charles Hotel was standing, a noted place for travelers, its barroom the most frequented place in the city, and it is still a popular hotel. Hotel de la Marine, near the old Market, was a rendezvous for the adventurers of the time. In 1857, many Sicilians were killed in this house during the Know Nothing riots. Built in the early 1800's, in 1815 it was known as the Navy Hotel, and advertised a coffee house, public baths, *table d'hôte* and boarding-house; also entertainments, such as rope dancing in costume, to the tune of Yankee Doodle, by a man who not only wore the costume of an old woman, but also set off fireworks while dancing on the rope.

Another early house, the Tremoulet, opposite the river-landing at the corner of Old Levee and St. Peter's Street, afterwards became Baron Pontalbas' residence, and again in 1814, was "a respectable lodging house."

Early homes were generally built around *patios*. From New Orleans to Baton Rouge there was a succession of handsome houses, always with one or more guest rooms for friend or travelers finding themselves in the neighborhood. This explains why there were few taverns. The Shell Road was opened between 1830 and 1832.

In 1820, many strangers came to New Orleans from the west, on flatboats down the river, bringing grain and cured meats. Bandits and gamblers came as well. The city was first lighted in 1821 by twelve large lamps, and about this time, sycamore and elm trees were planted on the levee front, the Place d'Armes and Circus. The following year paving was begun, so that it would no longer be necessary to pass through deep mud in bad weather.

Lafayette was entertained here, but at a private residence.

In the Parish of West Feliciana, in the Natchez district, there were two important towns. One, Bayou Sara, once the most important shipping point between New Orleans and Natchez, has now largely been submerged by the vagaries of the Mississippi River. The other, St. Francisville, was at one time considered for the State capital. Outside this town, the main street becomes the road to Natchez, and a branch of the old Natchez Trail turns off to Pinckneyville and Fort Adams.

A quarter of a mile off this second road stands a private residence, long ago an inn. Its exact age can not be stated, for many records were destroyed years ago by the burning of the Court House, but it is believed that it must have been built before 1810, since it is in Spanish style, and the Spaniards almost all left this section after that year. The grandfather of the present owner acquired the property in 1824.

Large brick pillars support the second-story gallery, and are surmounted by wrought-iron posts and an ornate railing. From this second-story gallery, an open staircase used to descend to the lower floor, but it has been replaced by a narrow winding flight at the end of the gallery, protected from the weather, as the old one was not. The lower floor is entirely paved within with bricks. It comprises a large dining-room, with smaller rooms at either end, and has a large old fireplace, with cupboards on either side. The glass doors of these match the panels in the old entrance door. A beautiful old lawn is filled in springtime with blossoming jonquils, narcissi, daffodils, and similar flowers, which have been increasing there for more than a hundred years.

This exhausts the list of old Louisiana inns which it has been possible to locate.

One would hardly expect to locate any inns in Texas when it is realized how new that country is. The early traveler, A. A. Parker, who journeyed through a part of the State in 1836, speaks of a few taverns, but in the next breath, mentions log and mud houses, so survivors are out of the question. August Santleben, who established the first stage connection between the United States and Mexico in 1867, speaks of El Paso roads as "infested with Indians," and such stage stops as he mentions were always made at ranch houses. His earliest recollections of San Antonio are of a town with a business section around two squares, the residences extending a couple of blocks in each direction beyond, and a population of four thousand, including many Mexicans and Indians; a poorly built town, he calls it, of one-story adobe and mud houses, many of them nothing more than huts.

## Chapter XIII

### *Inns in Ohio, and Erie County, Pennslyvania*

THE National or Cumberland Road, or the Old Pike, as it was called, the first road built by the Federal Government, was originally intended to run from Cumberland, Maryland, to Wheeling, in what was then Virginia, now West Virginia, or, in other words, to connect the Potomac and Ohio Rivers, as the old Nemacolin's Path, used by traders from the earliest days, had done. This road was, however, extended beyond Wheeling into Ohio, almost to Springfield; after that its construction was turned over to the states themselves.

As was to be expected, the building of the road, bringing new settlers westward, caused many taverns or inns to spring up, and by 1830 these were frequent along its entire course. Many of these old buildings remain, transformed into modern residences, and a few survive as inns or tea-rooms.

Before the National Road was laid out, an old road, now the Maysville Pike, formerly Zane's Trail, ran from Wheeling through Zanesville, Ohio, and on to Maysville, Kentucky.

There were still standing a few years ago several old taverns near Cambridge, Ohio. A man named Graham made the first settlement here in 1798, stayed for two years, keeping a tavern and a ferry, and then was succeeded by George Beymer, from Pennsylvania.

Inns existed all along the National Road in Ohio; many

[238]

were log cabins, long since replaced by modern buildings; a few have been preserved.

Zanesville is quite a tavern center. The Sign of the Orange Tree was opened here in 1807, and in it the State Legislature met for one session. Two years earlier, the settlement had what a traveler then described as "one log cabin, a kind of excuse for a tavern," but an earlier traveler, in 1799, when the place was known as Westbourne, mentions a log cabin opened as a tavern by Mr. M'Intire, who "introduced the luxury of comfortable beds." This cabin stood at what is now the corner of Market and Second Streets. M'Intire was a leading citizen. When he opened his tavern, there were several grog shops, and it seems as if the later traveler must inadvertently have gone to one of these. There, travelers could have supper of a kind, and with feet to the fire might sleep on the floor, or on such skins and rugs as they brought with them.

At Hendrysburg, the Pioneer Tavern, built in 1826, is still open as a hotel, outwardly little changed. Built by John McCartney, this was one of the inns opened to accommodate travelers by stage-coach. When the railroad came, it was used as a farm dwelling, and the automobile has restored it to its earlier use.

Fultonham had an inn built in the 1830's, by Lyle Fulton, and kept by him and his descendants for many years. Here horses were changed on the stage line from Somerset to Zanesville. The settlement, originally called Uniontown, was changed to its present name in honor of the innkeeper, who was the first Postmaster. When, in the '60's, the house was sold to Ham Norman, a well-known showman, he had it razed, and built one of the square houses so popular in that era.

Five miles south of Zanesville, a large stone house, now a dwelling, was once a tavern. Five miles west of Zanesville is the Headley Tavern, still open.

Built about 1802 for a dwelling, when the National Road was opened, Usual Headley decided to open it as an inn, and it remained such until 1865. The grandfather of the present owner then bought it, but for some years before its reopening four years ago, it had been unoccupied.

The present proprietors have furnished it with articles of its early days, and also those used in this section of the country. In one room may still be seen the original hand-hewn beams of walnut, and in almost every room some of the old wooden pegs which originally fastened the beams remain. The old dining-room and barroom have great fireplaces with hand-carved mantels; the kitchen fireplace is built of stone blocks. There is, too, a somewhat rare winding staircase, decorated on the risers in a hand-painted grape design.

Half a mile west of Headley's, the Blue Lion was once a tavern.

A cabin of hewn logs, with a stone chimney, was opened in 1802 on the site of the later Franklin House, Newark. The following year, the Reverend John Wright, a missionary, came to this tavern on a Saturday. He was a Presbyterian, and the only family in the settlement belonging to that church was so poor that the clergyman went to the tavern, which was soon filled with people come to a horse race. Later, having patronized the landlord's bar, these swore that the minister must either drink with them or be ducked in the horse trough. Since he refused to drink with them, they did duck him, whereupon he decided that he had best look up his fellow Presbyterian. The latter and his wife made the minister welcome, but they had but one bed, and although they begged him to take this he would not, so slept on the floor. The next day, after the horse race was over, his tormentors apologized.

North of Newark, Mount Vernon was founded in 1803 by three men who owned the land on which the town now

HEADLY TAVERN, ZANESVILLE, OHIO

[*See page* 239.

PIONEER TAVERN, HENDRYSBURG, OHIO

[*See page* 239

OLD INN, CAMBRIDGE, OHIO

[*See Page* 238.

stands. One of these, Benjamin Butler, from Pennsylvania, kept a log tavern on what is now the corner of Wood and Main Streets.

In the village of Lafayette is a charming old inn known as The Red Brick Tavern. In consequence of the opening of the National Road, this was built in 1837 by Stanley Watson, who also built himself a residence, but often entertained distinguished guests at his inn which was run by John McMullen. Among these guests was Martin Van Buren, at the time that he was running against William Henry Harrison for the presidency. A grand dinner, with guests from all the country around, was given Van Buren in the tavern, and Mr. Watson's sister-in-law, Mrs. Minter, who assisted in the entertainment, decided that this was the occasion for using her new gold-banded china, which she had been keeping for some worth-while guest. Pieces of this very set were shown not long ago in the tavern, while it belonged to a descendant of the original owner, and the room occupied by Van Buren is pointed out.

Another story is told of the rival candidates. About the time that Van Buren usually drank tea with the neighborhood aristocrats, Harrison arrived at the Red Brick Tavern one day, with his right arm in a sling, the result of much handshaking. Leaving the coach, he entered the house and ordered drinks for the entire company, of which only one refused to partake, the driver. Explaining that he never drank when on duty, Harrison then threw a dollar into the man's hat, which was passed among the crowd to take up a collection "to provide drinks for the driver when not on duty." Is it strange that Harrison won the election?

The Red Brick is an attractive tavern. The beautiful old doorway, of walnut, painted white, with Doric columns, is noticeable. A wide hall runs through the center of the house, with rooms on either side; the two rooms at the left were the state parlor and bedroom, those on the right, the barroom and office. In the former rooms old fireplaces with carved mantels, very lovely, remain. All of the wood-work in the house, of walnut, oak, and ash, was brought from Zanesville.

Behind the old barroom, a long dining-room and kitchen occupy the lower floor of a two-story addition. In this kitchen was placed the first cook stove brought into the county. It aroused much curiosity, this "invention of the devil," as some pronounced it, for it would "keep people from doing an honest day's work."

After the coming of the railroad seemed to have ruined its tavern business, the old house was offered for sale, but was finally bought in by the Mrs. Minter of the gold-banded china, and remained in her family until her granddaughter sold it to the present owners. They have furnished it in the style of its early prosperous days, and have succeeded in recovering a few of the original articles, such as the hat-rack on which many distinguished men once hung their hats, and the old bell which used to hang above the tavern, used to call the guests to dinner.

By 1832, the National Road was finished as far west as "the second covered bridge at the foot of the Masonic Home hill," near Springfield, and its later construction then turned over to the states. Four years later, it reached Vandalia, Illinois, and soon afterward, St. Louis, Missouri.

The Buena Vista Tavern is still standing in Springfield, on Main Street, part of the old road. In Champaign County, is the brick tavern which used to display the sign: O.K. Mr. Slager, of the Springfield Historical Society, explains thus the origin of the familiar expression.

It seems that at a political meeting in Champaign County, a banner was displayed, on which was lettered: "The People is Oll Korrect." This was abbreviated to our present: O.K.

Xenia was another early Ohio settlement, and in 1803 had three licensed taverns. After 1812, James Collier built a brick tavern on Detroit Street, which was "the grand hotel of the place." In the west room corner was an old-fashioned bar, the upper part enclosed with wooden slats, with a little window through which drinks were passed "in half pint glass cruets." Five and a half miles west of Xenia, was a log cabin tavern, where the first county court was held.

In Dayton, fortunately for lovers of old buildings, an actual old-time log cabin stands.

Early easterners coming into Ohio traveled through the New Jersey forests on horseback, or in wagons, to Fort Pitt, the present Pittsburgh, and there took flat-bottomed boats down the Ohio River, traveled for days to Fort Washington, which in 1789 was a settlement, now Cincinnati. Here, in 1794, George Avery had a tavern at the corner of Main and Fifth Streets, opposite a frog pond. The square mile on which Cincinnati stands was purchased for forty-nine dollars, and by 1805 the settlement had nine hundred and fifty inhabitants.

From the Ohio, emigrants could continue their river trip up the Miami to the site of Dayton, where three rivers met, all of which in those days were navigable. It took ten days to make the trip upstream.

The first settlement here was made by the sturdy pioneers in 1796, when fierce Indians were frequently seen in the neighborhood, and bears, panthers, and wolves abounded.

Newcom's Tavern was built in 1797, of hewn logs, chinked with mortar. It consisted of two large rooms on the ground floor, with a half story above, and was dwelling, tavern, and Dayton's first schoolhouse. By 1805, McCullom's Tavern, the first brick building in the settlement, was open, and more fashionable than Newcom's. McCullom's remained a hotel until 1870, then was used for business purposes, and in 1880 torn down. In the war of 1812, it was headquarters for collecting the blankets which "Mothers, Sister, Wives," were begged to contribute for the Army's use.

For one hundred years, Newcom's stood on the corner of Main Street and Monument Avenue, although clapboards had long covered the old log structure, and for years it had been a grocery store. A woman, Miss Mary Davies Steele, is chiefly responsible for its preservation, for she started the discussion of Dayton's centennial, and in connection with this, the movement grew to buy and preserve the old landmark. This was finally done. The clapboarding was torn off, the building removed to its present site on the river, and a Historical Society formed to make of the old tavern a museum, and to furnish it throughout with relics of its early days.

Visitors may now form an excellent idea of pioneer life. Near the old open fireplace where the first meals were cooked is a collection of pioneer cooking-utensils, firedogs, tongs, et cetera. Stools, spinning-wheels, four-post bedsteads, with old quilts, even the chair used by one of the original settlers, Benjamin Van Cleve, stands in the very room in which he taught the first school. Hand hominy mills, sausage fillers—many are the interesting articles which the Society has been able to assemble here.

When in 1818 the first stage line connecting Dayton with Cincinnati was established through Franklin, Middletown, and Hamilton, and it was proposed to run a weekly service, many declared that it could never pay. However, in another year, two trips weekly were made; other lines connected Dayton with Columbus, Sandusky, and Cleveland, and by 1828 there were twenty coaches making daily trips over the first route. With the river on three sides, this meant ferrying, until the first wooden bridge was built across the Miami in 1819. The first canal boat reached Dayton in 1829.

The towns connected by stage with Dayton were all fairly new settlements. Sandusky, or St. Dusky, was visited in 1745 by English traders, and a post established there, but as late as 1817 it was called Portland. About 1825, the land

[244]

on which Cleveland stands was purchased by colonial cap-
italists for thirty cents an acre. One log cabin stood there
in 1797. On what is now West Second Street, Lorenzo
Carter, a pioneer settler, was an early tavern-keeper. Of
him it is told that when his children set fire to his first log
house, he calmly went out, cut down trees, and built a larger
one. Indians used to frighten his wife by coming into the
tavern's main room, gathering around the fire, and remaining
there all day, paying no attention to her. Gilman Bryant
tells of the costume he wore at an early ball at this tavern.
He dressed his hair with a coating of candle grease and
flour, having no powdered wig, donned a suit of gingham,
a wool hat and heavy boots, and rode on horseback four miles
to fetch his partner, Miss Nancy Doan. She sat behind her
escort, spreading her under petticoat over the horse's back,
and holding up her calico dress to keep it clean.

Miss Doan's father became a tavern-keeper, and Doan's
Tavern, on Euclid Road, was well known. He was a prominent citizen, and not only kept a tavern, but had a factory, a
general store, kept the Post Office, was a Justice of the
Peace, and conducted religious services in his home.

The first broad road in this Western Reserve country was
built by the Connecticut Land Company over an old Indian
trail, and was known as the Euclid Road. Planked in 1840,
in 1860 it was graded, trees set out, and became Euclid Avenue. Erie County, Ohio, is but a part of the five hundred
thousand "fire lands" granted to the State of Connecticut
for sufferers from fire at the hands of British soldiers.

The fare paid on some of the Ohio stages was according to
weight. Between Dayton and Cincinnati, it was eight cents
a mile. Once the stage lines were established, they prospered, and before long they were daily leaving Cleveland in
every direction from the old Franklin House, where now
stands the Rockefeller Building.

Canestoga wagons were for many years the only means

of transporting freight west of Cincinnati and Pittsburgh. These great wagons, carrying from five to eight tons, and drawn by six or eight horses, traveled over roads which to-day would be considered impassable, their drivers camping out wherever darkness overtook them.

Chillicothe had two taverns in 1799; the first, General Wayne, opened by Joseph Tiffin, on the corner of Walnut and Water Streets; the other, The Green Tree, kept by Thomas Gregg, at the corner of Paint and Water Streets.

What is probably the oldest tavern now in use in the Middle West is located in Painesville, between Cleveland and Erie, Pennsylvania. The Randell was built in 1812, and if, at sight of it, the traveler remarks its resemblance to a New England inn, this is not strange, for it was built by a New Englander, Joseph Rider of Connecticut.

When first opened, it was merely "a house by the side of the road," on the old Indian trail between Buffalo and Cleveland. Ox-teams, traveling at the rate of ten miles a day, brought its first patrons. Then came the stages from Cleveland, changing horses first at Wickliffe, then at Randell's, and successively at Unionville, Ashtabula, Conneaut, Girard, then Erie. These coaches brought many guests to the tavern, and an old register shows that sometimes as many as one hundred and fifty were entertained at the same time.

On the walls now hang a framed waybill of the old stage company, with rates of fare to Buffalo and other points, and extracts from old day books, showing the prices of the period. One of these notes in 1850 a charge of $1.50 for four days' board. Other items are: five days' board, self and team, $4.50; a quart of brandy, 75 cents; and for eight weeks' board, $16.00.

Although railroads interfered with the old tavern's prosperity for a time, the automobile has now restored it.

The house was for five generations occupied by the original family, and first known as the Rider Tavern, then the West Painesville Hotel. In 1922, the old inn was re-modeled, but without changing its exterior lines. The old pillars, replicas of those at Washington's Mount Vernon home, still stand, one with the builder's initials, J.R., cut in it   Old mantels, the original hand-rail of the staircase, and on many doors the old hand-made latches, still remain, while four-post bedsteads with old quilts, rag rugs, and wall-papers copied from old ones, all suggest the past, even with those modern conveniences essential to the present traveler. In the living-room, with its colonial furniture, mirrors, and ornaments, the office, once the tap-room, or on the veranda, running the entire length of the house, one feels the atmosphere of bygone days.

These are some of the most accessible of the Ohio taverns. Continuing along the modern road which, like the old, fol-lowed the lake shore, in Erie County, Pennsylvania are more old inns.

Oldest of all, the Presque Isle Tavern, a mere shack on the beach of the bay, was set up in 1795 by Colonel Seth Reed, and in it Louis Philippe was entertained. It, like one built in Erie by the Colonel's son, Rufus, the following year, has long since gone.

Ryan's Tavern, also known as Taggart's, with a large drove-yard, is now a residence; another Erie hotel, the Buehler, later known as the Duncan, then McConkey House, built in 1800, in which the county was organized and the first courts held, was replaced a few years ago by a store.

The Eagle Hotel (1826), a stone building beside the site of the old Fort Leboeuf, is still used as a hotel. So is the Weigerville Hotel, now within Erie limits.

The Dickson House, built before 1812, on the southeast corner of Second and French Streets, has been purchased by the city as a memorial. Here Perry lived while assembling his Lake Erie fleet, and the house is filled with mementoes of him and of the city's early days. This was a station on the "Underground Railway," and there are secret chambers in its thick walls. Here, too, the dinner served to Lafayette on a big bridge over a gully near by, was prepared.

Swan's Tavern and the Nicholson Hotel, at Swanville, are now residences. On the Ridge Road, a mile east, the old Nicholson Tavern, with its drove-yard, was recently razed, but the Nicholson House, of brick, west of Asbury, on this same Ridge Road, is now a modernized residence, occupied by descendants of the Nicholson family.

Four miles west of Erie, on the Ridge Road, Willis' Hotel is now a residence, and so is the dilapidated old Half Way House, "midway between Buffalo and Cleveland." Traces of the old sign, lettered in black across the front, may still be seen.

Reed's Hotel (1810), at Waterford, where Lafayette stopped, was burned; Brown's (1810), at North East, has been remodeled, and is now open as the Haynes House.

The Old Kentucky Home, at Westminster, where the famous "Peacock Dinner" was given by Hon. William L. Scott of Erie, also burned down.

The Wattsburg House, Wattsburg; Fairview House, Fairview, and the Martin House at Girard, are all open as hotels.

It is stated that at one time there were eighteen or more taverns between Erie and Girard.

## CHAPTER XIV

### *Inns of New York State*

ALONG THE OLD INDIAN TRAIL following the shore of Lake Erie, later the stage road, and now almost the same route popular with automobilists, one will hardly find any surviving old inns. This was frontier country. A hundred years ago, when a New Englander came west to look over some lands in this section in which he was interested, he traveled almost entirely by sleigh. Arrived at Niagara Falls, where he had friends, they insisted that his wife and child remain, although they had thus far borne the trip, while he pushed on into the wilderness.

Following the Niagara River, about half-way between Buffalo and Lewiston, at North Tonawanda there still stands an old log cabin which was probably used as a tavern. This road was originally an old Indian trail, and between Lewiston and Queenston there was an early ferry used by travelers going westward through Canada.

Lewiston had two old taverns, both of which disappeared many years ago; one kept by Thomas Hustler and his wife, Betsy, at which James Fenimore Cooper boarded, drawing his characters of Sergeant Hollister and Betsy Flannigan, in *The Spy*, from his landlord and landlady. At the other, the Kelsey, Lafayette stayed on his visit to Lewiston in 1825. The Frontier House claims him, but as this was not open until 1826, although begun a year earlier, the claim seems debatable. It has, however, entertained such celebrities as Jenny Lind, Henry Clay, and Washington Irving.

[249]

The attractive centenarian is still open, with broad, deep veranda, and a signboard hanging near the street quite as it may have hung when the house was opened.

As early as 1794, the Genesee Road extended from old Fort Schuyler westward to the Genesee River, and in 1798 was extended to the State line. But before this there had been travelers over the old trail, although after the Erie Canal was built this was long the popular route for travel. Even after the railroad came, little stretches of it were owned by different companies, so train connections between these were poor, and for a time the canal still prospered.

The old Iroquois Trail ran from the Hudson to Niagara Falls, through Oneida, Onondaga, Cayuga, Canandaigua, Avon, Le Roy, near Batavia to Lewiston, and the first stretch of the Mohawk Trail, consisting of sixteen miles from Albany to Schenectady, was built in 1797 by two young engineers. So, in coming east from Buffalo, one follows, at least in part, these old roads.

Batavia, county seat of Genesee County, was not "set off" as a town from Northampton until 1802. Three years later, Timothy Bigelow, in his *Tour to Niagara Falls*, mentions here a "nearly finished building which is to contain a court house, a jail and a hotel under the same roof." He stayed at Russell's Tavern, whose proprietor insisted that his sheets were *clean*, for they had been slept in only a few times since they were washed. Luke's Tavern also stood here at the time.

The earliest tavern between Buffalo and Avon was about a mile east of the present town of Le Roy. Charles Wilbur came here in 1797, and opened a tavern in a log cabin. A year later, he sold this to Captain John Ganson, who was in the Revolutionary Army and fought at Bunker Hill. In the earliest days of this tavern, Indians frequented a spring near the house, and the nearest neighbors were "the desperate characters at Big Springs," and a few at Avon, where

Captain Ganson had first located. Early travelers frequently mention Ganson's. John Maude, in his *Visit to the Falls of Niagara in 1800*, says: "Proceeded on my journey 297 miles (from Albany) Ganson's Tavern. When my friend L. passed this place last year, Ganson's was a solitary house in the wilderness, but it is now in the midst of a flourishing town in which twenty-one families are already settled. A new tavern and a number of dwelling houses are building."

Five years later, Timothy Bigelow was not complimentary:

"July 22nd, 1805. Gansen's is a miserable log house. We made out to obtain an ordinary dinner. Our landlord was drunk, the house was crowded with a dozen workmen, reeking with rain and sweat. . . . We hastened our departure before the rain had ceased."

When the new roads were opened, many immigrants flocked to this section, the Ganson log cabin was replaced by a larger frame house, and when the first landlord died in 1813 and was succeeded by his son, John, it became one of the best known houses between Albany and Buffalo.

On the site of what was long the Eagle Hotel in Le Roy, —the village received this name in 1813,—was an early tavern known as Auntie Wemple's. A frame house followed this, kept by Richard Stoddard, and the brick building, part of which is now the Post Office, the rest a lodging-house, was built by James Ganson, another son of the first tavern-keeper, and continued as a hotel until 1920.

Before 1810, Richard Stoddard built a frame house on the site of the Wiss House. This was first used as a store, later as a tavern, kept by Rufus Robertson. Enlarged, it became the Globe and Eagle Hotel, with a brazen sign of the bird surmounting a globe. Many years ago it was given the name under which it is still open, after an early landlord, Wiss.

Half a mile west, on the main road to Buffalo, Captain

John Lent opened a tavern in 1813 which later became a private residence, and is now an exclusive lodging-house. The first frame house in Le Roy was Captain John Austin's Tavern, and survives as the wing of a private residence. Still another tavern in the village was opened by Hinds Chamberlain, and continued at least until 1810, later becoming a dwelling.

In this period, Le Roy was an important place. The largest town between Buffalo and Canandaigua, ten stage-coaches passed through it daily, besides many emigrant wagons going west and south. Many of the houses along the road were regularly licensed taverns, while others kept travelers over night, or furnished them with meals, which were sometimes scanty, as the following anecdote told by Mr. Sampson in an account of old times in Le Roy, published in a local paper, will show.

"A weary and hungry traveler on a jaded horse, rode up to the door of one [tavern] not a hundred miles hence, and asked for entertainment for the night. The landlady from within having assented, the following colloquy ensued:

"Traveler: 'Can you furnish provender for my horse?'

"Landlady: 'No, we have none.'

"Traveler: 'Can you furnish me with supper?'

"Landlady: 'We have no bread. My husband started for the mill this morning and will return to-morrow.'

"Traveler: 'Can you furnish me with a glass of whiskey?'

"Landlady: 'We have none. My husband took his gallon bottle, and will bring some when he returns.'

"Traveler: 'Madam, can you tell me what you do keep for the entertainment of travelers?'

"Landlady: 'We keep a tavern, sir.' "

At Fort Hill, east of the town, a tavern stood at the top of the hill, as the grandson of its proprietor, the former now a man of eighty or thereabouts, recalls. A three-story brick building in Pavilion was a stage-coach hotel; and one of stone in Caledonia, now the Post Office and Masonic Temple, was another. Almost every four corners then had its stage-coach inns, many of which are still standing as private residences.

Continuing eastward, a few years before the first tavern was opened in Le Roy, two Englishmen, Moffett and Kane, the "desperate characters" mentioned, had established one at Big Springs (Caledonia). Suspected of robbery and murder, they were driven away by Avon settlers, and were succeeded by Peterson and Fuller.

In Avon, Gilbert Berry built a log house in 1789, traded with the Indians, finally opening a ferry, entertaining in his cabin such travelers as passed along the old trail.

Hartford had Hosmer's; Bloomfield, Hall's Tavern, both mentioned by early travelers. For some years, the road west from Albany ended at Canandaigua, "a beautiful village," with Blossom's Tavern.

Geneva had Powell's; and at Cayuga was a tavern kept by Harris, who "boasted that he could keep beef fresh in summer for four or five days by hanging it as high as possible, after wrapping it in flannel." Halfway between Cayuga Bridge and Auburn was Colonel Godwin's place, and Auburn had an inn at least as early as 1819, while Bodine's was near by; at Skaneateles was Andrew's Tavern, and Tyler's at "Onondaga Hollow"; Streethar kept a tavern at Sullivan, and Laird at Westmoreland, where "the country was thickly settled with handsome houses." The latter place had also an inn kept by Mrs. Cary, "with six or seven charming daughters, sometimes called Mother Cary's chickens." They were very handsome and accomplished, and "helped to make the house attractive."

Syracuse in 1811 had but one house of any kind, Cossett's Tavern, where later stood the Syracuse House. South from here, on another road, at Cortland were two old taverns. On the site of one, the Eagle, was built the Messenger Hotel, now open; on the other, the Cortland House, burned, but replaced by a new one now open under the same name. Dusenberry's Tavern, at which André and his escort stopped on their way to West Point, was near.

In Orange County, at Warwick, Baird's Tavern (1760) is now a private residence.

Returning to the old road from Albany, at Manlius Square, beyond Syracuse, was a stage house kept by Manlius more than a hundred years ago; Vernon, at the same time had one kept by Stuart, and at Quality Hill was another, kept by Mr. Webb, "most polite of tavern keepers, who might have been a dancing master."

The town of Utica was settled in 1789, and when Bigelow visited it, he met several persons—probably in Trowbridge's Tavern—who, in the course of conversation, declared that Adam could not have been the first man, or else "he lived much longer ago than 5,000 years as the Scriptures declared [?], for it took more than 5,000 years for the Mohawk River to have broken through the rocks."

West of Little Falls was Spraker's Tavern, and in the village itself, Carr's, "a very good house," remarks Bigelow.

Johnstown, named for Sir William, was on the main line of travel, and had many taverns. The first was built before 1772, on the northeast corner of William and Clinton Streets, where a private residence now stands. This was Tice's, owned by the Tory Major, Gilbert Tice, associate of the Johnsons and Butlers, and who went with them to Canada. It was probably in this house that Governor and Lady Tryon stayed when they came to attend the dedication ceremonies of the new Tryon County Court House. Lafayette is also said to have stopped here in 1778, when he came for a friendly conference with representatives of the Six Nations. From Tice's the first shot west of the Hudson River in the Revolution was fired by the Tory sheriff of the county. The house was torn down early in the nineteenth century.

The Black Horse stands at the corner of Montgomery and William Streets, so it was most desirably located. Michael Rawlins, at that time proprietor of Tice's, bought the lot in 1778, and probably built and first conducted the tavern. In 1793, it was bought and became popular as "Jimmie Burke's Place," its house and barn often being filled to overflowing when Court was in session, for it was on the main road from Montgomery (then Tryon) county to Johnstown. Probably Sir William Johnson often stopped here, and many a colonial ball was given within its walls. The Johnstown Daughters of the American Revolution purchased the old inn, and now use it as a Chapter House.

A third tavern near the Court House was opened about 1812 by Jacob Yost, who was carried off into Canada by a band of Indians and Tories, during the Revolution. This house was later known as the Sir William Tavern. At that time there were thirteen taverns in Johnstown, all of them prosperous until the Erie Canal was opened.

Another inn on Montgomery Street was kept by Fon Claire, a former captain in Louis Philippe's Martinique regiment. Later he built his Union Hall, on East State Street, and ran this until 1811. His old house became the Potter, and continued under that name until it burned in 1867.

The Yellow Tavern was a famous one, with two ball-rooms, but this was not opened until 1849, with an inaugural ball in honor of James Polk. A business block has now replaced it.

When Henry Yanney came with his uncle from New Jersey, he opened another Black Horse, in 1796, one mile south of Johnstown, one of the largest, finest inns of this section.

In Amsterdam, the house built by Sir William Johnson for his son-in-law later became Pride's Tavern. This is

[255]

probably the Revolutionary inn at which Lafayette is said to have stopped, around which Conrad's Hotel was built, preserving a portion of the old house. Beale's was "a good house" in Schenectady, but it will not now be found. On State Street, however, a tablet affixed to a house marks the site of Robert Clench's Inn, where the civil and military authorities entertained Washington in 1782, and another tavern, or perhaps the same one at a later date, was kept by Mr. Givens, whose son went to West Point and became a major. Truax's, four miles, Downs', nine, and Humphreys', eleven miles east, were taverns here.

As early as 1792, Benjamin, father of Stephen A. Douglas, built a log house at Ballston, for the accommodation of invalid visitors, near Old Spring. The place, later known as Ballston Spa, soon became popular, even fashionable, and in the early nineteenth century had "two taverns and a number of boarding houses, Bromeling's, Aldrich's, McMasters', etc." It remained fashionable until after the development of steamboat traffic, and later was superseded by Saratoga.

In Albany there were many taverns and hotels. From early Dutch days, there was a settlement here, first known as Fort Orange. In colonial and later times, eight turnpikes passed through. One, the Catskill Turnpike, ran from Otsego Lake to the Susquehanna River, where a boat crossed to Wattle's Ferry on the opposite side. This name has long since been abandoned. An old military road ran from Lake George south to the Hudson River; Albany was, as mentioned, one terminus of the old Boston and Albany turnpike, so there were many travelers passing through the town.

In 1819, Benjamin Silliman, in his travels, describes crossing the Hudson six miles above Albany to Troy, on a ferryboat propelled by two horses, harnessed facing in opposite directions. The horses stood on the flat surface of a large, horizontal, solid-looking wheel, working it like a treadmill. This wheel was attached to two vertical wheels like paddles,

FRONTIER HOUSE, LEWISTON, NEW YORK

[See page 249.

SALLY TOCK'S INN, STONERIDGE, NEW YORK

[*See Page* 260.

SALLY TOCK'S INN, STONEBRIDGE, NEW YORK

BLACK HORSE TAVERN, JOHNSTOWN, NEW YORK

[*See page* 255.

BEEKMAN ARMS, RHINEBECK, NEW YORK

[*See page* 263.

which moved the boat. The invention of a man named Langdon, this must have been thought a marvelous successor to the old hand-propelled dugouts or rowboats.

In his *Stage Coach Traveling 46 Years Ago,* Thurlow Weed (1870), tells how passengers in these stages frequently walked, or used rails to help extricate the coach from bad places along the road. Stage drivers of those days, he says, "were as peculiar, quaint and racy as those represented by the senior and junior Weller, in 'Pickwick Papers.'" Passengers also helped to pass the time by telling stories. The turnpike from Albany to Schenectady was opened in 1802, but a local line had then been in operation for nine years.

In 1809 there were two hundred and sixty-five taverns in Albany alone, but an early historian remarks that in 1803 there was only one tavern better than "such as no gentleman of the present day would put his foot in." This was the Tontine Coffee House on State Street, built in 1750 near the first house, which had been built by Mr. Gregory in 1650. One of his family kept the Tontine, which had no bar, liquor being sold only with meals. "All travelers of consequence, all foreigners of distinction," put up at the Tontine. John Lambert, an English traveler in 1807, writes of it: "We had excellent accommodation at Gregory's, which is equal to many of our hotels in London. At the better sort of American taverns or hotels, very excellent dinners are provided, between two and three o'clock. They breakfast at 8 o'clock upon rump steak, fish, eggs, and a variety of cakes, with tea or coffee. The last meal is at 7 in the evening, and consists of as substantial fare as the breakfast, with the addition of cold fowl, ham, etc." He gives the rates as from $1.50 to $2 a day. "Brandy, Hollands and spirits" were free, other liquors extra. He declares that "Americans live in a much more luxurious manner than we do, but their meals, I think, are composed of too great a variety, and of too many things to be conducive to health. Formerly, pies,

[257]

puddings and cider used to grace the breakfast table, but they are now discarded from the gentler houses, and are found only in the small taverns and farm houses in the country."

In 1806, Gregory built and ran the Eagle Tavern, so it is possible that it was at this, not the Tontine, where Lambert stayed. This later house, as shown in an old print, was a square, three-storied house, with a two-storied ell. It was burned in 1848.

The Staats House (1667) formed part of the Lewis Tavern, at which the English traveler, Maude, stayed in 1800. The building was removed when Pearl Street was widened.

Not one of the following hotels existing about a hundred years ago, and mentioned by John J. Hill in his reminiscences covering 1825 to 1855, is standing now, although a few are within the memory of old residents: on State Street, the American House, Bement's, Franklin, Western; on South Market Street—not the present Market Street—the Columbia, National, Fort Orange, Exchange; on North Market the City Hotel, Temperance, and Mansion—the latter formerly an Albany merchant's residence—and the Lafayette House. Nor do the "country taverns on the hill," the 5th Ward, Northern, and Congress Hall, remain. There is apparently not one old tavern surviving in the city of Albany.

An old road known as the Albany and New Scotland was in use at an early day, and along this were many taverns. Some of these were: one of the six houses at Becker's Corners, six miles south of Albany; Elishana Janes' Tavern at South Bethlehem; Hagadorn, the first settler in what is now Hurstville, kept a tavern in his log cabin; at Berne (not given this name until 1825), Henry Engle opened in 1817 his Corporation Inn, which had been Eli Whipple's residence; and three years later, Elnathan Stafford was keeping a tavern at East Berne, or Werner's Mills, and buying his liquors in Philadelphia. At South Berne, in 1822, Alexander McKinley, a wagon-maker, opened a tavern, keeping a trained bear, a moose, and life-sized figures of noted criminals to attract custom.

Clarksville, being midway on this turnpike, was an important stage stop, and here taverns were kept by Samuel Ingraham, Joseph Bright, Harmanus Bogardus, Christian Houck—a kinswoman is landlady of Kinderhook's Grey Swan—David Chesebro and one Jenkins. In 1795 Moses Smith, Nic Lapaugh, Henry Pierce and Jan Leuvens were tavern-keeping in Chesterville or near by, and so was William Beardsley, who, when elected sheriff, removed to Albany.

Part of Richard Kloet's Tavern at Watervliet stood for a number of years after it had been made into a private residence. In this tavern one day an Indian became angry, and hurled his tomahawk at Kloet. Fortunately it missed him, but embedded itself in a rafter, where the mark was for years pointed out. General Morgan's soldiers camped near this tavern.

No old inns, according to local histories and old residents, remain in Kingston, which was burned by the British in 1777. Only one house is said to have stood, built in 1676 by one of the early Dutch settlers, and used as the Senate House when Kingston was New York's capital. It is now a kind of museum, a long, low, stone building, in the heart of the city.

Twelve miles away, at the little village of Stoneridge, off the railroad, is an old inn, although one would never guess its earlier usage in passing it, for it has been converted into a charming summer home. The original very thick walls stand, although painted, and with porches added. At the rear of the small front entry from which the stairs mount, is a small room; to the right, a large one, with great rafters supporting the ceiling, a large fireplace, and a number of quaint wall-cupboards. This was probably the tap-room.

From it a half flight of stairs leads up to a spacious old parlor, where dances were held, and from a narrow hall beside these stairs, others descend to the old basement kitchen, now the modern dining-room of the residence. Here is an enormous fireplace; again the thickness of the walls is proof of their age. Before the present owners bought it, the house was for several years a tea-room. The owner keeps for her house the old inn name: Sally Tock's. Here Washington's staff stayed while he was entertained at the private residence opposite, a large stone house still standing.

Between Stoneridge and Old Hurley, at the crossroads, is an old stone house which looks as though it, too, had been an inn, but it was not possible to learn if this were true.

New Paltz, twenty miles from Newburgh, is an old settlement, but the only inn building surviving there is now known as the Hasbrouck Memorial House.

Newburgh, too, was largely destroyed by the British. On the north side of Broad Street, Martin Weigand kept a log house tavern, which General Wayne made his headquarters. General John E. Wool was born in the house. Joseph Albertson kept a tavern at Liberty and Broad Streets, and another, which was Lafayette's headquarters, stood on the corner of Water and Third Streets. In 1767, the village was petitioning for more taverns, although there were then less than thirty houses in the settlement.

The chief means of crossing the Hudson in this vicinity at that time was by ferry to Verplanck's Point, then called King's Ferry, opposite historic Stony Point.

West Point has an almost century-old inn, built in 1829, but it is to be torn down within a year, and a new one will stand on Storm King Highway.

Coming south from Albany, along the east bank of the Hudson, the old road did not closely follow the river. All along were taverns, many more than on the west bank. Of several at Schodack and near by, one at Schodack Centre is

[260]

still standing. The old Post Road here joined the Boston and Albany turnpike. In New York State, few old taverns seem to have borne other names than those of their proprietors.

The attractive town of Kinderhook, with its broad, shady streets, was an old tavern center, and several of the buildings survive. The present Kinderhook Hotel is not old, but it replaced one burned in 1880. In The Grey Swan, opposite, a square and very old building forms part of the rear of the present hotel. Two years ago, while making repairs, a local builder discovered what he believes proves that this old part was Kinderhook's first Reformed Church, which makes it very old indeed. An old resident says that it next became a school-house, and later it was Major Hoes' Inn. Part of a very old cornice, with the dentil pattern, which was seldom used on early dwelling cornices but was used on churches, remains, but only one section, the rest crumbled to pieces and was removed. A succession of landlords kept this house and added to it. The predecessor of the present one had had the hotel for almost fifty years.

Farther down the street, so altered into a two-family house that one would never suspect it, is an old stage-coach inn, and almost opposite it a frame house called Martin Van Buren's birthplace. It is not, however, for it was built only about seventy years ago, but the story and a half stone house in which Van Buren was born, and which his father kept as a tavern, did stand on this site, and possibly the stone foundation is old. The Van Buren Inn is mentioned as early as 1759.

On the highroad to Hudson is a two-story house, built of bricks imported from Holland in 1770, as a date close under the eaves, almost undecipherable now, states. This was first the residence of Dr. Quilhot, then a tavern, and was given the name of the Benedict Arnold Inn after that general was brought there wounded. It is much modernized, its old

[261]

fireplaces have been removed, but the old rafters in hall and living-room may still be seen, as may the marks where a piece of an inner door-jamb was cut away to allow Arnold's stretcher to pass, and then later replaced. The house has been a dwelling again for many years.

Kinderhook had a Mansion House which old residents can not now locate. In 1798, Elijah Hudson attracted attention to his inn here by advertising that he would provide lodging and clean sheets for one shilling, in answer to the advertisement of a Tarrytown inn that "lodging and clean sheets, 3 sh; dirty sheets, 1 sh." might there be had.

A few miles north of Kinderhook, Quackenbos kept a tavern at about this same time, and Claverack—the old Claberack—once the county seat, had an inn, a two-story stone building which is now a private residence.

Hudson was off the old Post Road, but it had several taverns. The earliest, the King of Prussia, was built by Colonel John McKinstry; another was the Hudson; and a third, Kellogg's, stood on the site of the Worth House, built in 1837. At this inn, as many as two hundred stage-coach passengers often stopped for meals in a single day.

The old Post Road passed through Blue Stores, as the village is still known, having taken its name from the old tavern, so called because its front was painted blue. The road runs through Clermont as its main street, and on to the old settlement of Red Hook, where once were several taverns. One survives, the Red Hook Hotel, kept until his death a couple of years ago, at the age of ninety-eight, by Mr. Ellsworth, one of the 'Forty-niners. His descendants still keep the house open.

On the left-hand side of the road up from the Rhinecliff ferry to Rhinebeck, there stands at the entrance to the Kip estate an old stone house, formerly the Kip Tavern, now a dwelling. The old highroad probably passed directly in front of it, and it is but a stone's throw from the present road. A gate-post close by bears two dates: 1686-1898, and the tavern was built either at the earlier date or perhaps later, in 1709. Outwardly, save to have kept it in excellent repair, the house seems little changed.

On the ship coming to the new country with Peter Stuyvesant came a German, William Beckman, from the Rhine Valley. His son received a grant of land here from Queen Anne, in 1703, and he named his property Rhinebeck. Where the present Beekman Arms stands, on the Post Road, was built a tavern by William and Arent Traphagen, in 1700, on this, the first piece of land sold from the original Beekman or Beekman grant. (There is some confusion of dates here, for Queen Anne did not ascend the English throne until 1703.) If the inn really was built in 1700, it is the second oldest in the United States open continuously as such, even as, had any of the early buildings of the Canoe Place Inn at Hampton Bays, Long Island, survived, it, instead of the Elm Tree Inn in Farmington, would be the oldest tavern building, although the tavern in Connecticut would still be the oldest existing house *used* as such.

The old portion of the present Beekman Arms consists of the present living-room or entrance hall, into which the old hallway has been thrown, the large room on the left, and part of the present kitchen. All three rooms had old fireplaces. The one in the kitchen has been removed, but in a basement room beneath is an old oven which the present proprietor is somewhat at a loss to account for, since the room is only five feet high, and one can hardly imagine cooking being done where the cook could not stand erect. If the floor was raised, or the ceiling lowered, it must have been done many years ago. The right wing was added about a hundred years ago, the other by the present proprietor when he took the house twelve years ago. It was then in a deplorable state, having been used as a common saloon, but he has restored and added to it so as to preserve the old style, replacing the ugly double piazzas with a pillared portico across the front.

No one who examines the thickness of the original outer wall can doubt the great age of the house. The old rafters still support the ceiling of the entrance hall; upstairs the parlor is low-ceiled, and outside swings a signboard in imitation of the old one. This inn, open for six months of the year, is Rhinebeck's only ancient hostelry still in the business.

On East Market Street, four houses beyond the Roman Catholic Church, is a long, low building, now occupied by three or four families. Painted yellow, with a porch supported by columns, it does not at first glance look old, but in 1804 it was an inn, known as Tammany Hall, and here Aaron Burr made his headquarters when running for governor against General Morgan Lewis. The latter made his headquarters in Potter's Tavern, as the Beekman Arms was then called. Later, Tammany Hall was known as the Bowery. De Chastellux further mentions the Thomas Inn.

Staatsburg, another old town, doubtless had taverns, and just beyond the center of the town is a stone house, with an added floor perhaps, which resembles the old tavern buildings, but no definite information as to its history could be learned.

Long before 1753, there were in Poughkeepsie a court house, a church, "a tavern or two, and the beginnings of a village" on the hill. The Colonial Assembly authorized the laying out of a post road, but for a long time, travel through here was chiefly on horseback.

An inn stood on the corner of what are now Market and Main Streets, and in 1790 its landlord is mentioned as William Rider. In 1803, it was known as Baldwin's, then as Cunningham's, later as Myer's, when a breakfast was given here to Lafayette. In 1829, it was rebuilt and called the Poughkeepsie Hotel, and now stands as the Pomfret House, but its days are numbered, for the city recently purchased

NEWCOM'S TAVERN, DAYTON, OHIO

[*See page* 243.

*Photo by Otto White.*

OLD INN, QUEENSVILLE, INDIANA

[*See page 269.*

the property, and will raze the building to extend Market Street.

Stephen Hendricksen's Tavern was replaced by the Forbus Hotel, in front of which Lafayette was welcomed on his visit. Its site is now occupied by the modern Nelson Hotel.

The Farmers' Hotel stood in 1806 on Cannon Street, but was long ago torn down; Voice Hinckley was another early tavern-keeper "between Cannon Street and the church."

At Fishkill, Madame Egremont's Tavern was pronounced tolerable by the Marquis de Chastellux, on his early travels from Litchfield, Connecticut, into New York State. He also mentions Colonel Griffin's, five miles east of Fishkill, and at Dover, a drovers' inn, where he stopped for the night, and found two hundred and fifty head of cattle around the place, "the least troublesome of the company." However, learning that all the beds were taken, and preparing to sleep on the floor, some of the drovers engaged him in conversation, and learning that he was a Frenchman and an officer, protested that they could not allow him to do such a thing. He in turn assured them that, as a soldier, he was accustomed to hardships, but they persisted, and he was then given a room with beds for himself and his aides.

In 1730, John Rogers built a large house, two miles north of the site of Continental Village, where he kept a well patronized tavern, for at that time there was only an Indian trail beyond, through the Highlands to the Westchester line, and few travelers cared to pass over that trail at night.

Epenetus Crosby was an early tavern-keeper in Patterson, on the road running south to Cowl's Corners, and Haviland and David also had taverns, the latter near the field where the General Trainings were held.

Samuel Washburn's Tavern at Carmel was the only one for a long distance; later, John McLean opened one on the road to Lake Mahopac; and Conklin's is mentioned as being three miles from Carmel, on the road to Patterson. Dr.

# Early American Inns and Taverns

Robert Weeks built a hotel in Carmel early in the nineteenth century, but about 1850 this was razed and a residence built on the site. At Coldspring Landing was Abel Peake's, and at Milltown, Joseph White's.

Peekskill derived its name from Jan Peck's or Peek's, Kill, or stream. This worthy had a tavern in New York City, but his license was revoked because so many of his customers got drunk, and also because Jan "tapped during church hours." Later, the license was restored, but he finally retired to the land he owned in Peekskill, and it is not stated whether or not he kept a tavern there.

Tarrytown taverns are given by Irving as the origin of the town's name, for the Dutch *tarried* in them so long. Elmsford had an early tavern run by Captain Storms. The British partly burned his house during the Revolution, but he promptly rebuilt it. Later, the Ledger House stood on its site. Not far away to the north, at Four Corners, was the Hotel Flanagan. When its landlord joined the Revolutionary Army, his wife ran the hotel, and to her is ascribed the invention of the cocktail. But this honor is also claimed for others.

On Getty Square, Yonkers, the Getty House, although entirely remodeled, still is outwardly much as it was one hundred or more years ago, save that stores now stand beside it, and the park and pump which originally were in front have long since gone.

Diagonally across the Square still stands a hotel, Square in shape, in name and in location. It, too, is an old one.

An early popular Yonkers house, the Arlington Inn, was burned down in 1916, and the Masonic Temple now stands on its site. Another old hotel, the Park Hill Inn, was also burned, and an apartment hotel replaces it.

The Abbey Inn, although but recently opened as a hotel, stands on an old estate covering many acres. After the death of its owner, Mr. Lilienthal, the house was used as a residence for those studying for the priesthood, but it has now been converted into a picturesque inn, resembling a mediæval stone castle.

This concludes the list of New York State taverns which the writer has been able to locate, but doubtless many more existed, some of which may be still standing.

## Chapter XV

### Some Middle West Inns

RESEARCH and inquiries have failed to bring to light many surviving old taverns in Indiana. Doubtless there are some now transformed into residences, or, like the one in Queensville, rapidly falling to pieces.

Indiana had her early taverns, for in 1792, licenses might be revoked for selling liquor to the Indians, to minors, or for failing to provide "good and wholesome food for man and beast, keeping ordinary liquors of good and salutary quality," etc.

Until 1784, Indiana was part of Virginia, and most emigrants came into the future State by way of Red Banks, now Henderson, Kentucky. An old Indian trail ran from Fort Wayne through to Detroit, Michigan, but for years, Indiana was very thinly settled, and in 1800 had less than five thousand inhabitants.

Vincennes, one of the oldest settlements in the State, was first known as the Post, later named after a commander who was massacred by the Indians. It perhaps had a tavern, but apparently nothing of it remains.

Before the Civil War, thus bringing them to the respectable age of seventy years or more, there were several hotels in Madison. These seem never to have been called inns or taverns. On the river bank, as early as 1840, there stood a rambling brick building, known until 1870 as the Washington House. This still stands, used as a cheap tenement.

[268]

# Some Middle West Inns

The Western, and the William Tell, also on the banks of the Ohio, both once well-known houses, have been torn down. The Central Hotel dates from about the same period, and is still open. Just which of these early hotels if any is Pugh's Hotel, mentioned as existing in 1836, it has been impossible to learn. Present residents are unfamiliar with the name. The Arlington House occupies the site of an older hotel on the corner of Main and Seventh Streets.

The Jefferson Hotel, built in the 1850's, was originally known as the Madison. After being a hotel for some twenty-five years, it was turned into a girls' school. In 1885 it was again opened as the Madison Hotel, and twenty-five years ago the name was changed to the present one, under which it is still operated.

On the road from Madison to Indianapolis, three miles north of Mount Vernon, stands a poor old building in Queensville. Needless to say, it is not now occupied, but in 1840, when the building of the railroad from Madison to Indianapolis stopped because of lack of funds, Queensville became the terminus, and its tavern prospered. Later used as a private residence, it was finally deserted, and fell into its present dilapidation.

To quote its courteous Postmaster, ". . . when the city of Rochester [Indiana] was young, more than sixty years ago, a tavern was conducted at the juncture of Main and Third Streets, the landlord being Banner Lawhead. This place lives only in the memory of several aged citizens as a place of many pleasant festivities."

The Central House was an old Rochester tavern, and stood on the corner of Main and Sixth Streets. Its site is now a filling-station.

Rochester was on the stage-coach line, and one of the stage inns, six miles north of the city on the Michigan road, still stands, though it is now a farmhouse. This was the Ralston House, popular with the young people of the neighborhood.

[269]

A social dance was held here, so Mr. Bitters tells, on the memorable cold New Year of 1864, and there are now living in Rochester some who remember attending this party. Some of the young men's ears were frozen, and their horses nearly died on the way home, for the thermometer descended to 32° below zero.

A pioneer home, five miles south, on the Peru-Rochester road, owned by Mr. Thomas Shelton and still standing, was not an actual inn, but many travelers, including Indians of the two tribes then numerous in this section, were entertained in it.

A few miles south of Fulton, on the Michigan road, was an old inn where stage horses of the line between Indianapolis and South Bend were changed. The road was so bad, the coaches with their load of passengers so heavy, that many horses died under the strain. This inn was burned fifty years ago.

Ten miles east of Rochester, at Akron, Andrew Strong kept the first hotel, now replaced by a modern one.

Two old tavern buildings are still standing in Le Gro, and one in Laurel. The former were patronized when the canal between Fort Wayne and Lafayette was in use. Another may still be seen in Wabash; and at Pierceton, the Ryerson House, once a tavern, now a residence, is at least seventy-five years old. Its proprietor in the '60's committed suicide by cutting his throat. A former old resident here remembers seeing great trains of covered wagons bound westward.

Columbus, almost on a straight line westward from Cincinnati, Ohio, had until two years ago a veteran inn, the Jones House, on the corner of Washington and Second Streets, built about 1828 and run by John F. Jones, who was elected sheriff of Bartholomew County. He resigned the office in 1832, because, as he publicly stated: "by reason of the fact that the county jail was insecure, and the number of persons that were imprisoned for debt," he had no other recourse than to convert a portion of his hotel into a prison.

This house was the office and headquarters for the Voorhees stages running between Indianapolis and Madison, until the first railroad to Columbus was opened. Mr. Jones removed to Greencastle in the '50's, and his daughter ran the hotel until after the Civil War. Later, various persons owned and operated it, and its name was changed to the Western Hotel. Two years ago the building was torn down and replaced by a garage.

Although Richmond was an important stop on the National Road, no inns remain here, nor, to the best of an old resident's belief, in the county.

A filling-station occupies the site of the old Chapman Tavern, built in Greenfield about 1834, but its figure of an old rooster, said to have originated the Democratic Party emblem, has been carefully preserved.

It may surprise many to learn that the oldest site of a tavern or hotel in Illinois which has continued as one, lies in the heart of Chicago. No one who passes the towering Sherman House here would connect it with an old tavern, yet none the less, there has been a hotel on this site for ninety years. The first one known was built in 1836, by the Hon. Francis C. Sherman, and called the City Hotel, although it is said that as early as 1825, a blacksmith shop, with living-quarters above, stood here, and it is quite possible that travelers were then entertained. There is also the possibility that a small tavern was here before Sherman built his first house. An early picture shows the first building to have been a three-story structure of considerable size for its day; this was replaced by a four-story and basement hotel, called the Sherman House. In 1861, a six-story building again replaced an earlier one, and others were built, always

[271]

on the same site, in 1873, and 1910, the latter again enlarged.

A residence on Milwaukee Avenue was Dickinson's Tavern, built in 1842.

Early histories of the State mention no inns before 1800. The traveler was either accommodated in some private dwelling, or slept in his boat, for rivers furnished almost the sole means of communication between points in Illinois during early territory days. The first record of anything approaching an inn prior to 1800 was when John Kinzie built himself a mansion, in Chicago, its furniture largely brought from Montreal, and added to this residence a sixty-foot lodging for "voyagers and Indians."

In a history of early days in Chicago are mentioned several taverns: Wolfe's, opened in 1829; the Green Tree, 1830, and the Sauganash Hotel, 1831, but no one seems sure of their sites, and certainly nothing of them remains.

The Sauganash was kept by Mark Beaubien, married to an Indian girl, and, as his name indicates, himself a Frenchman. The father of twenty-three children, he played the fiddle and was a general handy man. Later, he kept the Mansion House on Lake Street, and still later, a tavern on the plank road, near Neperville. The first record of a theatrical company in Chicago mentions it as playing in the Sauganash Tavern. All of the plank roads into Chicago had taverns along them.

By 1833, Chicago had a population of one hundred and fifty, and four hotels. The Lake House, built in 1836, was four-storied, cost one hundred thousand dollars, and had the city's first printed bill of fare. This and the Sherman House were the most pretentious in this part of the country.

The oldest Illinois hotel, of which the original building stands, is the Hunter House in Alton, built in 1819 by Major J. C. W. Hunter, and, at least until recently, still open. Lincoln stayed here at the time of his last debate with Stephen A. Douglas.

[272]

# Some Middle West Inns

Belvidere, in Boone County, had the American House, which Margaret Fuller Ossoli visited, and pronounced "the best hotel between Chicago and the City of Oregon!" This was recently torn down; and the Doty Tavern (1836), has been replaced by the Opera House.

At Dixon, then Dixon's Ferry, was built in 1837 the Nachusa Tavern, by a stock company formed under the authorization of the State Legislature; the word *nachusa* in the Indian language signifying white-haired, this name had been given John Dixon, the first proprietor. When built, this was the largest hotel west of Chicago, and stood on the trail between Galena and Peoria. Enlarged and remodeled, part of the old building stands in the present hotel of the name.

Geneseo's present Geneseo House does not look old, for it was overhauled, refitted and modernized seven or eight years ago, but the building was erected in the '40's. Its numerous chimneys are due to the fact that in early days every room had its stove.

Shawneetown, said to be the oldest town in the State, was founded by the Government, eight years before the State of Illinois came into existence. Moses M. Rawlings built the Rawlings House, where Lafayette stayed in 1825, but this was burned in 1904, although replaced by a building practically identical. In 1925, Lafayette's visit was re-enacted in the hotel.

Towns along the Mississippi, and Shawneetown, on the Ohio River, were the earliest in the State. The first settlers came to Cairo in 1818, then the place was abandoned, and the town may be said to have been founded in 1836. Five years later it had a hotel, no longer in existence, but the present one was built by a company incorporated by the first Legislature, in 1857, and opened in 1859 under the name St. Charles. In 1880 it was bought by the Hallidays, its name changed, and as The Halliday it is open to-day.

[273]

During the Civil War, General Grant made his head-quarters here, and many dances were given to army officers in the dining-room. Alfred Tennyson Dickens visited Cairo and the hotel in 1911 but found it greatly changed from the days when his father styled it "a detestable morass." Going north, at Lebanon, is a two-story frame building, now a private residence which was the Mermaid Hotel, visited by Charles Dickens, and mentioned in his *American Notes* as "very clean and good." Its exact age is not known, it may be one hundred years old. The first proprietor, a retired sea captain, named it, and when questioned, replied that he gave it that name because he "believed in 'em." A large swinging sign bore what purported to depict one of " 'em."

Edwardsville's Wabash Hotel building, at which both Lincoln and Douglas stayed, stands, but has been made into apartments.

When Dickens visited Belleville he described its hotel as "half cowshed, half kitchen," but rebuilt and remodeled, it was recently reported as still open.

Garden Prairie had the Ames Tavern; at Grand-de-Tour, the hotel visited by Margaret Fuller Ossoli is reported to be still open; Princeton had an old inn; and near Newbury stands a farmhouse which was once an old tavern; but Peoria's inn, built in the '40's, was burned down.

Even using the word old comparatively, there are not many old taverns in Iowa. But one historian states that even as late as 1832 there were not fifty white people in all that is now the State.

Isaac Campbell cleared a farm and kept a public house in 1821, near what was called Des Moines Rapids, near the present city of Des Moines. Dr. Samuel C. Muir built a cabin on the site of Keokuk, and in this town two former taverns are standing.

On Main Street, Dubuque, was built in 1834 the Bell Tavern, so called because at the top of the building was hung a bell, "the first annunciator ever sounded in the county." Stores now occupy its site. Ten years later was built the Waples Hotel, later the Julian, and now the Julian Dubuque Hotel. In 1849, there were eight or ten hotels in the town, and later a magnificent structure was planned, to cost one hundred thousand dollars, but this burned down before it had been finished, and stores were built on the site. Part of the present Key City Hotel was built in 1854, and a hotel has stood on that site ever since. Still another hotel, first called the Lorrimer, then the Wales, was burned down. An early house was kept by Mark Beaubien, who may or may not have been the early Chicago innkeeper, or one of his numerous family.

Iowa probably had its share of log cabins in the early days, either inns or at least houses that furnished food and lodging to passing travelers.

Although a frontier country, the northern states along the Great Lakes had early taverns. Until 1805, Michigan was part of the territory of Indiana. Detroit, an early settlement, was first a French army post, but by 1800 there was a village of three hundred houses here. The first inn mentioned was the Steamboat Hotel, long since gone, as is the American Exchange. One inn has, however, been preserved, by the same man who has restored the Wayside Inn at Sudbury, Massachusetts, to its former estate. Mr. Henry Ford recently purchased an old inn which when built was in the country, although it is now within Detroit city limits. This is the Botsford-Jennings-Martindale House.

On Grand River Avenue stands this long, low, two-storied house, little changed outwardly, although it has been moved back from its old site. Built in 1836 by Stephen Jennings, this, the stage-coach stop and change for the four stage horses, was opened when overland travel from Detroit was at its height. Previously there had been no real roads, merely lanes, out of the settlement. In 1845, a plank road

[275]

was built, with ten toll-gates, and a charge of two cents a mile was fixed on all horse-drawn vehicles. The tavern prospered then, but later, after Milton Botsford had bought it, stage days went, and the prosperity of the old inn went with them.

When Mr. Ford bought it in 1925, the son of this Mr. Botsford, then a man well past sixty, told some interesting reminiscences of his father's days as landlord.

He recalled the first oil lamps introduced in the old tavern, and the fear of some of "the boys" when one was placed in the barroom, lest it explode. This barroom has been restored to its former appearance, although kegs and bottles are empty now, but the big open fireplace is as it used to be. Mr. Botsford recalled that his father used to buy whiskey for sixteen cents a gallon, and sell this quantity for twenty-five cents.

A two-story piazza runs across the front of the inn, from which, on the lower floor, two doors admit, one into the barroom, the other into a hall from which open the sitting-room and more formal parlor. This entrance is a fine old door, with the sidelights of a colonial inn, although of much later period.

The rooms are now refurnished with articles of the period when the inn was built. Behind the parlor is the dining-room, finished with wide panels, some of them twenty-two inches broad, and in the natural color of the wood, although probably originally they were painted white, as was customary. At the end of the hall is the old kitchen, with big fireplace and brick oven, and upstairs is the old ballroom, in which the new owner has already inaugurated old-time dances. The house is again a tavern in the sense that meals will once more be served, but it is also a museum, for many interesting things have been assembled.

Dearborn had an early tavern kept by Conrad Tenyat, who was graduated in the same class with Martin Van

Buren at the grammar school in Kinderhook, New York.
Fifteen miles from Detroit was the Half Way House.

Other taverns in various parts of Michigan are mentioned
in early accounts of travel. In Nankin, Doctor Adams built
himself a residence in 1828, which, after additions had been
made, became a tavern. Near the Post Office in this town,
a "large hotel" was built in 1832, by James Cahoon, and a
little earlier, a hotel painted red, near the Schwarzburg saw-
mill. This house burned, and the mill was later abandoned.

During the 1830's, there were several taverns along the
road from Flint to Pontiac, one of these in Groveland. This
Half Way House was kept by a man to whom an early
traveler gives this pleasant character: "He was a genial,
pleasant landlord, and as we sat by his cheerful fire, built
under a stick chimney on one side of his log house, cracking
jokes . . . we had no more idea of hardships than the
favored traveler of the present day."

The Howell House (1833) in Jackson, was burned in
1857. In 1838, E. F. Gay built his Temperance Hotel, the
first of its kind in the town, but in spite of its name, rather
a rough place. Howell's Old Stage House followed in 1840,
and Union Hall five years later, but the latter was burned.

West of Jackson, at Tekonsha, Calhoun County, an old
inn built in 1837 is still standing. The first landlord, Samuel
Hemenway, was also the town's first merchant. More than
sixty years ago it was purchased by a Mr. Blake, whose
daughter still lives in the old house, which is no longer an
inn. The ballroom on the third story may still be seen, although it no longer echoes to old-time dances.

The first tavern in Lansing, a log cabin, was built in 1847;
later, the Lansing House on the opposite side of the street,
succeeded it. The National, another early hotel, burned;
the Michigan House became a private residence; and the
Franklin Hudson was turned into stores.

Mrs. Ferrey, Curator of Lansing's Museum, tells of a

Civil War time landlord, who took the only daily paper in the town. His fellow citizens used to gather in his barroom to hear him read the latest news. His pronunciation was sometimes unique, as when he announced that: "The Massachusetts Zouaves charged on the Black Horse Cavalry, and they lost all their equipment as they eritreated across the Pot-o-mac."

At Cambridge Junction, in the southern border county of Lenawee, two old taverns stand where the Chicago and Monroe turnpikes cross. The frame house was built by Sylvester Walker, in 1832, and was known as the Walker Tavern. It was open until 1854, when its owner built the "new" Brick Tavern across the road.

The original two-story frame house, with its broad piazza, is now open as a museum, filled with antiques, some originally belonging here, others with interesting histories. Old oil paintings hang on the walls, old cooking-utensils are in the kitchen; there are three-cornered dish closets, even the old post box in which stage drivers used to deposit the mail they brought, remains built into the wall.

This tavern also has its murder chamber. Those interested in the gruesome may, it is said, even see the bloodstains on the floor of the room in which the murder occurred, and the furniture in this room is said to be that then in use. The story is as follows:

One night a traveler rode up on a black horse. He carried a great deal of money, which fact became known, possibly through his own garrulity. He was assigned the room now shown, but did not put his horse in the stable, instead, tying it to an oak tree in the woods behind the house. The following morning the traveler was found dead in his bed, stabbed with a dagger, and a large pool of blood had collected on the floor. The excited discoverers of the corpse left the room for a short time, and when they returned, the body was gone. The horse too had disappeared.

[278]

## Some Middle West Inns

The Reverend Lyster, who built and dedicated many early churches in southern Michigan, preached from the old bar, which still stands as used in 1835; old mugs, jars, and other liquor containers have been assembled here. A hotel register, an early checkerboard, such as may have been used by the guests who gathered here of a winter evening; bed-irons, and quaint candlesticks, with pictures dating back to 1820, are other interesting articles on view. The barber shop has specimens of cosmetics used here in 1840, and curious old shaving mugs. The dining-room contains china of the period, and the log-joisted kitchen, with its ladder leading to a loft above, also contains old furniture.

The Brick Tavern across the road, a much larger, three-story house, has a ballroom which has been the scene of many festivities in the past. In this house meals are now served to travelers. It has entertained many distinguished persons, among them Daniel Webster, Harriet Martineau, and James Fenimore Cooper. The latter made quite a stay at the Walker Tavern, making notes for his *Oak Openings*.

Doubtless the exploring of old highroads would find other inns in this region, although so many of the old landmarks have vanished.

In spite of the fact that many early taverns in Wisconsin were log cabins, or very primitive buildings, a number survive. How primitive they were may be judged when one reads that in the northern and western parts of the State, there were in 1840 to 1850 no bathing facilities in the taverns. A sink, small handbasin, soft soap, and an ancient comb were provided for toilet purposes. Unheated sleeping-rooms had small windows, corded beds, and for mattresses, sacks filled with straw. In very cold weather, warming pans might be used; sheets and pillowcases there were, but by no means always clean, and often the taverns were so crowded that the guests drew lots to see who should sleep on the

[279]

kitchen floor. Tallow candles furnished the lighting until superseded by kerosene lamps.

Food was abundant, although many dishes such as vegetables were absent. There were prairie chickens, quail, pigeons, and pies for dinner, the pies often made of green tomatoes or dried pumpkin, or apples. Buckwheat cakes with maple syrup or sorghum were served for breakfast, and one large salt-cellar placed in the middle of the long table at which the guests sat. These guests were usually heavy drinkers, and when they gathered around the big fireplace in the living-room, were expected to contribute to the general entertainment by narrating their own or their friends' adventures.

Mr. H. E. Cole tells of an early traveler who arrived at one of these inns just after a meal was over. The cook was not pleased at being obliged to prepare another meal, and angrily pulled a skillet from under the stove. As she did so, the family cat jumped out of the skillet, and the cook, without even wiping it out, proceeded to cook eggs in it.

Mr. J. H. A. Lacher states that in 1861, Wisconsin, north of an imaginary line drawn from Green Bay to La Crosse was, save for a few villages, almost an unbroken wilderness. When emigration began about 1846, there was not a really good road in the section, and the first stage line was not started until 1848.

Fort Atkinson's early tavern, the Green Mountain House, opened in that year, was later part of the Hotel Fort, then replaced by the Black Hawk Tavern, now open. From Fort Atkinson, in 1844, Mr. and Mrs. Sylvanus Wade moved to Greenbush, and two years later land was granted to Wade by President Polk. The pioneer had served in the War of 1812, his grandfather in the Revolution. The family journeyed with several teams, household belongings, cattle, hens, even a cat and her kittens, across a mere blazed trail, to the small log house which Mr. Wade had bought from

NACHUSA TAVERN, DIXON, ILLINOIS

[*See page* 273.]

THE WALKER TAVERN, CAMBRIDGE JUNCTION, MICHIGAN

[See page 278.

THE WALKER TAVERNS, CAMBRIDGE JUNCTION, MICHIGAN

TAVERN, SAUK CITY, WISCONSIN

[*See page* 284.

WADE HOUSE, GREENBUSH, WISCONSIN

[*See page* 281.

the original settler. Their nearest neighbor then was fourteen miles away.

Here the family lived, and many travelers westward stopped at the log house, with its gradually added rooms, and some took up land in the vicinity. One of Mr. Wade's granddaughters recently gave some interesting reminiscences to a local paper of things that she had heard from her parents or grandparents.

Black and red currants, high-bush cranberries, plums, crabapples, grapes, strawberries and raspberries all grew wild; partridges, prairie chickens and pigeons were plentiful, but so were wolves, and to protect cows and chickens from them it was necessary to build strong enclosures. Indians also frequently visited the little cabin, but never molested the family, for Mr. Wade always gave them food, and traded beads and calicoes for venison and maple sugar.

One room that was added was large enough for dancing, and people came from twenty miles around to dance. Music was not lacking, for Mr. Wade and his eldest son played the bass viol, and a New York lawyer, an early settler, the violin.

Six years after his arrival, Wade built the hotel still run by his grandson. Stages had been passing then for several years, and when the plank road was opened, a Milwaukee company ran coaches drawn by four horses three times daily in both directions. There were other lines as well, so that business was brisk, and by 1848 there were two hotels.

The Jefferson Hotel, in Jefferson, of the same county, is still the town's best hotel, and stands on the site of an older tavern.

Another old-timer still open, at Hale's Corners, the Julius Dreyfuss Tavern (1834), was originally called the Western House. Built of hand-hewn walnut and white oak, the doors, window-frames, flooring, and split poplar laths are all hand-made. On the main road to Milwaukee and the southwest, its first large barn soon proved too small to accommodate the teams of oxen and horses of farmers stopping for the night. Even when a second barn was built, often there was not stall room for the animals, and they must be bedded down on the floor. The original barn still stands.

The present owner's parents bought the house in 1873, and his mother introduced the chicken dinners for which the house is still noted; dinners such as she herself had often enjoyed on the Shell Road leading out of her native city, New Orleans.

In earlier days, patronage was chiefly from farmers taking their produce to Milwaukee. They tell of one man from Whitaker, who came downstairs one morning, walked up to the old zinc-covered bar still in its place, and calling for the usual "eye-opener," delivered the following:

> "Our fathers of old, they lived like goats.
> They washed their eyes and then their throats.
> But we, their sons, have grown more wise,
> We wash our throats and then our eyes."

Green Bay and Prairie-du-Chien both claim to have had the first tavern in what is now Wisconsin. In the former town, one was opened in 1825 by the Hon. John P. Arndt, from Pennsylvania. His wife was a very good cook, and her German dishes were much appreciated. In 1829 the Washington House, no longer standing, was opened, and six years later the Astor House, named for its owner, John Jacob Astor. This was "a large three-story, square building, with green blinds and a cupola, mahogany furniture, elegant carpets and silver service." It was burned in 1858. Nothing remains of the old tavern in Prairie-du-Chien. Kincaid's, in Truesdell, known in the '40's, is also gone.

As soon as it was opened, the stage route from Sheboygan

[282]

to Fond-du-Lac became a great thoroughfare, and especially when the plank road was put down. Stages left Fond-du-Lac at seven in the morning, and made their first change of horses at "Newton Kellogg's excellent tavern," twelve miles east.

Most of the heavy traffic from Milwaukee passed through Waukesha, and here there were more taverns than in any other section of equal size in the territory. There were eleven in the first four and a half miles west of Milwaukee, and nine in a short distance northwest. The Cottage Inn (1845) has not survived in Milwaukee, nor would one find the Forest House, northwest of the city, which was kept by Matthew Kilminster, an Englishman. He and his musical family were brought to this country by P. T. Barnum, and when the tavern was opened, entertained their guests with music.

Nor would one find the Prairie House, in Waukesha, most of whose landlords were New Englanders; but seven miles southwest, the Treadwell Tavern (1851), still stands in Genesee, its exterior much changed. On what was the Janesville plank road, now a county highroad, stands the Uncle Jesse Smith Tavern, a fine old three-story, cobblestone house, now a farm dwelling, but still retaining the old spring-floor ballroom. In Theresa, Dodge County, the Rock River House (1858), was standing a few years ago.

The McConnell Tavern at Okauchee, seventy-five years old, has been reopened. The Mukwonago House (1845) is still open, although the Henry Camp Tavern, about the same age, is now a private residence. Another old tavern some seventy-five years old, on the same Janesville highroad, the Leonard Martin, is now a farmhouse, as is one at Big Bend, the Aaron Putnam, which does not look like a tavern now, but was built for one in 1842. Others are at Wilmot and at Mequon, built about 1848.

The town of Milton, and its college, near Janesville, were

both founded by the Honorable Joseph Goodrich, the first landlord, merchant, Postmaster and Treasurer of the place. He built a log cabin sixteen by twenty feet, in which he lived with his family of thirteen, kept the tavern, and a store. In 1845, he built a large gravel (grout) house, and kept this as a tavern until 1867, when it became his private residence. It is now a tenement, and the original house is standing as well.

In Racine County, the Union House (1842), Rochester, is still a hotel, a rear addition containing a dance-hall, added in 1856. The Waterford House in the town of that name is another old-timer, now in use as a residence.

At first, almost all the taverns in this section were log or frame houses, but by 1850 they were being built of stone, gravel, or brick, substantial, with spring-floor ballrooms such as are found in the earlier New England taverns. These spring-floors are said to have caused some difficulty to "persons slightly inebriated, as they had no supports in the middle." The ballrooms were also used for society and Masonic lodge meetings.

In Sauk City, the Sauk City Hotel, built in 1850, later enlarged and called the United States, is still open. Richland City's Union Hotel is gone, but the King's Tavern, on the Baraboo-Prairie-du-Sac road, still stands. James Webster in 1843 built himself a log cabin on the Baraboo River, and since there was no other house, began furnishing travelers with food and lodging, until his became the first tavern in that section.

The Washburne Tavern, between Baraboo and Delton, was in existence as early as 1845, and the Harris House (1846), near Black Hawk, is still standing.

Watertown had many taverns. The American (1847), is gone, but the Commercial and the Buena Vista are still hotels. The Sandwich House, Fairfield, was standing two years ago. Built in 1845, the name was intended to be Sand

Hill, but the signpainter made a mistake, and the name remained as he had painted it. Business was at one time so brisk here that the landlady cut up and cooked an entire ox in ten days.

The Empire House (1854) in Prairie-du-Sac became the Briggs House, when bought and run by N. H. Briggs, and later, by his son, uncle of the popular cartoonist, Claire Briggs, of "When a Feller Needs a Friend" fame. The latter came from Reedsville, where his uncle also had a hotel, the Exchange House, long ago burned down.

On the Warner Memorial Road, between Baraboo and Devil's Lake, the road curves because the owner of a pioneer tavern, the Baraboo House, at the corner of what are now Lynn and Walnut Streets, refused to either sell or move his house. Built in 1847, it was later occupied for a time by Ringling's Circus employees, and then replaced by a brick building which became a grocery store.

Spring Green House, in this section, came to an untimely end. One night a guest arrived, and the next morning, when presented with an itemized bill: Supper, 25 cents; lodging, 25 cents; breakfast, 25 cents; declared that he had no money and departed. The landlord, furious, tore down his sign and chopped it up.

The picturesque Ferry House (1847) at Merrimack, removed from the original site, will probably soon be razed. The Red Tavern, between Kilbourne and Manchester, a noted stop when lumber trade and immigration were brisk, was standing recently.

The Cottage Home in Dalton is another survivor. During the Civil War, a southern sympathizer, known locally as the Copperhead, lived near. One day he met some young members of Company E, Wisconsin Volunteer Infantry, who made the tavern their headquarters. They surrounded the Copperhead, took him to the barn and ordered him to salute the flag. When he refused they strung him up, then letting

him down, again ordered the salute, which was again refused. Not until they had nearly killed him did the Copperhead yield.

In Iowa County, the town of Mineral Point was, in 1836,
ten times as large as Milwaukee, but one would now look in
vain for the tavern, consisting of several connecting log
cabins, kept here in 1828 by Colonel Abner Nichols, a
Cornishman; Hood's, kept by a miner's wife, or the "large
tavern" built in 1833 by Colonel John Moore, who came
here from North Carolina.

In Grant County, the Empire (1842), at Hazel Green,
is still open as a hotel. Opposite, another tavern used in the
'40's and '50's is now a private residence. Cassville's Hotel,
begun in 1836 but not opened until 1855, is still in operation.

Black River Falls, in Jackson County, had in 1846 a
tavern where they served fried salt pork with fried bread
for breakfast and supper, and for dinner, "for a change,"
pork, bread and beans. It is no longer open.

Other Wisconsin inns, the Burlington House (1839), Burlington, was standing recently; the Burr Oak at Juneau
stood until 1925; and the Buena Vista (1847), now called
The Cobblestone, is open at East Troy, in Walworth County.

Although the territorial government of Minnesota was
not established until 1849, several taverns were open by that
time.

A quaint old book published in 1853, the travels of Mrs.
Elizabeth F. L. Ellet, describes a trip which she took with
friends the year before, including Minnesota in their itiner-
ary. Although frequently guests in private homes, they also
stopped at some taverns.

In St. Paul she found the Rice Hotel and stages, almost
pioneer sight-seeing buses, ran three times daily between
that city and St. Anthony, giving passengers views of the
falls, several pretty lakes, and so forth. "Surveys have

been made," she wrote, "for a road from St. Paul to Fond-du-Lac, and even a railroad is talked of. This will bring Minnesota 800 or 900 miles nearer New York, and open the riches of the Northwest to our citizens." She found three public houses in Stillwater, and two taverns at Taylor's Falls.

The oldest hotel in Stillwater of which there are records, the Sawyer House, built in 1856, burned down two years ago. The first in Taylor's Falls, the Chicago House, was begun in 1851, but not finished until the following year. In 1870 the name was changed to the Dalles House, under which name it continued open until 1920, when the building was condemned for hotel purposes, but still stands. There was, however, at the time that Mrs. Ellet visited the place, the Barlow House, a private boarding establishment.

## Chapter XVI

*Kentucky, Tennessee, and Missouri Inns, with one in Kansas*

O LD KENTUCKY suggests the name of the pioneer ex-
plorer, Daniel Boone, and rightly; one of Kentucky's two oldest towns—save for French settlements in the western part of the state—was named
for him. Fort Boonesboro, his original camp, was founded
by him in 1775, and in the same year, Harrodsburg. The
former settlement lived for but a few years, although its site
may be distinguished.

A very old Indian trail led into what must indeed have
seemed a wilderness, and it blazed the way for what was
later known as Boone's Wilderness Road. This trail, the
Virginia Warriors' Path, ascended the beautiful Shenandoah
Valley, through what is now Danville, Kentucky, to the Falls
of the Ohio, site of Louisville, and after the Indians, was
used by traders, explorers, and early immigrants. Boone's
Trail followed the old trail through the Gap, to the new
settlements of Boonesborough on the Kentucky River, Crab
Orchard, and Danville, to Louisville. Colonel Logan and
his party went west by this trail.

Harrod's (Harrodsburg), Logan's, and Boone's forts
were important posts along this route. Accounts of Boone's
and Logan's adventures give thrilling pictures of early
pioneer days. Boone began exploring this country in 1769,
and only eight years later the first Kentucky court was held
at the new settlement of Harrodsburg.

[288]

HARRISBURG TAVERN, HARRISBURG, WISCONSIN

WASHBURNE TAVERN, DELTON, WISCONSIN

[*See page* 284.

THE HILL HOUSE (NOW BROWN PUSEY COMMUNITY HOUSE), ELIZABETHTOWN, KENTUCKY
[See page 295.

THE OLD MUNFORD INN, MUNFORDSVILLE, KENTUCKY
[See page 295.

# Kentucky, Tennessee, and Missouri Inns

In the old Harrodsburg Inn here, Lafayette is said to have played a game of billiards—and lost it.

Not far north of Harrodsburg is Shakertown, and its inn, built in 1871 and noted for good cooking, is open, but the Shakers have disappeared.

Mrs. W. T. Lafferty, in an interesting paper prepared for the Filson Club of Lexington, and incorporated in Kerr's *History of Kentucky*, gives an account of the early taverns in the State. She says in part:

"A large assembly room was always a feature in early Kentucky taverns. In one corner was the bar, the kitchen adjoined, and bedrooms were usually upstairs. If all the beds were occupied when a late traveler arrived, he spread a blanket down beside any bed he chose, or if this space were filled, he lay downstairs on the floor, his feet to the fire. In the morning, guests washed at a watering trough, and passed the towel from one to another."

Kentucky tavern laws, Mrs. Lafferty tells, provided that any one wishing a tavern license must petition the County Court, and would then, provided he gave bond guaranteeing good conduct, be awarded a license for one year. Tavern rates were fixed by the courts at least twice a year, and if an innkeeper overcharged his guests, he was fined thirty shillings for each offense.

Until 1815, when plans were drawn up for its improvement, little had been done for the Old Wilderness Road, which must at times have been almost impassable. Andre Micheaux, an early traveler who visited Kentucky in 1793, wrote of the lack of inns and bridges, the time lost in waiting until a sufficient number of travelers had assembled, that they might afford each other mutual protection against the dangers of the road.

Fortesque Cuming, an Englishman, who in 1808 or 1809 came by boat from Pittsburgh to Maystown, where he found a tavern kept by Mr. January, and then rode on horseback to Lexington and Frankfort, stopping at the principal inns along the road, complained that sheets were not in general use, "save in English inns, or places of fashionable resort." However, all of his comments were not disparaging, for in Washington, at Mr. Elbert's Tavern, Cuming praised the grace and intelligence of the "tavern ladies." In that town, he hired a horse for fifty cents a day.

In Millersburg, Captain Waller was "his obliging and interesting host." In Paris, he stopped at an inn whose hostler had served Washington as a personal servant through all his campaigns, and so well that the great man freed him and at his death left the former slave a plot of land near Mount Vernon.

On his way to Frankfort, Cuming stopped at Daily's Inn, which was unique. Daily was a mulatto who raised his own garden produce, had ice in summer—in those days most unusual—and during meals, played on the violin to his guests. He was so polite, kept so neat a house, and served such deliciously cooked food, that his inn was very popular, and greatly preferred to a rival establishment kept by a white man, known as Cole's Bad Inn. Cole is said to have been the grandfather of Jesse James, and Mrs. James was raised in his house. Local tradition also says that after the "bad inn" was deserted, a number of skeletons were found in the cellar, and were believed to be those of unfortunate travelers, killed by a villainous landlord.

Frankfort, in Cuming's day, had the Golden Eagle Tavern; and in Lexington he stopped at Joshua Wilson's Inn, "formerly and still known as Postlethwaite's." The Phœnix Hotel now stands on the site of the old inn, and since the days of the first one, save for brief intervals when the house was burned down, an inn has been open here.

Captain John Postlethwaite was a revolutionary soldier, who came to Lexington from Pennsylvania and built a tavern in 1800. He was noted for his courtesy, "always

[290]

wore neatly fitting small clothes and grey silk hose, and immaculate ruffles. He greeted each guest graciously upon his arrival, and by his cordiality and dignified demeanor, won each for his friend." In 1804, he rented his tavern to Wilson, who came to Lexington from Bardstown. For a time, the Post Office was in Postlethwaite's Tavern, the owner engaging in banking, and becoming one of the town's most prominent citizens. He married the daughter of Kentucky's fifth governor, Charles Scott, and several times served as town trustee.

The original tavern is described as a low, rambling log house, filled with fine cherry and walnut furniture, made by local cabinet-makers, and so beautiful that guests often commented on it. Rag rugs covered the floors, tallow candles furnished illumination, but guests were lighted to their bedrooms by negro slaves, of whom there were many.

This was not Lexington's first, but evidently its most noted, tavern. In 1801, there was a grand celebration in honor of Thomas Jefferson's election as president. There was a one o'clock dinner, to which one hundred and sixty ladies, with five hundred gentlemen, sat down, and sixteen toasts were drunk, assuredly not in water. After the dinner and speeches, "the sprightly dance" employed the guests until sunset, when part of the company repaired to Captain Postlethwaite's Tavern, where the evening was concluded with an elegant ball." [1]

Postlethwaite kept the tavern from time to time, leasing it for comparatively brief periods only, until his death in 1833. He once sold it to Sanford Keen, of the Lexington Jockey Club, but Keen died before he had paid for it, and the widow finding it impossible to run it, the executors returned it to the captain. During Keen's occupancy, it burned to the ground, and was rebuilt. After Postlethwaite's death, the name Phœnix was given the house, and a sign represent-

[1] John William Townsend, in the Lexington *Herald*.

ing that bird rising from its ashes was painted on the side of the tavern. The new proprietors advertised "a reading room and private parlor for gentlemen, and convenient parlor and chambers for families," and assured patrons that "the Bar and Cellar shall always be furnished with the best genuine red and white wines, Irish whisky (10 years old), and other liquors of the best quality."

Later, it was bought by John G. Chiles, of Virginia, who first established the Harrodsburg Inn. Under various owners, Lexington's old tavern continued popular until on May 14th, 1879, when the town was full of visitors to the races, it again burned down. A number of thrilling rescues were made, including that of the hotel cat from a third-story window, by a brave fireman who saved the animal by mounting a ladder against a tottering wall.

The present Phœnix Hotel was begun the following year.

Many distinguished guests have stopped in the first tavern or its successors. One day a gentleman with his daughter and her husband engaged rooms, but did not give their names. A small boy of the town recognized the older man as Aaron Burr. It was after the famous duel, and the boy had seen a waxwork representation of this, and so recognized Burr. President Monroe and General Jackson, with their suites, were entertained at a fine dinner, Louis Philippe of France stayed in the old tavern, and in 1825, Lafayette spent what must have been two most strenuous days there.

The tavern was then known as Mrs. Keen's. After the great Frenchman was shown his apartments, "fitted up with great taste and elegance, and adorned with a profusion of flowers," he was treated (?) to a "Literary repast" by the students of Transylvania University, who recited original odes in French, Latin, and English, the gallant Marquis replying in the same languages. He was entertained (?) at the Lafayette Female Seminary by more recitations, et cetera; attended a grand dinner given by the Masonic Lodge;

[292]

went to a ball; and sat for his portrait to Jouett, which portrait is now in Frankfort.

When, in June, 1925, the sesquicentennial of Lexington was celebrated, the proprietor of the Phœnix displayed in electric letters a notice that on May 26th, 1825, General Lafayette was a guest in the hotel. The French Ambassador and his daughter had come for the celebration, and the sign attracted much attention, and, one may be sure, many complimentary remarks from the Ambassador.

On Main Street, a bank now occupies the site of Brent's Tavern, where, in 1805, while Aaron Burr was in Lexington, the New Empire plotters held a conference. Nearly opposite, at 140 West Main Street, stood the Sheaf of Wheat, where the first local celebration of St. Patrick's Day was held in 1790.

One more note, before leaving Lexington. William Pitt Fessenden, an early visitor during the races, speaks of two drinks then popular, known as hailstones and snowstorms. "A hailstone," he explains, "is a brandy julep, a snowstorm a weaker one. The way they drink these things in Kentucky is a caution to sinners."

South of Lexington, beyond Toddville, where a road leads to Harrodsburg, is Burnt Tavern, at Bryantsville. The old farm here was owned by the Reverend James Smith, a Virginian, and the hotel was given its name after the building on the grounds had twice burned. It was a famous old roadhouse in stage-coach days, and one wing, saved during the second fire, is now more than a hundred years old. The owner's son, Henry Smith, was one of the first governors of Texas.

Rates at Cynthiana's Eagle Tavern in 1795 were: dinner, one shilling and threepence; breakfast and supper one shilling each; bed, "in clean sheets," six pence; and whisky cost eight pence for half a pint. Near Covington may be found several old taverns, one known as Tackett's; the ruins of another, Callaghan's, whose host was famed for fried chicken.

Olympian Springs had a hotel before 1805, and in 1822 the Olympian Hotel promised its guests the best food the country could produce, calling attention to the venison they served; the bar, with choice liquors; and also advertised that they had "as fine a PACK as ever went in a chase."

In Bardstown is a stone inn, one of the oldest buildings in town, still in use. It is close to the Post Office, and is considerably more than a hundred years old, for in 1787 the city council held its meetings here.

Two old inns survive in Elizabethtown, one still used as a hotel. This, now Smith's Hotel, with a reputation for good food, stands on the site of a log house, built from trees hewn in 1798 in the public square by Major Thomas Crutcher. This house stood on the corner of the public square and Main Street. On each side of the door was a lion rampant, and above, the inscription: At the Sign of the Lion. When bricks were first made in Elizabethtown, in 1801, Daniel Wade, who then owned the tavern, built on a brick addition. The third proprietor after Wade razed the log house, and built a three-story brick hotel which was then known as the Eagle House.

In 1869, fire started in the stables at the rear, and wrecked part of the hotel. After this, it was remodeled, and has been either a hotel or boarding-house ever since. The fine front entrance is gone, and most of the first floor is now occupied as a store.

A slave, Jerry Wade, belonging to one of the early proprietors, at his master's death purchased his freedom for one thousand dollars, went to Louisville, became an esteemed employee at the Galt House there, and amassed quite a fortune.

Another Elizabeth tavern was the Hill House, built for a residence in 1818 to 1820, but after the owner's death,

[294]

run as a tavern by his widow, known affectionately as "Aunty Beck." Jenny Lind stayed here, on her trip to the Mammoth Cave, and sang from the front doorstep to the assembled populace, where assuredly the colored people were well represented.

General Custer and his officers lived for some time at the Hill House, as did many other notables, passing through Elizabethtown by stage on the old Louisville and Nashville turnpike.

After Mrs. Hill's death, the house changed hands a number of times, remaining a hotel until, in 1923, it was purchased by two Chicago physicians, Dr. W. A. Pusey and Dr. Brown Pusey, and given as a memorial of their aunt, Mrs. Hill, and their parents and grandparents, to the citizens of Cardin County for community use. Modern improvements have not detracted from the appearance of the old two-story brick building, and in the rear, a charming old-fashioned garden has been laid out.

In Munfordsville, south of Louisville, the quaintest of old inns stands. In 1800, this log house was built of thirty-foot walnut logs, cut in the neighboring forest. The original cabin had but four rooms, two on each floor, and a large stone chimney. Afterwards two ells were added, but these have since been removed, so the old house, no longer a tavern, presents much the original appearance.

Helen Fitz Randolph in her book, *The Mammoth Cave and the Cave Region of Kentucky*, quotes a traveler as follows:

"It was as late in the season as June the 8th, of the early '50's, but we found a roaring hickory fire in the Inn at Munfordsville, and the neighbors around it, talking politics of course. The tavern in Kentucky is not only the resort, but the respectable resort of the masculine inhabitants of the village at all hours. One seldom drives up to a tavern without alighting amid a group (oftener a crowd), and titles flying from mouth to mouth, inform you that all the judges, generals and colonels possible to the size of the population are among the company. The stranger is received with courteous acknowledgment. . . . Our landlord was quite a superior and intellectual looking man, and when supper was ready, he waited on table, conversing with great ease as he handed around the hot cakes, and seating himself at the head of the table when all were helped, he discussed the religious topics which chanced to come up very intelligently. A judge drove the stage-coach in which I crossed the country from Harrodsburg—the wealthy nabob of Elizabethtown was the 'stage agent' who helped us into the coach and arranged our baggage."

To Miss Fitz Randolph I am indebted for descriptions of the next two taverns.

Halfway between Louisville and Nashville, on the Dixie Highway, is the old unfinished Bell's Tavern. Built of bricks made by slaves, many distinguished men stopped here on their way to visit the Mammoth Cave, discovered about 1809. It was a rendezvous for Kentucky politicians, and a favorite stopping place of Henry Clay. Its landlord, Billy Bell, served venison, wild turkey, and pheasants, fish from the river, and his favorite drink, "peach and brandy."

It was burned in the '50's, and plans were made for replacing it with a fine stone house, but before this had been completed the Civil War broke out, and to-day only vine-covered walls and window arches stand, roofless. Franklin Gorin, owner of the Mammoth Cave property, and keeper of the inn built there soon after the cave was discovered, married a daughter of Landlord Bell.

The Mammoth Cave Hotel, a group of log cabins, stood for more than a hundred years, then it, too, burned in 1917. More than three years were needed to build the first group of cabins, because:

"The timbers . . . were hewed, the ends notched and

[296]

OLD HOTEL IN CUMBERLAND COUNTY, TENNESSEE

[*See page* 299.

THE ELK HORN TAVERN, ELK HORN, ARKANSAS

[*See page* 302.

Photo by J. W. McChesney, Marshall, Mo.

OLD TAVERN, ARROW ROCK, MISSOURI

[See page 307.

fitted together. The carpenters sawed through each log lengthwise, one plank at a time. Tradition says that the men could saw no more than 75 or 100 feet a day, and received $1.25 a day for their labor. All flooring, ceiling and finishing material was prepared in this way.

"Shingles were shaved with a 'shaving horse.' The blocks of cedar were boiled in huge kettles, and then cut one at a time . . . attached to the roof by wooden pegs."

Whose mouth does not water at thought of the food and drink which Miss Fitz Randolph mentions as characteristic of these two old inns, only nine miles apart?

"Venison steak, bass fried in corn meal, mast-fattened bacon, cured with hickory wood fire, snapbeans cooked with green corn, pone bread from the skillet on the hearth, and cider and rum, French brandy and home made wines."

Until 1909, the famous Galt House stood in Louisville. In 1842, when Charles Dickens stopped there, the landlord was Mr. Throckmorton, "a high strung southerner." He knew the most important men in the city, and many in the State as well, so he called on Dickens and proffered his services, letters of introduction, and other courtesies. Mr. Dickens is said to have replied as follows:

"Sir, are you the publican who keeps this inn?"

"Yes, sir," replied Throckmorton.

"Then," said Dickens, "when I have need for your services, I will ring for you." [2]

On the western border of the State, in Paducah, laid out in 1821, were many old inns, several of which are still standing.

Earliest of these was probably Hays' Fox House, built in 1826, on north First Street, between Broadway and Jefferson Streets. A little later, the Indian Queen, the first brick building in Paducah, was opened, and in the '30's and '40's, "Doc Thomas' Inn," at First and Jefferson Streets, was pop-

[2] John M. Lansden, *Journal of the Illinois Historical Society.*

ular. This faced on the Ohio River, and was a popular meeting place. Brick business buildings now replace it.

The Southern Hotel, nearly eighty years old, still stands on the corner of First and Broadway. When built, this three-story house was Paducah's most imposing building, and was called the St. Francis. After the Civil War the name was changed to the Richmond, then to the Southern, by which it is now known.

Bristol, in the northeastern corner of Tennessee, was early an important town, on the direct stage route from Baltimore to New Orleans. Along this road stages changed horses every twelve or fifteen miles, so taverns sprang up, but not many survivors will be found.

An old tavern at Abingdon, Virginia, fifteen miles north of Bristol, was torn down quite recently. Ten miles west of Bristol, the old Deery Tavern is still standing in Blountsville, although it was damaged a number of times during the Battle of Blountsville, in 1863. An old bell, used to call guests to meals, still hangs outside, and bears the date, 1806. Nails, hinges, and locks throughout the house are all handmade, and there is a fine old mantel in the rear parlor.

Sixteen miles west of Blountsville, the Kingsport Tavern stands, but is a private residence. This was a famous house, built very soon after the Revolution by Richard Netherland.

Continuing westward, in Rogersville is the Rogers Tavern (1790). Of this house it is told that once when it was crowded with travelers on a cold night, a noisy, troublesome man vowed that he would have a room to himself. Andrew Jackson was there, took him by the neck, and piloted him to the corncrib, the slats of which, two inches apart, let in an abundance of cold air. Jackson threw the disturber into the crib, and declared that he would kill him if he ventured out before breakfast time.

Gambling was prohibited in this tavern, and if any diso-

[298]

beyed, a kettle of burning feathers placed in a closet beneath their room soon ended their game.

Twenty-five miles west of Rogersville, at Bean Station, is another old tavern, also with marks of cannon balls of the Civil War, and one also stands in Knoxville.

Southwest of Bristol, on another road, the old Chester Inn stands in Jonesborough, but is no longer a hotel. It was built between 1820 and 1830 by Robert I. Chester, after whom both inn and county were named.

Jonesborough was the first town in the State of Tennessee, and the first capital of that unique commonwealth known as the Lost State of Franklin, formed in 1784, when North Carolina ceded her western lands in what is now Tennessee to the United States, but did not provide for the eastern section. That part promptly set up a republic of its own. John Sevier was its governor for four years, until, after some bloodshed, the affair was adjusted.

In Crab Orchard, Cumberland County, is another of the old inns at which President Jackson used to stop on his journeys to Washington. A long, low, two-story building, with a porch across the entire front, it is no longer occupied. The chimney on its western end fell just as a group on the platform of the near-by railway station were pointing to it and discussing the old building's condition.

Daniel Webster is said to have stopped at this inn while hunting in the Cumberland Mountains, although this story seems to have been based merely on the initials: "D. W." cut in a tree near the Crab Orchard station.

In Nashville, although no old ones survive, taverns there were a-plenty, for this was an important center. In 1801, the United States made a treaty with the Choctaw Indians, providing for a road from Nashville to Natchez, largely following the old Chickasaw trail. The following year, this road was completed from the northern terminus to Nash-

[299]

ville. The present Hillsboro Turnpike follows almost the same route as the old road.

Until after 1800, Nashville had only log cabins, but in 1787, tavern rates were fixed by the Davidson County Court, among these having: "½ pint whisky such as will sink tallow, 2 shillings; bowl of toddy made with loaf sugar and whisky, 3 shillings, 6 pence; dinner and grog, 4 shillings."

Later, breakfast, dinner and supper were to be twenty-five cents each, lodging, six and a quarter cents, and stabling a horse for twenty-four hours, thirty-seven and a half cents. "Every house was an inn, where all were welcomed and feasted."

In 1808 Granny White came into eastern Tennessee from North Carolina, keeping a tavern and establishing a good reputation for her cooking, and especially for her cakes. When she had made enough money she moved west again, and set up another tavern on the road to Franklin, near where the Natchez Road crossed this. Its site was not far from the historic Lea home, which afterwards and for more than a century has belonged to the Overtons.

Thomas H. Benton, for thirty years United States Senator, knew Granny White well. She was very thrifty, and in one of his Senate speeches, Benton compared the general Government to her, always holding tightly to what she had, and always grasping for more.

Her tavern became the best known between New Orleans and Louisville, chiefly for its cooking.

On the road from Nashville to Andrew Jackson's home, the Hermitage, stood Mud Tavern, patronized by the president and other well-known men.

In 1786, Lardner Clark was a merchant and ordinary-keeper. Two years later, Black Bob opened the most aristocratic place in town.

The Nashville Inn was opened about 1798 by W. T. Lewis in his private residence, where he had previously entertained many travelers, at a time when there were no inns. Stages made this their stop. It was on the north side of the Public Square, its site now occupied by a business building. In 1813, Andrew Jackson left it to cross the Square to the Post Office, and returning, passed the old City Hotel, where Benton and his friends were then stopping. In this hotel, Jackson, his friends and the Bentons engaged in a shooting fray, in which Jackson was seriously wounded by Jesse Benton. Afterwards they became greater friends than ever before.

The City Hotel also has yielded to business buildings.

In 1814, the Bell Tavern, at which many notables were entertained, stood, but it burned in 1856.

Four miles north of Franklin was Beech's Tavern, opened about 1820. Later, the Natchez Road was shifted to pass this tavern, and it was popular with travelers. It had not been an inn for many years when recently it was cut in two and made into residences.

Memphis, in 1805, was described as "quite a brisk town," by some early travelers who camped part of the time on their trip, and were, as was common in the south then as later, frequently entertained in private homes. Tavern was, in that locality and time, the usual term; inn not being heard much until later.

The Bell Tavern, first house built on the site of Memphis, survived until quite recently. Its exact age could not be learned, but as early as 1819, General Jackson, General James Winchester, and Judge John Overton met in it to lay out the town of Memphis, and it was in this tavern that Fannie Wright and Robert Dale Owen were entertained, when they came, about 1827, to found a training-school and home for freed negroes.

The Gayoso Hotel was opened in 1845, but the present is the third rebuilding of the house. It was named for Don Manuel Gayoso de Lomos, Spanish Governor of Louisiana,

Early American Inns and Taverns

who in 1795 built a fort on the site of the Memphis of to-
day. This hotel, too, has entertained many distinguished
people during its more than eighty years of existence, among
these John C. Calhoun, Stephen A. Douglas, Jefferson Davis,
Andrew Johnson, General Grant, Theodore Roosevelt, and
the Grand Duke Alexis.

In the entire State of Arkansas but one old inn, and that
in the northwestern corner, has been located, nor has this
been used as an inn since the Civil War. It stands in good
condition, however, and is occupied by the family who owned
it during its last days as an inn.

This, the Elk Horn Tavern, was built in 1833, by Jesse
Cox. He was succeeded by his son, and after the latter's
death, his daughter and her husband purchased it.

The old tavern took its name from a pair of huge elk
horns, which were fastened to the top of the house, the
animal having been killed by the carpenter and builder.
This house was a stage stop.

During the three days of March 6-8, 1862, a battle raged
near here, and at one time, General Curtis of the Union
Army, with forty thousand troops, was encamped here,
while the Confederate General Pierce and his men were
camped to the south. The latter learned of General Curtis's
whereabouts, and surprised him near Elk Horn, by taking a
different route than had been expected. The battle lasted
until both sides had exhausted their ammunition, and is
known as the Battle of Pea Ridge. The present owner of
the old tavern tells that his wife's parents were living here
at the time, and that the last of the fighting went on in the
actual yard. A bill has been introduced in Congress to make
this section a National Park, so the old tavern may yet be
spared for many years.

Missouri's Old Road was a military highway, established
by the Federal Government, and it extended from Springfield to Boonville. In 1831, a ferry was established at the

point where this road crossed the Osage River, when surveyed and charted. Doubtless there was a tavern.

St. Louis, Missouri, is a very old settlement, but one could hardly expect to find a surviving old tavern in the large modern city. The nearest approach to a first inn was when, in 1815, Mr. and Mrs. Charless opened their large house for the accommodation of travelers, since there was no inn at that time in the town. Two years later, the Missouri Tavern was begun, and finished in 1819. Its owner, Major Biddle, traveled east to find the best landlord whom he could persuade to come out there. For more than a hundred years, this house was the pride of the Mississippi Valley; many balls and entertainments were given in it, many St. Patrick's Day celebrations held, and also, alas, many duels arranged.

The Planters was a well-known hotel when Dickens visited it in 1842 and declared that it "was built like an English hospital, with long passages and bare walls, and skylights above room doors for the free circulation of air." He pronounced it none the less "an excellent house, and the proprietors have most bountiful notions of providing the creature comforts. Dining alone with my wife in our own room one day, I counted fourteen dishes on the table at once," he concludes.

Dickens was by no means always uncomplimentary to conditions in our new country. Stage-coach travel he did not enjoy, and no one who reads his descriptions of several such trips can be surprised. But more than once he praises the inns or hotels, even as again he may be ruthless in criticism of others. Louisville, Kentucky's hotel was "excellent."

His inn at Upper Sandusky, for instance, a log inn, "tapestried with old newspapers, pasted against the wall" was in what then was a mere Indian village, but at Sandusky he found "a comfortable little hotel on the brink of Lake Erie."

[303]

# Early American Inns and Taverns

St. Charles was Missouri's early capital, and at the time that the Assembly met there, a tavern gave its members board for two dollars and fifty cents a week, but eggs were then selling for but five cents a dozen, pork was a cent and a half a pound, venison hams could be bought for twenty-five cents, although both sugar and coffee were one dollar a pound. Benjamin Emmons opened a hotel here in 1817.

Many believe that a still older city at one time stood thirteen miles west of this St. Charles; there is even a tradition that French Canadian refugees settled there in 1732, and certainly the town was in existence by 1769. On the other hand, St. Genevieve, in the county of that name, claims to be the oldest town in the State, but there are no authentic records to prove this claim. Some say that it was founded in 1732, others in 1759, but it is certain that for years, St. Louis merchants bought their supplies in St. Genevieve. The original town was three miles south of the present one, and had narrow streets and decidedly foreign-looking houses.

Across the river from St. Charles, there was a tavern kept by Lafreniere Chauvin, born in St. Louis and descended from a French family which had first settled in New Orleans. Charles Joseph Latrobe, who traveled through Missouri with Washington Irving, speaks of "a little French inn, with a small bowling green, skittle ground and garden," which reminded him more of the Old World than anything that he had seen in weeks.

At Myrtle, a tavern was kept by another Frenchman, Alexander Bellissime, who came to America with Lafayette and served under him. When the Marquis visited Missouri in 1824-5, he was welcomed by Bellissime with a military salute, and was greatly interested to meet here one of his old soldiers.

The Middle West did not take kindly to the word inn, as being "too English," so their hostelries were generally at first called ordinaries, then taverns.

[304]

OLD HOTEL, NEW MADRID, MISSOURI

[*See page* 307.

BEDWELL'S TAVERN, GREENVILLE, MISSOURI

[*See page* 305.

MC CARTY'S HOTEL, JEFFERSON CITY, MISSOURI

[*See page* 308.

# Kentucky, Tennessee, and Missouri Inns

On Boone's Lick Road, one Robert Weston kept a tavern, and it was noticed that horses put up in his stable never fed heartily. Finally, someone discovered that Weston greased the ears of corn between the kernels, to keep the horses from eating.

Zadock Martin opened a tavern in 1826, at the Falls of the Platte, and as this was on the main road from Fort Leavenworth, it was well patronized.

At Loutre Lick, called Missouri's first spa, one Van Bibber kept a tavern. He married a granddaughter of Daniel Boone, and had the reputation of telling his patrons marvelous tales.

Coming into Missouri from the southern part of Illinois, in Perryville, facing the Court House Square, is—or was in the summer of 1925—a dilapidated, unpainted building, the first hotel here, built in 1842 by Henry Hooss. Opened as the White Tavern, it became noted.

Wayne County, farther west, was once called the Free State of Wayne. The French and Spanish explored this territory, but Joseph Parish of Virginia is believed to have been its first settler. In 1801, he built a cabin on the St. François River, but for years the only town in the county was Greenville, a frontier post, to which goods were brought by ox teams from St. Genevieve. Until 1836, there was no provision for delivering mails. Later, it became a night stop for coaches between St. Louis and Arkansas, and in the '40's, Bedwell's Tavern, a two-story, frame house, with a piazza across the front, was the stage house. As the stage driver drew up, cracking his whip loudly to announce his arrival, meals were being prepared of bear meat, pheasants, and corn pone, with supplies for various kinds of toddies and punches. Even to-day, Greenville has no railroad.

During the summer of 1925, Mr. Louis La Coss made an extensive trip throughout Missouri, taking pictures of old landmarks, talking with old residents, and bringing to light

[305]

much interesting and curious history of the early days. His articles appeared in the St. Louis *Times Democrat* and supply an invaluable history of the State.

During this same summer, there was living in Versailles, Morgan County, a veteran hotel-keeper, Mrs. Elizabeth Martin, then ninety-nine years old, surely the oldest of landladies. She came to this section in 1853 with her husband and four children, emigrating from Virginia, and lived in one part of the town for seventy-two years.

"Versailles in those days was little more than a clearing," she told Mr. La Coss. "There were three or four houses, and the streets were grown up with weeds. The second day we were in Versailles, a woman came to me with a proposition. She had been running a sort of hotel, but she was tired of the job. She wanted to rent it to us. We struck a bargain, and took over her place on the basis of $100 rent per year, the only stipulation being that we hire a negro servant who had been with her for years. That did not tax our resources much, as he received nothing but his board and a place to sleep.

"So without warning, we became hotel keepers. Of course we didn't have much—a couple of extra beds and a dining table, where our paying guests took potluck with us. But we made it go, and at the end of the year we had done so well that the woman wanted her property back. By that time, we saw a future in the business, so Mr. Martin raked and scraped together $300, with which we bought this hotel." This was for the land, on which he built a large house, now part of the hotel building.

Mrs. Martin had some exciting adventures during the Civil War, for soldiers of both armies passed through the town, and she fed many.

"We gave them rough food but good," she remarked, "and we had many promises of payment, but precious little money did we have in those days."

This hotel at Versailles is still open.

House- and barn-raisings were the pioneers' chief amusements, these always followed by a supper and dance. Mr. La Coss quotes a Benton County pioneer as to early conditions:

"We traveled in truck wagons, with wheels made from logs, and drawn by oxen. Our plows were bull tongues fastened to forks cut from young trees, our houses were log cabins, daubed with mud, with stick and mud chimneys and clapboard doors—no schools, no churches, no courts, no voting. Both men and women wore home-made clothing with not much cotton in it. Tall nettles were gathered from the rich bottoms, allowed to decay, and then worked up like flax, and made into cloth. Game was plentiful. Frequently, my father killed three deer before sunrise."

New Madrid is another old town, and it originally stood within the Kentucky line. The vagaries of the Mississippi River, the fierce earthquakes of 1811 to 1812, followed three years later by floods, shifted it to Missouri. In 1781, French traders had come here, but the first settler was George Morgan, a Revolutionary soldier. A seventy-five-year-old hotel, the New Madrid, still survives, the two-story piazza in southern style lending dignity to the plain frame building, which none the less was once considered quite a fine house.

Doniphan, in Ripley County, had a tavern in 1843, but this town was almost wiped out during the Civil War.

The first house built in 1837 in Gallatin, Daviess County, and owned by Jacob Stollings, was used as a hotel.

Arrow Rock, Saline County, has a most picturesque old tavern, owned now by the State of Missouri, its preservation entrusted to the Daughters of the American Revolution. Save when this organization closed it to make needed repairs, the old house had been open continuously as a tavern, and is to continue as one. Built in 1830 by Judge Joseph Huston's slaves, of bricks which they had burned, all of the woodwork is hand-sawn and -hewn black walnut. It contained both a barroom and a public hall. This was not only a stage-coach stop, but a popular meeting place for politicians during reconstruction days. Washington Irving, Kit Carson, and several governors were distinguished guests.

The old fireplaces are still preserved, and the Daughters intend that the house shall be as nearly as possible what it was in the early days. Upstairs one may see the canopied beds, and other walnut furniture; one bed is even shown as having been occupied by Washington.

Mr. La Coss discovered the old Shawnee trading-post, a long, two-storied frame building, with double piazzas across the front, near the site of Westport, Jackson County. This was a very early trading-post at the junction of the Missouri and Kaw Rivers.

Independence was, in 1824, the headquarters for wagon trains trading with Mexico, and was the last outfitting post.

St. Joseph's chief hotel and several streets are named for its founder, Joseph Ribidoux (1826), and his second wife and children. This town became the headquarters and starting point for the famous Pony Express to San Francisco. The stables are now a garage.

In Jefferson City, one may see a two-story, red brick building, now an apartment house, which was for years McCarty's Hotel, dating from 1837. Its proprietor came from Virginia, bringing with him a negro, and the house became noted for good cooking. During the late war, the Government used it for a hospital.

Bowling Green's old Mann's Tavern survived only until 1873, when it was replaced by a business building.

Kansas City's first hotel was built in 1849, on the bluff overlooking the river, between Delaware and Wyandotte Streets. It was called the Western, the American, then the Gillie House, but has vanished with the city's rapid growth.

Inquiry has brought to light but one surviving inn or

tavern in the state of Kansas. There may be others, for the territory was organized in 1854. This lone inn stands out in the country, four or five miles from Fort Riley, on Whisky Lake (in that dry state!), and was popular with officers from the camp and Fort during the war, for it is charmingly located among the hills.

Finally, in Washington, when it was a territory, far to the west in the little settlement known as Moclif's, stood a little gray shack, which was patronized for meals, for lack of any other place, by a group of young men. One day its owner discussed giving this shack a name, and consulted with the young men as to a suitable one. Without hesitating, one of her boarders suggested: The Limit, and with no thought of the possible application, the landlady promptly adopted it. As The Limit it was accordingly known until the little group of patrons had dispersed to the ends of the earth.

# BIBLIOGRAPHY

AFOOT AND ALONE—Stephen Powers. Columbian Book Co., Hartford, Conn., 1872

AMERICAN PIONEER, THE—Published in local Ohio magazines in 1842

ANNALS OF ANNAPOLIS—Ridgeley. Annapolis, Md., 1840

ANTIENT TOWNE OF NORWICH, CONNECTICUT, THE—Mary E. Perkins. The Bulletin Co., Norwich Conn., 1895

AUTOBIOGRAPHY OF A PIONEER—Rev. Jacob Young. Poe & Hitchcock, Cincinnati, O., 1860

BALTIMORE PAST AND PRESENT—Brantz Mayer. Baltimore, Md.

BLUE GRASS TOURS. The Motorway Series, Henry MacNair, New York City, 1925

BYWAYS AND BOULEVARDS IN AND ABOUT HISTORIC PHILADELPHIA —F. B. Brandt and H. V. Gummere. Philadelphia, 1926

CENTURY OF BANKING IN NEW YORK, A—Henry W. Lanier. George H. Doran Company, New York, 1922

CHRONICLES OF BALTIMORE—John Thomas Scharf. Trumbull Bros., Baltimore, Md., 1874

CHRONICLES OF BALTIMORE COUNTY—John Thomas Scharf. L. H. Everts, Philadelphia, 1881

CLEVELAND GOLDEN STORY—James Wallen. Wm. Taylor, Son & Co., Cleveland, 1920

CROWN INN, THE—William C. Reichel. King & Baird, Philadelphia, 1872

CUSTODIAN'S HISTORY OF THE MUNROE TAVERN—Carrie E. Bacheller, Lexington, Mass.

FRANKFORD [PENNSYLVANIA] HISTORICAL SOCIETY PAPERS— William B. Dixon and others

[311]

# Early American Inns and Taverns

FRAUNCES TAVERN—Henry Russell Drowne.  New York, 1919

GREATEST STREET IN THE WORLD, THE—Stephen Jenkins.  G. P. Putnam's Sons, New York and London, 1911

GUIDE BOOK TO HISTORIC GERMANTOWN—Charles F. Jenkins. Site & Relic Society, Germantown, Pa., 1902

HISTORIC HOUSES, SOUTH CAROLINA—Harriette Kershaw Leiding. J. B. Lippincott Co., Philadelphia, 1921

HISTORIC PLACES IN DAVIDSON, WILLIAMSON, MAURY AND GILES COUNTIES, TENNESSEE—Issued by the Nashville Auto Club, Nashville, Tenn.

HISTORIC POINTS IN DELAWARE—Compiled by the Colonial Dames of Delaware

HISTORIC VIRGINIA HOMES AND CHURCHES—Robert A. Lancaster, Jr.  J. B. Lippincott Co., Philadelphia, 1915

HISTORICAL ENCYCLOPEDIA OF ILLINOIS.  Munsell Pub. Co., Chicago, 1900

HISTORICAL SPOTS IN NEWPORT, RHODE ISLAND—Edith May Tilley.  Newport Historical Society

HISTORY OF ALBANY AND SCHENECTADY COUNTIES, NEW YORK—Howell Zenny.  W. Munsell & Co., New York, 1886

HISTORY OF THE CITY OF NEW YORK—Van Rensselaer.  The Macmillan Co., New York, 1909

HISTORY OF DELAWARE—Henry C. Conrad.  The Author, Wilmington, Del., 1908

HISTORY OF DELAWARE—John Thomas Scharf.  L. J. Richards & Co., Philadelphia, 1888

HISTORY OF FRANKFORD, [PENNSYLVANIA]—Guernsey A. Hallowell

HISTORY OF HUDSON, NEW YORK—Anna R. Bradbury.  Record Printing & Publishing Co., Hudson, N. Y., 1908

HISTORY OF LANCASTER COUNTY, PENNSYLVANIA—Ellis & Evans.  Everts & Peck, Philadelphia, 1883

HISTORY OF KENTUCKY—Edited by Judge Charles Kerr.  American Historical Society, 1922

HISTORY OF LANCASTER COUNTY, PENNSYLVANIA—H. M. J.

# Bibliography

Klein. Lewis Historical Pub. Co., New York and Chicago, 1924

HISTORY OF LITCHFIELD, CONNECTICUT—Alain C. White. Enquirer Print, Litchfield, Conn., 1924

HISTORY OF NEW HAMPSHIRE TOWNS (BOSCAWEN)—Charles Carleton Coffin. Republican Press Association, Concord, N. H., 1878

HISTORICAL COLLECTIONS OF NEW JERSEY—Barber & Howe. W. Barber, New Haven, Conn., 1868

HISTORY OF NORWICH, CONNECTICUT—Caukins. T. Robbins, Norwich, Conn., 1845

HISTORY OF PHILADELPHIA—Scharf & Westcott. L. H. Everts & Co., Philadelphia, 1884

HISTORY OF POUGHKEEPSIE, NEW YORK—Edmund Platt. Platt & Platt, Poughkeepsie, N. Y., 1899

HISTORY OF PUTNAM COUNTY, NEW YORK—Pelleatreau

HISTORY OF SCHENECTADY COUNTY, NEW YORK—Howell Zenny

HISTORY OF WESTCHESTER COUNTY, NEW YORK. Robert A. Bolton, New York, 1848

MARKET STREET, PHILADELPHIA—Joseph Jackson. J. Jackson, Philadelphia, 1918

MEMORIAL HISTORY OF CONNECTICUT

MISSOURI TAVERN, THE—*The Missouri Historical Review*—Walter B. Stephens. Columbia, Mo.

NEW BRUNSWICK [NEW JERSEY] IN HISTORY—William H. Benedict. The Author, New Brunswick, N. J., 1925

NEW ORLEANS AS IT WAS—Henry C. Castellanos

NORTH CAROLINA HISTORICAL PAPERS

NORWICH [CONNECTICUT] JUBILEE, THE—Compiled by John W. Stedman

OHIO BEFORE 1850—Robert E. Chaddock. Columbia University Monographs. Longmans, Green & Co., New York, 1908

OHIO, ITS HISTORY AND ANTIQUITIES—Henry Howe. The Author, Cincinnati, O., 1848

OLD AND NEW LOUISIANA—Edward King

[313]

# Early American Inns and Taverns

Old New England Inns, Little Pilgrimages Among—Mary Caroline Crawford. L. C. Page & Co., Boston, 1907

Old Ordinary at Hingham, [Massachusetts] The—Elizabeth H. Russell. Reprinted from *The House Beautiful*, August, 1925

Old Pike, The—Thomas B. Searight. The Author, Uniontown, Pa., 1894

Old Providence—Issued by the Merchants' National Bank of Providence, Rhode Island

Old Sun Inn, The—William C. Reichel. King & Baird, Philadelphia, 1877

Old Times in Tennessee—Joseph C. Guild. Eastman & Howell, Nashville, Tenn., 1878

Pioneer Roads and Experiences of Travelers—A. B. Hulbert. A. H. Clark Co., Cleveland, 1904

Providence in Colonial Times—Gertrude S. Kimball. Houghton Mifflin Co., Boston, 1912

Random Recollections of Albany—Gorham A. Worth. J. Medole & Son, New York, 1884

Red Brick Tavern, The, Lafayette, Ohio—Carrie M. Zimmerman and Mary Trimble Keifer. The Authors.

Reminiscences of Albany—John J. Hill. J. Medole & Son, New York, 1884

Sauk County [Wisconsin] Inns—H. E. Cole. News Publishing Co., Baraboo, Wis., 1925

Scharf's History of Westchester County, New York. L. E. Preston & Co., Philadelphia, 1886

Souvenir History of Chester, Pennsylvania—H. Graham Ashmead

Stage Coach and Tavern Days—Alice Morse Earle. The Macmillan Co., New York, 1900

State Historical Papers of Iowa, Michigan, Missouri, New Jersey, Wisconsin, Etc.

Story of Dayton [Ohio] The—Charlotte Reeve Conover. The Otterbein Press, Dayton, O., 1917

# Bibliography

TAVERNS AND STAGES OF EARLY WISCONSIN—J. H. A. Lacher. State Historical Society, Madison, Wis., 1915

TAVERNS AND TURNPIKES OF BLANDFORD [MASSACHUSETTS]— Sumner Gilbert Wood. The Author, Blandford, Mass., 1908

TEXAS PIONEER, A—August Santleben. Neal Publishing Co., New York, 1910

TOURIST GUIDE TO CONNECTICUT, A—Issued by the Mattatuck Historical Society, Waterbury, Connecticut

TRAVELS THROUGH THE UNITED STATES IN 1807-8—Edward Augustus Kimball

250TH ANNIVERSARY OF WESTFIELD, MASSACHUSETTS

WASHINGTON HEIGHTS, MANHATTAN, ITS EVENTFUL PAST— Reginald Pelham Bolton. Dyckman Institute, New York, 1904

WAYSIDE INNS ON THE LANCASTER ROAD—Julius F. Sachse. New Era Press, Lancaster, Pa., 1915

Also, articles in the St. Louis *Times-Democrat* on the History of Missouri, by Louis La Coss, 1925; in the Winston-Salem *Union-Republican*, by William S. Pfohl; in the *Western Telegraph*, Washington, Pa., by Earl Forrest, etc.

Article written for the National Science Association of Staten Island, New York, by Ira K. Norris. Article in *Americana*, by Mrs. Frances A. Westervelt.

Article for the New York *Times*, by Perceval Reniers.

# A Record of Inns by Towns and States

* Indicates inns which are still open as hotels, tea-rooms, etc.; † those which have been taken over by clubs or societies but are open on certain conditions to visitors. Occasionally an inn marked * has been replaced by a modern one on the same site. The various names by which a house has been known are given.

## ALABAMA

*Blakely's*
  Burn's (near)
  Fowler's
*Fort Bainbridge*
  Tavern—Cook's
  Walker's (between Fort Bainbridge and Line Creek)
*Fort Dale*
  Inn
  A log cabin inn (near)
*Fort Mitchell*
  Crowell's—Johnston's Hotel
  Royston's Inn (14 miles away)
*Greenville*
  Taylor House
*Near Greenville, on road to Montgomery*
  Cooker's

*Near Greenville, on road to Montgomery*
  Longmyre's
  Mrs. Lucas'
  Macdavid's
  Macmillan's
  Mrs. Mills
  Peeble's
  Price's
*Leighton*
  Inn
*Line Creek*
  Tavern
*Montgomery*
  Bonum House (near)
  First Tavern
  Globe Tavern—Indian Queen
  Mansion House—*Exchange Hotel

[317]

# Early American Inns and Taverns

*Montgomery*
  Montgomery Hotel—La-
    fayette Tavern
  Wood's Tavern (beyond
    Bonum's)

*Murder Creek*
  Tavern
*Pole Cat Springs*
  Inn
*Uchee Bridge*
  Tavern

## ARKANSAS

*Elk Horn*
  Elk Horn Tavern

## CONNECTICUT

*Ashford*
  Perkins Inn
*Berlin*
  Fuller Tavern
*Bethlehem*
  Bellamy's "Racon" Tavern
*Brooklyn*
  Wolfe Tavern
*Canaan*
  Capt. I. Lawrence Tavern
*Centrebrook*
  Williams Tavern (1826)
*Cheshire*
  Beach Tavern
*Clinton*
  Inn
*Danbury*
  Brookfield Tavern
  Taylor Tavern

*Durham*
  Swathel Inn
*East Thompson*
  Jacob's Inn
*Essex*
  Hayden's
*Fairfield*
  Benson Tavern
  Hull Tavern
  Sun Tavern
*Farmington*
  *Elm Tree Inn
*Hartford*
  Bennett's
  Bull's Tavern
  Free Masons' Arms
  Wadsworth Tavern (3
    miles from Hartford)

[318]

# A Record of Inns by Towns and States

*Litchfield*
Grove Catlin's—Mansion House
Hanks Tavern
Phelps' Tavern (1st)
*Phelps House (2nd)
Sheldon Tavern
Red Tavern (formerly at Chestnut Hill, Connecticut)

*Manchester*
Buckland's
Green's
Olcott's
Richard Pitkin's
Woodbridge

*Meriden*
*Ye 1711 Club Inn

*Middletown*
Inn

*Milford*
Clark's Tavern

*New Haven*
Bunch of Grapes
Morse's—Franklin

*New London, Between, and Norwich*
Mme. Knight's Tavern

*Norwalk*
Norwalk Inn

*North Branford*
Oakdale Tavern (1769; near)

*Norwich*
Brown's
Major Durkee's
Hyde's
Lathrop's
Leffingwell's
Peck's
Teel House—
Sign of George Washington (1789)
Waterman's—Huntington's
Witter's

*Old Saybrook*
Pratt or Old Tavern

*Pomfret*
*Ben Grosvenor Inn

*Ridgefield*
Cannon Ball House—
Keeler's Tavern

*Saybrook*
Black Horse Tavern
Uriah & Ann Hayden's
*Ye Old Saybrook Inn

*South Windsor*
Bissell's Tavern
Stoughton's

*Straitsville*
Collins Tavern

*Suffield*
Suffield House

*Thompson*
*Vernon Stiles' Inn

[319]

# Early American Inns and Taverns

*Union City*
Porter's

*Wallingford*
Smith's

*Washington*
Coggswell Tavern

*Waterbury*
Tontine Tavern

*Watertown*
Watertown—Bishops
Tavern (1800)

*Windsor Centre*
Tavern

*Windsor*
*Betsy Kob Tea-Room

*Woodbury*
*Curtis House

*Woodstock*
Arnold's Inn
William Bowen Tavern
(1782)

*Worthington*
Fuller's

## DELAWARE

*Camden*
*Mifflin House

*Canterbury*
Caldwell's Tavern

*Dover*
Biddle Tavern—Capitol
Hotel
Harris Tavern—Steamboat
Hotel
King George—The George
John Rees'—The George
Washington Tavern

*Duck Creek*
Brick Inn (near Smyrna)

*Grubb's Landing*
The Practical Farmer

*Milford*
*Central Hotel

*Naaman's Creek*
*The Robinson House

*Newark*
Newark Hotel
St. Patrick's Inn—*Deer
Park Hotel

*New Castle*
Gilpin's
Old Packet

*Red Lion*
Red Lion

*Smyrna*
Indian Queen

*Wilmington*
Buck Tavern
Cross Keys
Foul Anchor
House That Jack Built—
Bull Frog Tavern

# A Record of Inns by Towns and States

*Wilmington*
    Indian Queen
    Sign of the Ship—Happy
        Retreat

Swan—Gibson House—
    Lynch House
White Hart—Washington
    House

## FLORIDA

*St. Augustine*
    Fatio House

## GEORGIA

*Savannah*
    Tondee's

## ILLINOIS

*Alton*
    *Hunter House
*Belleville*
    *Hotel
*Belvidere*
    American House
    Doty Tavern
*Cairo*
    St. Charles—*The Halli-
        day
*Charleston*
    Charleston House
*Chicago*
    City Hotel—*Sherman
        House
    Dickenson's Tavern
    Green Tree

Lake House
Mansion House
Sauganash
Tremont
Wolfe's
*Decatur*
    Harrell—Claudess—Hanks
        —*St. Nicholas
*Dixon*
    *Nachusa Hotel
*Edwardsville*
    Wabash Hotel
*Galesburgh*
    Gale House
*Garden Prairie*
    Ames Tavern

[321]

ILLINOIS (*Continued*)

*Geneseo*
  *Geneseo House
*Grand-de-Tour*
  *Hotel
*Lebanon*
  Mermaid
*Naperville*
  Tavern (near)
*Newbury*
  Tavern (near)

*Peoria*
  Peoria House
*Princeton*
  Inn
*Rock Island*
  Island City Hotel
*Shawneetown*
  Rawlings House—*2nd
    Rawlings House

## INDIANA

*Akron*
  Strong's—*Hotel
*Cambridge City*
  Tavern
*Center Township*
  Tavern
*Centerville*
  Lashlaey's
  Tavern (west)
*Columbus*
  Jones House—Western
    Hotel
*Dublin*
  Schoolfield's
*Fulton*
  Fulton Inn
*Germantown*
  Tavern
*Greenfield*
  Chapman's
*Indianapolis*
  Tavern

*Laurel*
  Tavern
*Le Gro*
  2 Taverns
*Madison*
  *Arlington
  *Central Hotel
  Honore's Hotel
  *Jefferson—Madison
  Pugh's
  Washington
  Western
  William Tell
*Pierceton*
  Ryerson House
*Queensville*
  Inn
*Richmond*
  Baldwin's
  Buhl's
  Cheeseman's—Vaughan's
  Gilbert's

[322]

# A Record of Inns by Towns and States

*Richmond*
- Harter's
- Jeffries'
- Justice's
- Kibbey's—Paige's
- Lacey's
- Nixon's—Huntington House
- Sign of the Green Tree
- Sloan's
- Starr's—Tremont Hotel
- Vaughn's

*Rochester*
- Central House
- Lawhead's Tavern
- Ralston House

*Sycamore Valley*
- Neal's
- Clawson's (1818; near)

*Terre Haute*
- Tavern

*Wabash*
- Tavern

## IOWA

*Des Moines*
- Campbell's Tavern (near)

*Dubuque*
- Beaubien's
- Bell Tavern
- Dickinson's Temperance Hotel
- *Key City Hotel
- Lorimer—Wales House
- Waples—Julian House—
- *Julian Dubuque Hotel

*Keokuk*
- 2 Taverns

## KANSAS

*Whisky Lake*
- *Inn

## KENTUCKY

*Bardstown*
- *Inn

*Bryantsville*
- Burnt Tavern

[323]

# Early American Inns and Taverns

*Covington*
    Callaghan's (ruins; near)
    Tackett's (near)

*Cynthiana*
    Eagle Tavern

*Elizabethtown*
    At the Sign of the Lion—
        Eagle House—*Smith's
        Hotel
    †Hill House

*Frankfort*
    Golden Eagle
    Cole's Bad Inn (near)
    Daily's Inn

*Harrodsburg*
    *Harrodsburg Inn

*Lexington*
    Brent's
    Sheaf of Wheat
    Wilson's — Postlethwaite's
    —Mrs. Keen's—*Phœ-
    nix Hotel (2nd)

*Louisville*
    Galt House

*Between Louisville and
    Nashville*
    Bell's (ruins)

*Mammoth Cave*
    Mammoth Cave Hotel

*Maysville*
    January's Tavern

*Millersburg*
    Waller's

*Munfordsville*
    Munford Inn

*Olympian Springs*
    Olympian Springs Hotel

*Paducah*
    Doc Thomas' Inn
    Hays' Fox House
    Indian Queen
    St. Francis—Richmond—
        *Southern Hotel

*Paris*
    Tavern

*Shakertown*
    *Shakertown Inn

*Washington*
    Elbert's Tavern

## LOUISIANA

*New Orleans*
    Mme. Fournier's
    Hotel de la Marine—Navy
        Hotel
    Le Veau Qui Tete
    *St. Charles Hotel

    St. Louis Hotel
    Tremoulet

*Opelousas*
    La Combe Hotel (1801)

*St. Francisville*
    Inn

# A Record of Inns by Towns and States

## MAINE

*Bath*
Shepard's Inn
*Durham*
Inn
*Fort Halifax*
Inn
*Freeport*
Old Codman Tavern—
Jameson—Old Codman
*Kennebunk*
Mousam House (1777)
*Kittery*
Bray's Tavern
James Carswell's Tavern

*Machias*
†Burnham Tavern
*Montpelier*
Seth Munson's Tavern
(near)
*Portland*
Inn
*Wells*
Jefford's Tavern (before 1750)
*York*
Pitt Tavern

## MARYLAND

*Annapolis*
Annapolis Coffee House
Blue Bells
*Carvel Hall
City Hotel
*Peggy Stewart Inn
*Baltimore*
Black Bear
Black Horse
Bull's Head
Fountain Inn—Carrollton
Hotel—*Southern Hotel
General Wayne
Golden Horn
Golden Lamb
Hand Tavern
Indian Queen

Kaminsaky's
Larsh's
Maypole
Myers'
Payne's
Rising Sun
Rogers'
Stenson's
Three Tuns
White Swan
Cook's Tavern (near)
Hawes' (near)
Red House (near)
*Bladensburg*
Indian Queen
George Washington

[325]

## MARYLAND (*Continued*)

*Boonesboro*
  Fowler's
  Galexin's
  Slifer's
  Fosnack's (near)
*Claysville*
  Kelley's
*Clear Spring*
  Kershaw's
  Kensel's (near)
*College Park*
  *Rossburg
*Cotocket*
  Gèlzendamer's
  Hagan's (near)
*Cumberland*
  American
  Black's
  Blue Springs
  Edwards'
  Evans'
  Kelso's
  Mahaney's
  Mallingly's
  Mountain City House
  Pennsylvania House
  Plumer's
  Shipley's
  Everstine's (5 miles west)
  Six Miles House (6 miles
    west)
  Clary's (8 miles west)
*Ellicott's Mills*
  Earlocker's

*Flintstone*
  Elbow's
  Huddleson's
  Piper's—Howard's
  Robinson's
*Frederick*
  Stone Tavern (Miller's)
  *Rose Hill Manor
*Frostburg*
  Franklin House
  Highland Hall
*Funkstown*
  Ashton's
  Wate's
*Grantsville*
  Gillis'—Sheers'
  Lehman's—Fuller's—
    Fuller House
  Shultz House
  Steiner's
  Thistle's—Delavain's—
    Deans (2 miles west)
  Haldaman's—Smouse's
    (3½ miles west)
*Green Ridge*
  Collins'
*Hagerstown*
  Wrench's Tavern
  Miller's (near)
  Newcomer's (near)
*Hancock* (near)
  Jacob Brosius
  Widow Downer's—Nico-
    demus House

# A Record of Inns by Towns and States

*Hancock* (near)
Mann's
Norris'

*Havre-de-Grace*
*Lafayette House

*Indian Spring*
David Miller's
Snider's (3 miles west)
Widow Bevan's (4 miles west)
David Barnett's (6 miles west)

*Keyser's Ridge* (near)
Cambridge's—Hunter's—Stoddard's
Fairall's

*West of Keyser's*
Augustine House
Fear's—Bane's—Carlisle's, etc.
Reynolds'—Waller's
Wood's

*Little Meadows*
Endsley's—Thistle's
Tomlinson Tavern

*Martin's Mountain*
Street's
Miller's (near)
Osford's—Hager's
Slifer's

*Middletown*
Riddlemoser's
Tetlow's
McGruder's (near)

*Negro Mountain*
Hobletzell's—Beall's—Street's

*Petersburg*
Bradfield's (near)

*Pine Orchard*
Dehoff's
Goslin's
Brown Stand (4 miles west)
Whalen's (8 miles west)
Warfield's (near)

*Piney Grove*
Fairall's—Cade's—Cross', etc.
Wagoner's—Bell's—Cade's (west of)

*Polish Mountain*
Fletcher's

*Poplar Springs*
Dorsie's
McPherson's (near)

*Pratt's Hollow*
Samuel Hamilton's
McGruder's

*Princess Anne*
*Washington Hotel

*Sand Springs*
Ward's—Welsh's—Sutton's—Conrod's
Beall's (west of)
Cheney's—Conrod's
Recknor's (west of)

[327]

# Early American Inns and Taverns

*Sideling Hill*
    Widow Ashkettle's (near)
*Snib Hollow*
    John Alder's
    Widow Turnbull's
*South Mountain*
    Miller's

Fowler's—Harris' (near)
Zettle's (near)
*Town Hill*
    Bevan's—Luman's
    Dennis Hobletzell's—
        Cessna's

## MASSACHUSETTS

*Acushnet*
    Old Tavern
    Jabez Taber Tavern
        (before 1710)
*Andover*
    Abbott's
*Amherst*
    Boltwood's—Amherst Ho-
        tel—*Amherst Inn (on
        site)
*Arlington*
    Cooper Tavern
    John Nash's (1785)
*Ashley*
    Wyman's
*Barnstable*
    *Barnstable Inn
*Bedford*
    David Reed Tavern
        (1727)
*Beverly Ferry*
    Old Ferry Tavern
*Billerica*
    4 old Taverns

*Blandford*
    Job Almy's
    Robert Black's—Col. Ab-
        ner Pease's
    Blair's
    Boies'
    John Gibbs'
    Luke Hall's
    Hatch's—Solomon Noble's
    Deacon John Knox's
    Parks'
    Pease's—Ashmun's—Scott's
        —Lloyd's—Mansion
        House—Sage's New
        Hotel
    Porter's
    Capt. Sloper's
*Blandford (north part)*
    Baird's — Bartholomew's
    Harroun — Sinnett's —
        Bruce Tavern
    Norton and Ely's
    Taggart's

# A Record of Inns by Towns and States

*Boston*
  Blue Anchor
  British Coffee House
  Bunch of Grapes
  Castle Inn
  Cole's—Hancock's (1634)
  Eagle
  Eastern Stage House
  Exchange House
  George, or St. George
  Green Dragon
  Hudson's (1640)
  King's Arms—State Arms
  Lafayette Hotel (1824)—
    Brigham Hotel
  Lamb (The) (1746)—
    Adams House on site
  Liberty Tree
  Oliver Cromwell's Head
    (1760)
  Orange Tree
  Pollard's
  Province House Inn
  Royal Exchange
  Sign of the New York
    Stage
  Wallace's
  Whig Tavern
  Wolfe Tavern

*Boston, near (Charles River Bridge)*
  Robbins' Tavern

*Brookfield*
  Ayers'

*Brookfield Inn
  Rice's

*Brookline*
  Punch Bowl

*Burlington*
  Winn's Three Spread
    Eagles

*Cambridge*
  Blue Anchor (1652)
  Porter's

*Charlestown*
  The Three Cranes

*Chelmsford*
  Manning Tavern

*Concord*
  Buss's—Willard's
  *Colonial Inn
  *Wright House

*Danvers*
  Bell's
  Berry Tavern
  Browne's Hall
  Deacon Gideon Putnam's

*Dedham*
  Lieutenant Joshua Fisher's
    (1658)—Ames'

*Deerfield*
  Frary House

*Dorchester*
  Robinson's

*Douglas*
  Moses Hill's (1793)

[329]

# Early American Inns and Taverns

*Duxbury*
 Collins'
 Southworth's
 Sprague's

*East Brookfield*
 Thomas Ball's
 Waite's

*Eastham*
 Captain Collings'

*Easton*
 Oldest House in Town

*Essex*
 Half Way House

*Fairhaven* (formerly *Ox-
 ford*)
 Sam Campbell's
 Elliott Tavern (1714)
 Marcy's Tavern (1730)
 Moore's Tavern
 Pratte Tavern
 Red Tavern (1760)
 South Tavern

*Fitchburg*
 Upton's

*Florence*
 Warner Tavern

*Gloucester*
 Ellery House

*Greenfield*
 Wells'

*Groton*
 Emerson's

 Keep's Ordinary—Central
 House—*Groton Inn
 Richardson's

*Hadley*
 White Horse

*Haverhill*
 Bliss Tavern—Coolidge's

*Head of Westport*
 Parker's Tavern
 Tavern

*Hingham*
 †Old Ordinary

*Ipswich*
 Bartholomew's
 Belcher's
 Compton's
 Leimpkins'
 Payne's
 Perkins'
 Peters'
 Ringe's
 Roberts'
 Ross's
 Stacey's
 Stewart's
 Treadwell's
 Wade's
 Whipple's (1693)
 White Horse—Deacon
 Moses Pengryn's
 *Ye Olde Burnham Inn

*Lancaster*
 Houghton's
 Old Brick Inn

# A Record of Inns by Towns and States

*Lancaster*
  White's
  Willard's (1690)
*Lexington*
  †Buckman Tavern
  †Munroe Tavern
*Littleton*
  Lawrence Tavern
*Lynn*
  The Anchor
*Marblehead*
  Old Tavern
*Marlboro*
  Black Horse
  *Williams Tavern—Gates House—Williams Tavern
*Marthas Vineyard*
  2 Taverns
*Medford*
  Admiral Vernon
  Fountain Inn
  Mead's
  Royal Oak—Porter Tavern
  Uncle Willis' Tavern
*Milton*
  Wilde Tavern (1770)
*New Bedford*
  Eagle Tavern
  George East Tavern (1780)
  Golden Bell
  Loudon's

  Nelson's Hotel (before 1808)
  Parker's
  The Swan (1780)
*Newbury (Newburyport)*
  Brewster's
  Calder's
  Coffyn's
  Dexter House
  *Garrison House (1775)
  General Wolfe
  Greenleaf's
  Lambert's
  Lunt's
  †Marsh's Blue Anchor
  Masons' Arms—Harrod's
  Plumer's
  Poore's (1798)
  Prescott's—Conkey Tavern (1758)
  Putnam's—Illsley's
  Richardson's
  Sewall's
  Sign of the American Eagle
  Sun Hotel
  Tracey House—Sun Hotel
  Washington House
  *Wolfe Tavern (1800)
*North Bloomfield*
  Benton's
*Northborough*
  Capt. James Eager's
  Martin's

*Northfield*
  Doolittle's
  Shelton's
*North Granby*
  Case's
*North Wilbraham*
  Washington Inn
*Oxford* (now *Fairhaven,*
  q. v.)
*Palmer*
  Scott's
*Paxton*
  Paxton Inn
*Pelham*
  Conkey's
*Plymouth*
  Bradford's Tavern (1703)
  Howland's
  Plymouth House (1825:
    burned)
*Plymouth Turnpike (on)*
  Pembroke Tavern (1800)
*Prescott*
  Conkey Tavern (1758)
*Provincetown*
  *Red Inn
*Reading*
  Old Tavern on Square
  Parker Tavern
*Roxbury*
  Greyhound Tavern
*Russell*
  East Part Tavern

*Salem*
  Black Horse
  Washington (1812)
*Shirley*
  Sawtell's
*Shrewsbury*
  Balch Tavern
  Baldwin's
  Farrar's—Pease's
  Harrington Tavern
  Old Arcade
*South Hadley*
  *College Inn
*South Lancaster*
  Bowers' Inn
*Smith's Mills*
  Tavern
*Spencer*
  Jenks'
*Springfield*
  Parsons'
*Sudbury*
  Red Horse—*Wayside
    Inn
*Sutton*
  Woodbury's
*Tewksbury*
  Subscribers' Hotel
*Truro*
  *Truro Hotel
*Upper Beverly*
  Old Bakers' Tavern
*Wareham*
  Fearing's

# A Record of Inns by Towns and States

*Wayland*
  Pequod Inn—Wayland
    Inn
*Westborough*
  Amsden Gale Tavern
  The Blue Anchor
  Brigham's—Westborough
    Hotel
  Samuel Forbush Inn
*West Brookfield*
  *West Brookfield Inn
*Westfield*
  Cook's Tavern
  Fowler Tavern
  Goodenough's—Morgan's
  Holcomb House
  Gad Palmer's
  Washington's Tavern
*West Newbury*
  Boynton's
  Pearson's

  Sawyer's
*Weston*
  Golden Ball (1751)
  Joel Smith's—Flagg's
*Winchester*
  Black Horse
*Woburn*
  Winn House
*Woodville*
  Wood's—Coolidge Tavern
*Worcester*
  Bay State House
  Central Hotel (1722)
  Exchange—United States
    Arms—Sykes' Coffee
    House — Sykes' Stage
    House—Thomas' Ex-
    change Coffee House—
    Thomas' Temperance
    Exchange

# MICHIGAN

*Cambridge Junction*
  †Walker Tavern
  *New Brick Tavern
*Dearborn*
  Tenyat's
*Detroit*
  American Exchange
  Black Horse Tavern
  Botsford—Jennings—
    *Martindale House

  Eagle Tavern
  Half Way House (near)
  Johnson's
  Lander House
  Mansion House
  Michigan Exchange
  National (1836)—Rus-
    sell—Pontchartrain
  Richard Smyth's (1805)
  Steamboat Hotel

# Early American Inns and Taverns

## MICHIGAN (*Continued*)

*Detroit*
Wales Hotel
*Galesburg*
Brick Hotel
*Groveland*
Half Way House
*Jackson*
Howell House
Old Stage House
Temperance Hotel
Union Hall
*Lansing*
Log Cabin Tavern
Franklin Hudson House
Lansing House
Michigan House
National

*Nankin*
Adams Tavern
Cahoon's Hotel
*Perrinsville*
3 Taverns
*Pine Run*
McLean's
*Saline*
Keats'
*Schwarzburg*
Tavern
*Tekonsha*
Heminway's
*White Pigeon*
Hotel
*Ypsilanti*
Whitmore's Tavern

## MINNESOTA

*St. Paul*
Barlow House
Rice's Hotel
*Stillwater*
Chicago—Dalles House

Sawyer House
*Taylor's Falls*
Taverns

## MISSOURI

*Arrow Rock*
*†Arrow Rock Tavern
*Boone Lick* (on road)
Weston's
*Bowling Green*
Mann's

*Doniphan*
Tavern
*Falls of the Platte*
Martin's
*Gallatin*
Stolling's

[334]

# A Record of Inns by Towns and States

*Greenville*
　　Bedwell's Tavern

*Jefferson City*
　　McCarty's Hotel

*Kansas City*
　　Western—American—
　　　Gillie House

*Loutre Lick*
　　Van Bibber's Tavern

*Medill*
　　Ensign's Tavern

*Myrtle*
　　Bellissime's

*New Madrid*
　　*New Madrid Hotel

*Perryville*
　　White Tavern

*St. Charles*
　　Emmons'
　　Tavern
　　Little French Inn (op-
　　　posite)

*St. Louis*
　　Charless' Boarding House
　　Missouri Tavern
　　Planters' Hotel

*Versailles*
　　*Hotel

## NEW HAMPSHIRE

*Boscawen*
　　Coich's
　　Corser's
　　Fowler's
　　Little's
　　Pearson's

*Charlestown*
　　Walker's

*Concord*
　　Stickney (1794)

*Dexter*
　　*Folsom Tavern

*Dorset*
　　Cephas Kent Tavern

*Dover*
　　Dover Hotel

*Dunbarton*
　　Clifford's

*Fitzwilliam*
　　Goldsmith's—Fitzwilliam
　　　Tavern

*Hillsboro*
　　†Pierce Inn

*Hopkinton*
　　Perkins Inn (1786)

*Jaffray*
　　Cutler's (1802)

*Keene*
　　Chandler's—Holland's
　　Dunbar's—*Crystal Cafe

[335]

# Early American Inns and Taverns

*Keene*
  Lyon and the Brazen Ball
    —Phœnix Hotel—
    *Cheshire Hotel
  Ralston's
  Richardson's
  Shirtleff's—Harrington
    Coffee House—
    *Eagle Hotel
  Wyman Tavern

*Kittery*
  Rice's

*Lyme*
  *Alden Tavern

*Newton*
  Eagle

*Pembroke (Suncook)*
  *Kimball Tavern
*Penacook*
  Penacook House—*Old
    Bonney Tavern
*Portsmouth*
  Bell—Purcell House
  Earl of Halifax—William
    Pitt—Stavers Inn
  *Rockingham Hotel, 2d
*Tarleton Lake*
  Tarleton Tavern (1774)
*Walpole*
  Carpenter's
  Craft's
*West Keene*
  Sawyer Tavern

## NEW JERSEY

*Alloway*
  *The Alloway
*Ardena*
  Our House
*Barnsboro*
  John Ford's
*Basking Ridge*
  Larzelaer's (near)
  White's
*Bergen*
  Half Way House
  Sign of the White Star
*Bergen Point*
  Van Tile's

*Blairstown*
  Blairstown Hotel

*Bordentown*
  Kester's

*Bound Brook*
  At the Sign of the Buck
  Black Horse
  Bull's Head
  Harris Tavern — Middle-
    brook Hotel — Bound
    Brook Tavern
  Stanbury's
  Tunison's

# A Record of Inns by Towns and States

Bridgeton (*Parrin's Bridge*)
    Hotel
Burlington
    Blue Anchor
Camden (*Cooper's Ferry*)
    Cooper's
    Fish House (near)
Chapel Hill
    Mount's
Chester
    *Chester Hotel
Chew's (*Chew's Landing*)
    John Cadd's
Clarksburg
    Old Willow Tree—
        Temperance House
Clinton
    Bonnell's
Deerfield
    Inn
Elizabeth (*Elizabethtown*)
    Cornelisse's
    Indian Queen
    Sign of the Roebuck (near)
Englishtown
    *Village Inn
Everettstown
    Tavern
Flemington
    Fleming's Castle
    Larison's Corners Inn
        (near)
    Inn at Unionville (near)

Fort Lee
    Burdett's
Franklinville
    George Cake's
Freehold
    Craig's Inn
    Monmouth House
    Union—Belmont House
Gloucester
    Hugg's
Greenwich
    Inn
Hackensack
    Ackerman's
    Albany Stage Coach House
        —*Washington Man-
        sion House
    Archibald Campbell's
    Hackensack House
    Hackensack Tavern
    Mrs. Watson's
    Douw's Tavern (near)
Hackettstown
    American House
    Leonard's Inn
    *Warren House
    Windsor Hotel—Wash-
        ington House
Haddonfield
    Creighton Tavern
    †The Indian Chief
Hancock's Bridge
    Hancock House (1734)

# Early American Inns and Taverns

*Harrington*
 Demarest's
*Hoboken*
 King's Arms
*Hohokus (Hopperstown)*
 Hopper's
*Hope*
 Inn
*Johnson*
 Log Gaol Tavern
*Jutland*
 Brick Tavern (near)
*Kingston*
 Van Tilburgh's
 Withington's—*Union
 Line Hotel
*Lambertville*
 Coryel's
*Lower Suankum*
 Paul Sears'
*Madison*
 Brant's Inn
 *Bottle Hill Inn
*Mannington Township*
 Deer Park Inn
*Medford*
 *Indian Chief
*Morristown*
 Arnold's—Freeman's—
 Hayden's
 Ford's
 Norris'—Dickenson's
*Mt. Ephraim*
 Edward Middleton's Inn

*Mount Holly*
 Arcade Hotel
 *Mills Street Hotel
*Moorestown*
 Old Inn
*Newark*
 Gifford's
 Major Samuel Sayre's
 Johnson Tuttle's
*New Brunswick*
 Ann Balding's
 Bellona
 Indian Queen—Bell—
 Parkway
 Red Lion
 Steamboat Hotel
 White Hart—White Hall
*Newton*
 Bassett's
 *Cochran House
 Cross Keys—Hoppaugh's
 —Ward House
 Dowling House
*North Plainfield*
 Washington Headquarters
 Inn
*Oldman's Township*
 Jericho Tavern
 Pedricktown Tavern
 Pennsville Tavern
 Pine Tavern
 Quinton Tavern
*Orange*
 Mumm's

# A Record of Inns by Towns and States

*Paterson*
  Godwin's
*Perryville*
  *Brick Tavern
*Perth Amboy*
  Crown Inn—*Packer House
  Brighton Hotel—*The Westminster
*Piscatrway*
  Tavern
*Pittstown*
  Old Century Inn—*New Century Inn
*Princeton*
  *Nassau Inn
  Tavern
*Repaupo*
  Sign of the Seven Stars
*Saddle River*
  Van Houten's
*Salem*
  *Green's
  Hall's (1691)
*Schooley's Mountain*
  4 Hotels
*Sharpstown*
  Inn
*Somerville*
  Wood's
*South Woodstown*
  Tavern

*Swedesboro*
  *Swedesboro Hotel
*Trap, The*
  Thompson's Tavern
*Trenton*
  Bispham's
  Legioner—Black Horse
  Sign of the Green Tree
*Union*
  Meeker Inn
*Upper Pittsgrove*
  Pole Tavern
*Washington*
  Windsor Tavern—Washington House—*Windsor Hotel
*Westville*
  Sign of the Buck— *Toppin Inn
*Woodbridge*
  Inn
*Woodbury*
  Death of the Fox
  Seven Stars Hotel
  Jesse Smith's—*Caul's Hotel
*Woodsboro*
  Pole Tavern
  *Washington House
  *Woodsboro House
*Woodstown*
  Niggers' Glory

# Early American Inns and Taverns

## NEW YORK

*Albany*
American House
Bement's
City Hotel
Columbia
Congress Hall
Eagle House
Exchange
Fifth Ward
Fort Orange
Franklin
Lafayette
Lewis' Tavern
Mansion House
National
Northern
Temperance
Tontine Coffee House
Western

*Amsterdam*
Pride's—*Conrad Hotel

*Auburn*
Inn
Bodine's (near)

*Avon*
Inn

*Ballston Spa*
Aldrich's
Bromeling's
Douglas's
McMaster's

*Batavia*
Luke's

Russell's

*Beckers' Corners*
Inn

*Berne*
Corporation Inn

*Bloomfield*
Hall's

*Blue Stores*
Blue Tavern

*Caledonia (Big Springs)*
Hotel
Tavern

*Canandaigua*
Blossom's

*Carmel*
Conkling's (near)
Luddington's
McLean's
Washburne's
Weeks'

*Cayuga*
Col. Goodwin's (near)
Harris'

*Chesterville*
Beardsley's
Lapaugh's
Leuvens'
Pierce's
Smith's

*Clarkesville*
Bogardus'
Bright's
Cheseboro's
Houck's

[340]

# A Record of Inns by Towns and States

*Clarkesville*
  Ingraham's
  Jenkins'
*Claverack*
  Claverack Inn
*Coldspring Landing*
  Peake's
*Continental Village*
  Rogers'
*Cortland*
  *Cortland House
  Dusenberry's (near)
  Eagle—*Messenger Hotel
*Dover*
  Inn
*East Berne (Werner's Mills)*
  Stafford's
*Eastchester*
  Crawford's Inn
  Romy Guion's
*Elmsford*
  Storms'—Ledger House
*Fishkill*
  Mme. Egremont's
  Griffin's (near)
*Four Corners (near Elmsford)*
  Hotel Flanagan
*Geneva*
  Powell's
*Hartford*
  Hosmer's

*Haviland's Corners*
  Tavern
*Hudson*
  Hudson Inn
  King of Prussia
  Kellogg's—Worth House
*Hurd's Corners*
  Tavern
*Hurstville*
  Hagadorn's
*Johnstown*
  †Black Horse Tavern—
    Jimmie Burke's Place
  Black Horse 2d (near)
  Fon Claire's—Potter's
  Tice's
  Union Hall
  Yellow Tavern
  Yost's—Sir William
*Kinderhook*
  Benedict Arnold Inn
  Major Hoes'—*The Grey Swan
  Hudson's
  *Kinderhook Hotel (2d)
  Mansion House
  Quackenbos' (near)
  Stage Coach Inn
  Van Buren Inn
*Le Roy*
  Auntie Wemple's—Eagle House
  Austin's

[341]

# Early American Inns and Taverns

Le Roy
    Chamberlain's
    Fort Hill Tavern (near)
    Ganson's
    Lent's
    Robertson's—Globe and
        Eagle—*Wiss House
    Wilbur's (near)
Lewiston
    *Frontier House
    Huston's
    Kellogg's
Little Falls
    Carr's
    Spraker's (west)
Mamaroneck
    *Lawrence Inn
Manlius Square
    Manlius'
Milltown
    White's
Newburgh
    Albertson's
    Lafayette's Headquarters
        Inn
    Weigand's
New Paltz
    Inn—†Hasbrouck Me-
        morial House
New Rochelle
    Besley's
New York City
    Astor House
    Black Horse No. 1

Black Horse No. 2—Mc-
    Gown's—Red House
Black Horse No. 3
Blue Bell (two)
Brannan's Road House
Broadway Hotel
Buck's Horn
Bull's Head No. 1
Bull's Head No. 2
Bunker Hotel
Burns' Coffee House—
    Province Arms — City
    Arms—Cape's Tavern
    —City Hotel
Cato's
City Tavern
*Claremont
Cook's
Creiger's—Martin—Burns'
    Coffee House (?)—
    Province Arms (?)—
    Atlantic Gardens
Cross Keys
Dove Tavern
Drover's
Giraerdy's or Gerritson's—
    Staat's Herberg
Golden Hill Inn
Greenwich Hotel (1811)
Half Way House
Hoyatt's or Hyatt's—Cox's
    Inn
Inn at 126th Street
King's Arms

# A Record of Inns by Towns and States

*New York City*
Kingsbridge Hotel
La Chair's Tavern
Madison Cottage
Mansion House
Martling's
Merchants' Coffee House
—Tontine Coffee House
Montagne's
Morris'—White House
Myer's Tavern
Nassau Street Tavern
Old Tom's—*Ye Olde
Chop House (2d)
Post Inn
Queen's Head—*Fraunces'
Tavern
Stone Bridge Tavern
Tammany Hall
United States Hotel
(1823)
Water Street "House of
Entertainment"
Wolfert Webber's
Ye Olde Chop House
(1st)
*North Castle*
Miller's Tavern
*Northampton*
*Fish House (1805)
*North Tonawanda*
Log Cabin Tavern
*Onondaga (Hollow)*
Tyler's

*Patterson*
Crosby's
David's
Haviland's
*Pavilion*
Inn
*Pawlins'*
Log House Tavern
*Poughkeepsie*
Farmers'
Hendrickson's—Forbes—
*Nelson Hotel
Hinckley's
Rider's—Baldwin's—Cun-
ningham's — Myer's —
Poughkeepsie House —
*Pomfret House
*Quality Hill*
Webb's
*Red Hook*
*Hotel
*Rhinebeck*
*Beekman Arms
Tammany Hall—The
Bowery
Thomas's
*Rhinecliff*
Kip Tavern
*Rye*
Byam River Tavern
†Square House
Straing's
Van Sicklen's

*Scarsdale*
 †Wayside Inn
*Schenectady*
 Beale's
 Givens'
 Robert Clench's
 Douw's (near)
 Humphrey's
 Truax's
*Schodack Centre*
 *Inn
*Skaneateles*
 Andrews'
*Sodom*
 Inn
*Somers*
 *Elephant
 Thorn's
*South Berne*
 McKinley's
*South Bethlehem*
 Elishana Janes' Tavern
*Stoneridge*
 Sally Tock's
*Sullivan*
 Streethar's
*Syracuse*
 Cossett's—Syracuse House

*Utica*
 Trowbridge's
*Vernon*
 Stuart's
*Warwick*
 Baird's Tavern
*Watervliet*
 Kloet's
*Westmoreland*
 Mrs. Cary's
 Laird's
*West Point*
 *West Point Inn
*West Troy Road*
 Pye's
*White Plains*
 Hatfield's
 Oakley's No. 1
 Oakley's No. 2—Carlyon
 Arms
*Yonkers*
 *Abbey Inn
 Arlington Inn
 *Getty House
 Park Hill Inn
 *Square Hotel

## LONG ISLAND, NEW YORK

*Coram*
 Goldsmith's—Temperance
 House

 Inn
*Greenport*
 *Clark House

# A Record of Inns by Towns and States

*Greenport*
Half Way House (on Jamaica Road)

*Hampton Bays*
*Canoe Place Inn (on old site)

*Hollis*
Goetz's

*Huntington*
Rachel Chichester's Tavern (Mother Chick's)

*Mattituck*
*Mattituck House

*Middle Islam*
Two Taverns

*Setauket*
Old Roe Tavern

## STATEN ISLAND, NEW YORK

*Bennett's*
Bloomingview

*Bull's Head*
Bull's Head

*Castleton Corners*
Bodine's

*Fort Wadsworth*
Cliff's (near)

*New Dorp*
Black Horse
Fountain House
Rose and Crown

*Port Richmond*
Port Richmond Hotel—Decker House
Steamboat Hotel

*Princess Bay*
Purdy's Hotel
Red Horse Inn

*Richmond*
Cucklestone Inn

*Rossville*
Blazing Star—Le Vaud's Hotel—O'Neill's

*Sailors' Snug Harbor*
Stone Jug

*St. George*
King's Inn—Pavilion Hotel

*Stapleton*
Planters' Hotel

*Tompkinsville*
Nautilus Hall
Union Garden

*Tottenville*
Ferry Tavern
Union Hotel

*West Brighton*
Swan

[345]

# Early American Inns and Taverns

## NORTH CAROLINA

*Barclaysville*
  Inn

*Danbury*
  *McCauless Hotel

*Edenton*
  Hornblow's Tavern—
    *The Bay View Hotel

*Hertford*
  The Eagle

*Hillsboro*
  Occoneechee Hotel—Cor-
    binton Inn—*Colonial
    Hotel

*Raleigh*
  Lane's
  *Peter Casso's Inn

*Southport*
  *Stuart House

*Winston-Salem*
  *Salem Tavern

## OHIO

*Bridgeport*
  Chambers'
  Cusic—Neal's
  McCaffrey's (near)
  McMahon's (near)
  Rhodes' (near)
  Woodman House (near)

*Cambridge*
  Brown's
  Bute's
  Cook's
  Ferguson's
  Grimes'
  Hershing's
  Hutchinson's
  Metcalf's
  Moore's
  Needham's
  Pollard's
  Tingle's

*West of Cambridge*
  Carran's
  Dixon's
  Grumore's
  Laird's
  Leeper's
  Lewis'
  McDonald's
  Scinefrank's
  Sutton's

*Champaign County*
  O.K. House

*Chillicothe*
  General Wayne
  Green Tree

*Cincinnati*
  Avery's

*Cleveland*
  Carter's
  Doan's

[346]

# A Record of Inns by Towns and States

OHIO (*Continued*)

*Cleveland*
Franklin House

*Columbus*
Neal House

*Dayton*
McCullom's
†Newcom Tavern

*Elizabethtown* (near)
Samuel Smith's
Craylor's
Widow Drake's

*Fairview*
Bradshaw's
Gleaves'
Armstrong's (near)
Ferrell's (near)
Taylor's (near)

*Fultonham*
Fulton Inn

*Hendrysburg*
*Pioneer Tavern

*Lafayette*
*Red Brick Tavern

*Lebanon*
Inn

*Middletown*
Hays'
Thompson's
Briggs' (near)
Speer's (near)

*Morristown*
Bynum's
Lippincott's

Hoover's (near)
Taylor's (near)

*Mount Vernon*
Butler's Tavern

*Muskingum County*
McCloud's
McKinney's
Wilson's

*Newark*
Tavern—Franklin House

*Norwich*
Suisabaugh's

*Painesville*
Rider Tavern — West
Painesville Hotel—
*Randell Tavern

*St. Clairsville* (near)
Chamberlain's
Hoover's
Neiswanger's

*Sandusky*
Hotel

*Springfield*
Buena Vista Tavern

*Upper Sandusky*
Log Cabin tavern

*Washington*
Beymer's
Black Horse
Colley's

*West of Washington*
Davis'
Griffith's
McCuen's

[347]

# Early American Inns and Taverns

### West of Washington
McMurry's
Nice's
John Shaw's
James Smith's
Slater's
Waterman's
Widow Slain's

### Xenia
Collier's
Log Tavern (near)

### Zanesville
Blue Lion (near)
*Headley's Tavern
McNutt's (near)
McIntyre's
The Sign of the Orange
    Tree
Tavern (5 miles west)
Probasco's (10 miles from
    Zanesville)
Tavern (5 miles south)

## PENNSYLVANIA

### Ambler
*Blue Bell Inn (near)

### Ardmore
Red Lion

### Barren Hill
Lafayette

### Baumstown
*Red Lion

### Beallsville
Bennington's—Gutter's
Greenfield's
Three Keys—Cluggage's
    —Denison's
Miller's—Chambers'—
    Demore's

### Berwyn
Peggy Dane's
Spring House

### Bethayres
Lady Washington

### Bethlehem
Crown Inn
Golden Eagle—*The
    Bethlehem Hotel (on
    site)
Inn for Indians
*The Sun Inn

### Birdsboro
Mansion House

### Braddock's Grove
Shaw's

### Braddock's Run
Risler's

### Bridgeport
Arnold's
Bar—Kimber House
Riley House

# A Record of Inns by Towns and States

*Broad Axe*
  *Broad Axe Inn
  Split Crow
  *Three Tuns (near)

*Brownsville*
  Beckley's
  Brasher House
  Hezlof's (1797)—Workman House
  Reynolds—Marshal House—Petroleum House

*Buckingham*
  *General Greene

*Centre Square*
  *The Wagon Inn

*Centreville*
  Constitution
  Lashley's
  Miller's—Riggle's—Dutton's
  Railley's—Welsh's (near)
  Riggle's—Colley's—Whitsall's, etc.
  John Rogers'—Bracken's—Jeffrey's

*Chad's Ford*
  *Battlefield Inn

*Chalk Hill*
  Downer's—Rush's—Shipley's—Olivine's

*Near Chalk Hill*
  McClean's—Rush's—Hadden's, etc.

Price's
Snyder's

*Chester*
  Blue Anchor—Hope's Anchor—White Swan
  Blue Bell
  Boar's Head
  Pennell's Tavern
  Stacey House
  Steamboat Hotel
  Pennsylvania Arms—*Washington Hotel

*Clay*
  Clay Hotel

*Claysville*
  Black Horse
  Bazil Brown's
  Bell's
  Callahan's
  Conkling's
  Dennison's
  McIlree's
  Purviance's
  Walker's
  Watkins'

*Coatesville*
  The Prussian Eagle—Speakman House

*Collegeville*
  General Wayne
  Washington (near)

[349]

# Early American Inns and Taverns

*Compass*
Inn

*Concordville*
Pineapple Inn

*Coon Island*
Canodes'—Brotherton's

*Near Coon Island*
Alexander's
American Eagle (1796)
Mrs. Sarah Beck's
Carr's—Gilfillan's
Isaac Jones'
Knode's
Lawson's
Widow Rhodes'—Gilfillan's
Rogers'—Jones
Valentine's
John White's

*Daylesford*
Blue Ball

*Douglasville*
Shirley Hotel

*Downington*
Downing's Stage
General Washington
Half Way House (near)
Swan (near)

*Doylestown*
Cross Keys
*Fountain Inn
Green Tree
The Ship

*Dublin*
Schoolfield's

*Dunk's Ferry*
Inn

*East Hanover Township*
Adam Harper's (1st and 2d)

*Easton*
*Barnet House
Green Tree Inn—*Franklin House
Kaeshlein House
Lefebvre Tavern (6 miles from)
Jacob Opp's Tavern
Swan—*Stirling
Uhler's Hotel
Vernon Ferry House
White's Hotel

*Edgmont Township*
*The Drove
President Tavern

*Elizabethtown*
The Bear

*Elm Grove*
Blackburn's
Samuel Carter's
Mrs. Goodman's

*Erdenheim*
The Wheel Pump (1779)

*Erie*
Buehler House
†Dickson House

[350]

# A Record of Inns by Towns and States

*Erie*
　*Eagle House
　Erie Hotel
　Half Way House (near)
　Presque Isle Tavern
　Rufus Reed's
　Ryan's—Taggart's
　*Weigerville Hotel
　Willis House (near)

*Esterly*
　*Black Bear Inn

*Fairview*
　*Fairview House

*Fayette Springs*
　Fayette Springs Hotel

*Flourtown*
　Black Horse
　*Wagon and Horse

*Fortside*
　Blue Tavern—*Fortside Inn (on site)

*Fort Loudon and Chambersburg Road, On*
　Bratton Hotel (near St. Thomas)
　Gillan Hotel
　Old Hotel (east of St. Thomas)
　White House
　Bart Zeiger's Hotel

*Frankford (Philadelphia)*
　Cross Keys—Mrs. Rice's
　General Pike

Golden Fleece—*Park Hotel
Jolly Post Boy
Robin Hood—Cedar Hill Hotel
Seven Stars—Lewis Hotel
Sign of St. George and the Dragon—Sign of the White Horse—Sign of the Bear—Sign of the Buck
Sorrel Horse (near)
Sun Tavern—Ale House
Wheat Sheaf (near)

*Gallagherville*
　Tavern

*Gap (The)*
　Clemson's Tavern—Continental
　Gap Hotel
　Mansion House
　Penn's Inn (near)

*Gardenville*
　Sign of the Plow

*Geiger's Mills*
　The Plow
　The Running Pump (near)

*Germantown (Philadelphia)*
　Green Tree—Widow McKinnett's—The Hornet
　Washington
　(And many others whose names are now forgotten)

[351]

## Pennsylvania (*Continued*)

*Girard*
  *Martin House

*Glassly*
  Stage Tavern

*Greenland*
  Tavern

*Gwynedd*
  *William Penn House

*Gulph*
  Bird in the Hand

*Hamburg*
  *American House
  *Washington House

*Hand's Pass*
  Cross Keys

*Hanover*
  McAllister's

*Harleyville*
  The Stag

*Hatboro*
  Crooked Billet

*Haverford*
  Old Buck

*Hillsboro*
  Beck's—Ringland's—
    Railly's, etc.
  Zeph Riggle's
  Wilson's—Phelps'—
    Powell's
  Youman's

*West of Hillsboro*
  Harting's
  Hughes—Upland House
  Miller's

*Plymire's*
*Ward's*

*Holmesburg*
  Green Tree

*Inheritance*
  Cross Keys (1754)

*Intercourse*
  At the Hat
  Duke of Connaught (near)
  Red Lion

*Irwinna*
  *Riverside Inn

*Jeffersonville*
  *Jeffersonville Inn
  The Trooper (near)

*Jenkintown*
  Barley Sheaf — American
    Eagle—Cottman House
  The Ivy (1682)

*Jockey Hollow*
  Brown's
  Probasco's
  Van Sickles'
  Wyatt's

*Keyser's Ridge*
  (west of)
    Auld's—Beckley's
    Brown's
    Reynold's
    Wilson's Black Horse

*King of Prussia*
  *King of Prussia

*Knauer's*
  Furlow's Hotel

# A Record of Inns by Towns and States

*Kutztown*
  Black Bear—*Hotel
     Eagle
  *Kemp House
*Lancaster*
  Balsamen Inn
  *Canestoga Inn
  Cross Keys
  Fountain Inn
  Globe—*Pennsylvania
  Grape—Michael's
  Hen and Chickens
  Hickory Tree
  Lamb Inn
  Manor House
  Miller's
  Pennsylvania State Arms
  Pitt Tavern
  Postlethwaite's
  Ship
  Shober's
  *Sign of the Wagon
  *Sorrel Horse
  Swan—Golden Swan—
     White Swan
*Laurel Hill*
  Cottage Tavern
  Slack's
*Leamon Place*
  Plow and Anchor—*Hotel
*Lebanon*
  *American House
  *Buck Hotel

*Lima*
  *Black Horse
*Lime Kiln*
  Oley Line Hotel
*Maidencreek*
  Half Way House
*Malden*
  Malden Tavern
*McConnellsburg*
  *Fulton House
*Media*
  Anvil
*Menataway*
  Pleasantville Hotel
*Mercersburg*
  Fegley's (near)
  *Mansion House
  *Washington Inn
*Merion Township*
  Flag
  *General Wayne Inn
  Green Tree
*Middletown Township*
  Polly Inn (1737)
*Monroe*
  Dennison's—Fry's
  General Wayne — Deford
     House
  McMaster's—Hair's
  Monroe House
  Morris' (near)
  Shipley House
  Skiles'

[353]

# Early American Inns and Taverns

*Monroe Springs*
   McKinney's
*Montgomery Square*
   *Inn
   *Spring House (near)
*Morgantown*
   *Morgantown Inn
*Morrisville*
   Robert Morris Inn
*Mount Augusta*
   Thos. Brownfield's
   Bryant's—Old Mc-
      Cullough Stand
   Bush House or Three
      Cabins
   Collier's
   Ewing's—Rush's
   Frazer's
   Inks House
   McCullough's (2d)
   Rush's
   Sheep's Ear
*Mount Hope*
   Logan House
   Mount House
*Mount Penn*
   Dengler's
*Mount Washington*
   Conway's
   Ewing's—Sanpey's
   Mauler's
*Nazareth*
   *Inn (on site of old one)
   Rose Inn

*Newbury*
   Bradfield's—Jennings'
   Snow's—Lenhart's—
      Thompson's—Letzger's
*New Hope*
   Two Old Inns
*Newton Square*
   Black Bear—Bull's Head
   Wayside Inn
*North East*
   Brown's—*Haynes'
*Palatine Bridge*
   Jesse Vincent's
*Pancake (near Washington)*
   At the Sign of Gen. Georg
      Washington—Rettig's
   Martin's Tavern
   Ringland's
*Paoli*
   Paoli Tavern
   General Warren—*The
      Warren Inn (near)
*Paradise*
   Sign of the Buck
   Sign of the Free Masons
   Sign of the Ship—*Para-
      dise Hotel
   Sign of the Stage
   Practical Farmer—
      Reynold's (near)
*Perkiomen*
   *Perkiomen Bridge Hotel

[354]

# A Record of Inns by Towns and States

*Petersburg*
Abram's—Skinner's—
Clary's, etc.
Hunter's—Walker's—Mc-
Mullen's, etc.—
Mitchell's (2d)
Mitchell's (1st)
Wentling's—Risler's
Connelly's

*Philadelphia*
Adam and Eveses Garden
Black Horse
Blue Bell
Boatswain and Call
Brig and Scow
Bull's Head No. 1
Bull's Head No. 2
Bunyan's Pilgrim
City Tavern
Clark's Inn—Coach and
Horses (1693)
Columbus (1798)
Crooked Billet
Death of the Fox
Dolphin
Durham Ox
*Eagle Hotel
Federal Convention Inn of
1797
Fish (The)
Four Alls (The)
Franklin Head
George Inn
Golden Lion—Yellow Cat

Guest's Inn
Hughes Tavern
Indian Queen No. 2
Indian Queen No. 1 or
Centre House
Lamb (The)
Lebanon Tavern
Man Full of Trouble (A)
Noah's Ark
Old London Coffee House
Peg Mullen's Beefsteak
House
Penny Pot House—Jolly
Tar
Pennsylvania Farmer's Inn
Poore Tavern
Purple and Blue Tavern—
The Quiet Woman
Raleigh Inn
Rising Sun No. 1
Rising Sun No. 2
Spread Eagle
Three Crowns
Three Jolly Sailors
Top Gallant
Two Sloops
Union Hall (1820)
United States Hotel—Man-
sion House — The New
Bingham (on site)
*Valley Green Inn
Washington Hotel—New
Theatre Hotel
White Lamb

[355]

# Early American Inns and Taverns

*Philadelphia*
  William Penn No. 1
  William Penn No. 2
  Wounded Tar
  Yellow Cottage
*Philadelphia, near (on Philadelphia-Lancaster Turnpike)*
  Barley Sheaf
  Irish Tavern (16 miles)
  Ludwick's
  Mendenhall Ferry Tavern
  Midway House (37 miles)
  Mills Tavern (16 miles)
  Plough
  Rainbow (39 miles)
  Sheep Drove Yard
  Sign of Admiral Warren
    (23 miles)
  Steamboat
  The Tun (47 miles)
  Unicorn (16 miles)
*Quakertown*
  *Red Lion
*Radnor Township*
  *Spread Eagle
*Rankinton*
  Spalding's—Rankin's
*Near Rankinton*
  Bedillion Tavern
  Andrew Caldwell's
  John Coulson's
  Robert Smith's
  Wilson's—John Miller's

*Reading*
  Cross Keys
  Federal Inn
  Franklin House
  *Mansion House
  Witman's
*Richmond Township*
  Eliason's
  Eslepp's
  Half Way House
*Ridley Park*
  White Horse
*Roney's Point*
  Bell's—Beck's
  Bentley's—Kimberley's
    (near)
*Sadsbury*
  Mount Vernon Inn
  Rising Sun—*Hotel
  Three Crowns
  White Horse
  Waterloo Tavern (near)
*Scarlet's Mills*
  White Bear
*Schaefferstown*
  Royal George—George
    Washington
*Searight's*
  Gray's—Risler's, etc.
*Near Searight's*
  Wilkes Brown's
  Brubaker's
  Abel Colley's—Grimes'—
    Green Tree

# A Record of Inns by Towns and States

*Near Searight's*
    Johnson's—Hatfield's—
      Johnson House
    Red Tavern
    Wallace's—Baily's

*Sinking Spring*
    *Centennial House

*Skippack*
    Skippack House—Farmers'
      and Mechanics

*Slaymaker's*
    Kinzer's (near)
    Slaymaker's Inn

*Somerfield*
    Blucher's
    Campbell's (log cabin,
      1824)
    Endsley Tavern (1818)
    Kinkead's

*Soudersburg*
    Tavern

*South Bridge*
    Widow Brownlee's—Hall's
      (near)
    Caldwell's
    Widow McClelland's

*Springmill*
    Ferry and Boathouse

*Stroudsburg*
    *Indian Queen

*Swanville*
    Nicholson Hotel
    Nicholson House

    Nicholson Tavern
    Swan's Tavern

*Swarthmore*
    *Lamb Tavern (near)
    *Rose Tree Inn (near)
    Black Horse Tavern
      (near)

*Torresdale*
    Red Lion

*Trappe*
    Fountain Inn
    The Lamb
    Shepherd's

*Triadelphia*
    Foster's
    Thompson's

*Trydeffr Township*
    General Jackson

*Uniontown*
    Margaret Allen's (1788)
    Brownfield's
    Hotel Brunswick
    Colin Campbell's—Salter's
      (1785)
    Matt Campbell's—Fulton
      —Moran House (on
      site)
    Clinton House
    John Collins'—Salter's—
      Wiggins', etc.
    Thomas Collins (1794)
    Culp's
    Gregg House (1798)

## PENNSYLVANIA (*Continued*)

*Uniontown*
  Jolly Irishman (1801)
  Manypenny's (1804)—
    Miller's
  McCleary House—
    Brunswick
  McClure's (1792)
  McNiman's (1802)
  National House
  Rowland's
  Pierson Sayers'
  Seaton House (1820)—
    West End Hotel
  Sellers'
  Slack's
  Spread Eagle
  Swan
  Walker House (1816)—
    United States—Central
  Weaver's — McClelland's
    McClelland House (on
    site)

*Near Uniontown*
  Grimes'
  Hunter's — Darlington's—
    Colley's
  Moxley's
  Old Hart
  Wiggins' Tavern—Half
    Way House—Moxley
    House

*Valley Forge*
  *Washington Inn

*Village Green*
  *Seven Stars

*Vintage*
  *Williamstown Hotel

*Warringtonville*
  Craig's Tavern

*Washington*
  Sam Acklin's
  John Adams' (1783-9)
  Black Horse—Gen. George
    Washington
  Buck Tavern
  Catfish Camp Tavern
  John Colwell's (1784)—
    Means'
  Commodore O. H. Perry
  Chas. Dodd's (1782)
  John Dodd's
  Donaldson's — Workman's
    —Parks'
  William Falconer's
  Farmer's Inn—Black Bear
  Fountain Inn
  Fox's
  Franklin
  General Brown
  General Wayne
  Green House
  Indian Queen
  Kirk's—Wilson's
  Lane's
  Dr. Lemoyne's—Good's
  Manuel's

# A Record of Inns by Towns and States

*Washington*
  Meetkirk's
  Mermaid
  Rising Sun
  Schmidt's Hotel
  Sign of the Buck—Huston's Home Inn — *George Washington Hotel (on site)
  Sign of the Cross Keys
  Sign of Gen. Jackson—Travelers' Inn and Stage Coach—National—Railroad — Auld House — Jackson
  Sign of the Globe
  Sign of the White Goose—Swan—Valentine's—Allison House—Hotel Siegel—*William Henry (on site)
  Spread Eagle—Sign of the Eagle—Mansion House Wilson's—At the Sign of Gen. Wayne
  John Wilson's Tavern

*Waterford*
  Reed's Hotel (near)

*Wattsburg*
  *Wattsburg House

*Wernersville*
  Brinckley's

*West Alexander*
  Lawson's

*West Ardmore*
  Prince of Wales

*West Brownsville*
  Huston's Tavern
  Vincent Owens'

*West Chester*
  *Eagle (near)
  *Green Tree
  Grove House
  Star Tavern
  Travelers' Rest
  *Turk's Head
  Washington (1787)
  White Hall (1796)

*Westminster*
  Old Kentucky Home

*West Sadsbury*
  Black Horse

*West Somerfield*
  Shellback

*West Whiteland Township*
  Sheaf of Wheat
  Ship
  Steamboat

*Whitpain*
  Wentz's

*Willistown Township*
  Green Tree

*Willow Grove*
  Red Lion
  *Willow Grove Hotel

*Winding Ridge*
  (near)
  Blucher's

# Early American Inns and Taverns

*Winding Ridge*
Wable's—Jones'—Augustine's
Welsh's—Dennison's—Paul's, etc.

*Womelsdorf*
*Central House
*Seltzer House
Seltzer Tavern (1st)

*Wrightstown*
*Anchor Hotel

*Yellow House*
Yellow House Tavern

*York*
Gen. Wayne's Headquarters Inn
*Ye Olde Valley Inn
Schultz House (near)
Tavern (5 miles from York)
Ten Mile House (10 miles from York)
Wolf's Tavern (5 miles from York)

## RHODE ISLAND

*Barrington*
Bowen Inn
Green Bush
Gifford's (1811)

*Bristol Ferry*
Inn

*Champlin's Corners (Warwick)*
David Arnold Tavern

*Charleston*
General Staunton

*Lime Rock*
Mowry Inn

*Newport*
King's Arms
Pitt's Tavern
Townsend's Coffee House
The White Horse

*North Kingston*
Haven's

*Pawtucket*
Ballou's Tavern

*Portsmouth*
Inn

*Providence*
Amidon's
Bull Dog
Golden Ball Inn—*Mansion House
John Whipple's Inn
Mowry Tavern—Abbott House
Sabin Tavern
Seahen's—Barker's
Turpin Inn

[360]

# A Record of Inns by Towns and States

*Quinswicket*
Eleazer Arnold's (1710)
*Smithfield*
Beer's
Brown's
Greenville Tavern (1730)

*Warren*
Inn
*Wickford*
Inn (Phillips' farmhouse)
*Woonsocket*
Arnold Tavern

## SOUTH CAROLINA

*Camden*
At the Sign of the Eagle
and Harp
Ballard's
*Charleston*
Broad Path Tavern
Quarter House

*Georgetown*
Oak Tavern
Winyah Inn
*Greenville*
McCullough House (near)
*St. Paul's Parish*
Rantowles House

## TENNESSEE

*Bean Station*
Bean Station Tavern
*Blountsville*
Deery Tavern
*Crab Orchard*
Inn (ruins)
*Franklin*
Beech's Tavern (near)
*Jonesborough*
Chester Inn
*Kingsport*
Kingsport Tavern
*Knoxville*
Tavern

*Memphis*
Bell Tavern
*Gayoso Hotel
*Nashville*
Bell Tavern
Black Bob's
City Hotel
Clark's
Granny White's (near)
Mud Tavern (near)
Nashville Inn (near)
*Rogersville*
Rogers Tavern

# Early American Inns and Taverns

## VERMONT

*Bennington*
  Catamount
  Walloomsac Inn
*Chimney Point*
  Chimney Point Inn
*East Poultney*
  Eagle Inn
*Newfane*
  *Newfane Inn
*North Bennington*
  Bert Henry Inn

*Sudbury*
  *Hyde Manor
*West Brattleboro*
  Hays Tavern
*Westminster*
  *Westminster Inn
*Windsor*
  †Old Constitution House
  —Patrick's

## VIRGINIA

*Abingdon*
  Ordinary
*Aldie*
  William West's or Watts'
  Ordinary
*Alexandria*
  †Braddock House
  Gadsby's—City Hotel
*Ashby's or Berry's Ferry*
  Ashby's Tavern
*Auburn*
  Nevill's Ordinary
*Boyd's Tavern P. O.*
  Shepherd's Inn
*Charlottesville*
  *Colonial Hotel
  Eagle Tavern—*The
  Monticello
  Rising Sun (near)
  Swan

*Free Union*
  Michie Old Tavern (near)
*Fredericksburg*
  Exchange—*Maury Hotel
  Indian Queen
  Mrs. Sukey Livingston's
  Coffee House
  †Rising Sun
*Gloucester*
  *Ye Olde English Tavern
*Greenwood*
  Inn
*Hanover*
  *Tavern
*Ivy*
  *Hardindale Inn
*Louisa County*
  Cuckoo Tavern
*Middleburg*
  Beverage House

# A Record of Inns by Towns and States

## VIRGINIA (*Continued*)

*Paris*
  Ashby's

*Richmond*
  †Swan

*Rony's Point*
  Dagg's

*Staunton*
  Clarksville Tavern

*Stony Point*
  Pinch-em-Slyly (near)

*Yancey's Mills*
  *At the Sign of the Green
    Teapot

*Yorktown*
  *Ye Olde English Tavern

*Williamsburg*
  The Raleigh

## WASHINGTON

*Moclif's*
  The Limit

## WEST VIRGINIA

*Clarksburg*
  Tavern

*Kanawha Falls*
  Stockton Tavern

*Lewisburg*
  Star Tavern

*Pleasant Valley*
  Blakely's

*Wheeling*
  Beymer's (1802)
  Widow Beymer's (No. 2)
  Bradfield's

McCortney's
Monroe House
Mosier's Tavern
Mosier House
Teeter's
United States Hotel
Virginia

*Wheeling (near)*
  Steenrod's (2 miles east)
  Rhodes — Beagler's (12
    miles east)

## WISCONSIN

*Baraboo*
  Baraboo House

*Big Bend*
  Aaron Putnam's Tavern

*Black Hawk*
  Harris House

*Black River Falls*
  Tavern

[363]

# Early American Inns and Taverns

*Burlington*
Burlington House

*Cassville*
*Hotel

*Dalton*
Cottage Home

*Delton (between, and Baraboo)*
Washburne Tavern

*East Troy*
Buena Vista—*The Cobblestone

*Fairfield*
Sandwich House

*Fond-du-Lac (12 miles from)*
Kellogg's

*Fort Atkinson*
Green Mountain House—Hotel Fort—*Black Hawk

*Genesee*
*Treadwell Tavern

*Green Bay*
Arndt's
Astor House
Washington House

*Greenbush*
*Wade's

*Hale's Corners*
Western House—*Julius Dreyfuss Tavern

*Hazel Green*
*Empire Tavern

*Janesville Road, On*
Leonard Martin's
Uncle Jesse Smith's

*Jefferson*
*Jefferson House

*Jumean*
Burr Oak

*Kilburne*
Red Tavern (near)

*Mequon*
*Hotel

*Merrimack*
Ferry House

*Mineral Point*
Hood's
Moore's (near)
Nichol's

*Milton*
Goodrich's Tavern No. 1
Goodrich's Tavern No. 2

*Milwaukee*
Cottage Inn
Forest House

*Mukwonago*
Henry Camp's
*Mukwonago House

*Okauchee*
*McConnell's

# A Record of Inns by Towns and States

*Prairie-du-Chien*
   Tavern
*Prairie-du-Sac*
   Empire House—Briggs
      House
*Reedsville*
   Exchange House
*Richland City*
   Union House
*Rochester*
   *Union House
*Sauk City*
   King's Tavern
   Sauk City Hotel—*United
      States Hotel
*Sauk County*
   Harrisburg Tavern

   Webster's (on Baraboo
      River)
   Spring Green House
*Theresa*
   Rock River House
*Truesdell*
   Kincaid's
*Waterford*
   Waterford House
*Watertown*
   American
   *Buena Vista
   *Commercial
*Waukesha*
   Prairie House
*Wilmot*
   Tavern

THE  END

[365]